TONY DAGRADI
A SPIRITUAL APPROACH TO JAZZ

THE LIFE AND WORK OF THE NEW ORLEANS SAXOPHONIST AND BANDLEADER

by David Lasocki

Astral Project Series, No. 2

PORTLAND, OREGON
2018

ISBN-13: 978-0983404866
ISBN-10: 0983404860

Copyright © 2014 and 2018 by David Lasocki

This version 1 March 2018

Cover design by Laura Serrano-Silva

Published by Instant Harmony, http://www.instantharmony.net

TABLE OF CONTENTS

Introduction 1
1. Before New Orleans 3
2. Early Days in New Orleans 17
3. *Oasis* 29
4. Astral Project, 1978–85 35
5. The Carla Bley Band 41
6. The Long View of Ramsey 51
7. Back to School; Sideman, 1984–89 63
8. *Images from the Floating World* and *Sweet Remembrance* 71
9. Astral Project, 1986–95 81
10. Quartets, Big Bands, and Trio 89
11. *Live at The Columns* and *Heart to Heart* 99
12. Astral Project, 1996–2000 107
13. New Groups and Instruments 115
14. Sideman, 1994–2005 121
15. Astral Project, 2001–05 131
16. After Hurricane Katrina 137
17. Teaching 147
18. What Now? 161
Discography 165
Bibliography 177
Index of Names 189

INTRODUCTION

Jazz—I mean modern jazz, not Preservation Hall-style traditional jazz—is alive and well in New Orleans. Most of the famous modern jazz musicians from the Big Easy, such as Wynton and Branford Marsalis, have long since moved to New York or elsewhere. Of the modern jazz musicians who remain, the ones who make the bulk of their living playing and teaching in the city don't have much of a reputation outside. Nevertheless, these musicians are creating their own styles of jazz, their own mixtures of the local and the national and the international, that deserve a hearing beyond the tourist clubs and bars of Frenchmen Street and Uptown.

For me, the finest of these musicians belong to Astral Project, a group that sprang to life as long ago as 1978 and is still going today. Tony Dagradi, saxophone, the leader; Steve Masakowski, guitar; James Singleton, bass; and John Vidacovich, drums, constitute "a band of geniuses." Each member is inventive and inspiring in his own right; the group as a whole is tight. If you're on their frequency, and it's a high one, you'll be blown away, into the astral plane and beyond.

Tony Dagradi is best known as the leader of Astral Project, which he has made his life project. As the bassist and composer Ramsey McLean said to me, "Tony *is* Astral Project. The rest of the people are in the band, but Tony *is* the band." And we will certainly survey his involvement with the group, based on my book *A Higher Fusion: The New Orleans Modern-Jazz Group Astral Project at 34*.[1] Nevertheless, he has had several other important threads in his forty-year career: serving a series of informal apprenticeships with experimental jazz, soul, and rhythm-and-blues artists in the 1970s; playing, touring, and recording with the great New Orleans rhythm-and-blues pianist and singer Professor Longhair, 1978–80; doing the same with the Carla Bley Band, 1980–85; partnering with McLean in the early 1980s; performing in a longstanding trio with James Singleton and John Vidacovich; making recordings as a sideman with many New Orleans jazz and popular musicians; and teaching at Loyola University of New Orleans as well as writing some important pedagogical materials on jazz saxophone. These threads will be the focus of the present book.

The book is based on about forty interviews with New Orleans musicians and their families, vast amounts of research in published writings, and the aural evidence of over two hundred recordings, commercial and live. It's a reference book in the sense that it surveys Tony's recordings as both leader and sideman, and it contains a discography. To make it more readable for those who find that surveys contain too much detail, I have placed them as far as possible in separate chapters, so that they can be readily skipped over. Of course, the book is also a detailed biography of a wonderful jazz musician, whose work speaks to me at a high musical and spiritual level. And let me add that the chapters on Astral Project, taken as a whole, also constitute an abridged version of *A Higher Fusion*, so they should suit readers who want the highlights and not the detail.

The printed version of this book (2018) adds a description of Tony's CD *Oneness* (2017).

Acknowledgements
My heartfelt thanks to:
  Tony Dagardi, Steve Masakowski, James Singleton, and John Vidacovich: for supporting this series of books with extended interviews, e-mail messages, and advice.
  Their spouses, Joan Dagradi, Ulrike Masakowski, Marcela Lineiro Singleton, and Deborah Vidacovich: for their interviews, e-mail messages, and support.

My wife Lilin Chen and our son Lucien Lasocki: for always being there.

My late mother, Margaret Lasocki: for providing me with a clothing allowance as a teenager that I spent on jazz records (and generously, still buying me clothes afterwards).

Scott Aiges, Rebecca Barry, Al Belletto, Olivier Bou, Stanton Davis Jr., the late James Drew, Mark DiFlorio, Andy Durta, Dave Easley, Patrice Fisher, Helen Gillet, the late Clyde Kerr Jr., Clarence Johnson III, Lula Lowe Lewis, Roger Lewis, Ted Ludwig, Ramsey McLean, Davy Mooney, Stanton Moore, Michael Pellera, Frank Puzzullo, Mark Sanders, Larry Sieberth, Jim and Mary Anne Singleton, David Torkanowsky, and Angelle Trosclair: for granting me interviews, in person or on the phone.

Jeff Boudreaux: for writing me some vivid memoirs of the period.

Laura Serrano-Silva for her wonderful cover and help with the illustrations.

The owners of the Green Mill and Snug Harbor: for "putting our names at the door."

Norman Kim and Marianne Weiss-Kim, Alice Redmann, and Katie Triplett: for housing us on our trips to New Orleans.

Randy Bayers, Tim Call, Bill Goss, Tim Green, Richard Henry, Wolfgang Kurth, Tommy Macintosh, Laurie Phillips, Carl Reisman, Richard Russell, Mark Sanders, Larry Sieberth, Tom Walsh, Luke Wroblewski, and WYES: for providing copies of live and rare recordings. Rosanna Fidler Stephens, my former reference intern: for copying live videos. David Pickett: for CD transfers of LPs and making me a gizmo that kept my LP player working longer.

Gary Potter, Evan Rothstein, and Allen Winold: for discussing drafts of chapters.

The Indiana University Libraries and the Indiana University Librarians Association: for their generous support of research time and money. My former colleagues in the Cook Music Library: for their understanding. The interlibrary loan staff: for their patience and fortitude. The university itself: for granting me a sabbatical that generated this astral project.

Sascha Feinstein: for insisting that I dig deeper inside myself when writing about Astral Project and its members.

Bernard Gordillo, who grew up partly in New Orleans: for research assistance—wading through New Orleans periodicals of the last thirty years, fishing out relevant articles and performance listings; transferring recordings; becoming as excited as I did about Professor Longhair; and acting as an enthusiastic sounding board for my ideas. Roll on the next project, bro'. Where y'at?

David Lasocki
Portland, Oregon
September 2014, March 2018

Note

1. David Lasocki, *A Higher Fusion: The New Orleans Modern-Jazz Group Astral Project at 34* (Portland, OR: Instant Harmony, 2012).

1. BEFORE NEW ORLEANS

Anthony Arnold Dagradi was born on 22 September 1952 at the St. Albans Naval Hospital in Queens, New York. Tony grew up in Summit, New Jersey, where his reverse-named father, Arnold Anthony Dagradi, worked at nearby Newark Airport as a mechanic for Eastern Airlines. (Eventually, the company was absorbed into Continental; he felt it treated its workers shabbily, and he left embittered.) Tony remembers that his parents enjoyed big-band music from the 1940s, which he heard in the background, and they were good dancers. His mother, née Matilda Albenga, "listened to a funny amalgam: Hank Williams, Harry Belafonte, *The King and I*, *My Fair Lady*."

> "The only person I knew who played an instrument was an old Italian uncle who played guitar a little. We would have these big family feasts on holidays like Memorial Day, and he would play the guitar and fall asleep on the couch. That was my musical family."

Tony's father didn't express any particular interest in music at the time.

> "Only later, when he came to visit me down here [New Orleans] and I was doing some gigs and he really enjoyed them, only then did I find out that he had thought of being a musician. He really liked the saxophone and the big bands that he was listening to. I didn't know that was such an interest from him."

Coming from an Italian family, albeit a second-generation one on both sides, Tony grew up Roman Catholic. "Went to the Catholic church, first communion, after-school catechism classes: went through the whole system. I liked it. Wasn't anything I was displeased with."

Tony's interest in music really stemmed from the fine band program in his elementary school. "When you got to fourth grade they took you in a room and let you try a trumpet, a saxophone, a clarinet, and a flute, and said, 'What do you want to play?' On the spur of the moment, I picked the alto saxophone." The choice seems have been arbitrary. "There was no magnetism one way or the other. Totally luck of the draw." He went through this program for a couple of years, without distinguishing himself in any way: "Just had this saxophone and showed up at the rehearsals and the lessons." At that stage of his life, he was more interested in baseball.

In seventh grade Tony had a life-changing experience:

> "I remember in junior high, they had what they called a stage band, a big band— five saxes, four trumpets, four trombones, and a rhythm section—made up of the older kids at the school. I was just watching them, and all of a sudden this kid in the saxophone section, who was playing a tenor, stood up and took a solo. I'd never seen that before. I thought, 'I like that; that was pretty cool.' I felt, 'That tenor, yeah: that's the one I want to play.' There was something about the horn, the sound. That started me off on a journey."

At the end of that academic year, the school instituted a new policy that students could no longer borrow instruments but would have to buy or rent. Tony took the school note home to his father, who asked him: "If I buy you an instrument, are you going to practice?" Tony replied: "If you buy me a *tenor* saxophone, I'll practice." True to his word, on the last day of seventh grade, Mr. Dagradi arranged for one of the music instructors at the school to take Tony over to a music store in Newark where he had paid for a saxophone.

> "I went with the guy, and we picked up the saxphone. I thought I was going to get a funky used saxophone: I would have been happy with that. But he had picked out a brand new, gleaming Selmer Bundy."

After that, Tony began to work hard on his music. He joined the stage band at Summit High School, which he found exciting, and at home he practiced, made transcriptions, and listened to records.

> "I found myself listening to a lot of big bands, and I thought that was jazz. That's jazz: I like it. I listened to the older bands, and we had records from the 40s. The more popular bands: Glenn Miller, Tommy Dorsey, those were around in the house. There might have been a Duke Ellington record, a Count Basie record, but I didn't really discover those guys until later. Not too much later, though, because I started to read about jazz, and Ellington was always held up as an important figure, so I definitely explored him. It was a lonely search, because it was the 60s and all my friends were listening to the Beatles and all the little pop groups that came out. I was definitely the odd person out there, because I was listening to jazz and everyone was dealing with Woodstock Nation. I had a reputation: 'He's into jazz, he's different.' As I was listening I would try to transcribe things. Nobody told me that was a good thing to do, but it's the most important thing you can do at any level."

Gradually, he developed his ear, which had been "good enough to get started."

> "I would do crazy stuff. I would listen to a big band and try to write down all the parts. I didn't know how hard that was. I didn't understand harmony, either. I would just try to pick out all the different notes to make those sounds. Sometimes I would miss, but at other times I would get pretty close. Then I would take those transcriptions into the band and have them play them. I would write out all the parts."

When he was 16 or 17, the stage band, "a notably good one for a high school," even made records of his arrangements.

> "Back then, it was hard to tell what the music was about. But it just happened to be a good group of people. They weren't great, they weren't heavy players, but they could get through the music. The band director lucked out, and I guess I lucked out."

In addition, Tony started composing for the band, and enjoyed hearing what he had written.

> "Big bands are a funny animal in jazz, anyway, because there are so many people up there, and only a few get to actually improvise. The person who has the most fun is the guy who wrote the arrangement, because he gets to hear everybody play his notes."

Naturally, Tony started listening to jazz records, especially by saxophone players. He recalls, "When I was looking for things, nobody would give me a list of the Top Ten, and I was asking people, 'What should I listen to?' I had a subscription to *Down Beat*, and I would read the reviews, and buy certain records because of the reviews." The first records he recalls listening to were by Cannonball Adderley and John Coltrane.

"The first Coltrane record I bought was *Giant Steps*, which I loved. But I said, 'This is pretty heavy. This is very advanced.' Because I was just learning how to play. Then Cannonball: I remember specific records, and I think if you talk to anybody, they'll have specific records that changed their lives. The Cannonball Adderley record for me was *Mercy, Mercy, Mercy*, which is still such a great record. Both of those are landmarks in jazz, and I was fortunate to stumble upon them. In my ignorance I found some good stuff to base my playing on."

Two records by Stan Getz made almost as great an impact on Tony.

"I probably bought *Sweet Rain* because of a review I saw, and I think that's the best record Stan Getz ever made. That was very influential on me in sound. And if you think of the rest of the band: Chick Corea was playing piano, and they recorded two of his tunes—'Litha' and 'Windows'—and they were very advanced harmonically, on the cutting edge of what jazz was at that time. I didn't understand it, but I really liked it. I said, 'I'll learn how to do that.' I was very attracted to how Chick Corea was comping on the piano. 'Wow, that's way different from Bud Powell.' And it was. It was based on McCoy Tyner and Herbie Hancock. I would transcribe things that Chick played on the record, and I didn't even know that was a good thing to do. I would transcribe solos, little bits of things. I figured out that Chick Corea was voicing his left hand in fourths, and I said, 'Wow, look at that. What is he doing? Why does that sound so good?' And I would play it on the piano. I didn't realize at first how he was applying the harmonies of the song to the chordal comping in his left hand: it took me a while to put that together. But it was something I immediately warmed up to. And the choice of compositions on *Sweet Rain* really inspired Stan Getz to play at the peak of his artistry. Getz was a very tortured individual: drug addict, alcoholic, volatile personality. I don't think he was ever too happy as a person. But in his playing you get this beautiful ethereal sax sound. So I absorbed that and took it for granted, in a way.

"Another record on a similar plane is *Focus*, which he did with an orchestra, and in my mind, and in a lot of people's minds, it's the best fusion we've ever had of improvisation with classical music. The perfect marriage of someone improvising and reacting to the orchestra, as if it were comping for him. The fusion is just coming from what he played. Because all he did was listen to what was written—a through-composed chamber-orchestra piece—until he evolved a part. Then he went into a studio, did one pass, and that was it. It was extremely successful."

Tony's band director from elementary through high school had been Joe Loreti, "a good musician—trumpeter—and very supportive. He gave me my first lessons: group lessons with three or four other guys playing alto." When Tony was obviously outgrowing him, Loreti recommended "Joe D." (Joe D'Addario, d. 1988), a multi-reedman who freelanced in theater orchestras and went to Summit one or two afternoons a week to give lessons on the saxophone, clarinet, and flute.[1] He provided Tony with a solid grounding on all three instruments.[2]

When Tony was a junior in high school, he told D'Addario that he wanted to learn about harmony and arranging. D'Addario directed him to a piano teacher in New York called Tony Aless, an experienced jazz pianist in a hard bop style. The young saxophonist would take the bus there on Saturdays for lessons. He recalls that he took in Chick Corea records to Aless, asking to learn this new style, "but he didn't know what it was. He couldn't show me voicings in fourths." What Aless could and did give him was a foundation in jazz harmony.

"I just wanted to learn about arranging. But he made me learn how to play piano: do Bach, and Chopin etudes, and develop some technique on the piano. I was doing all that and enjoying it. One important thing he showed me was reharmonization: substitutions of chords; taking a melody and writing a million different accompaniments to it. I thought that was cool. He had a very organized but very personal approach to harmony. It was systemized, but only the way he had organized it. He had a partner, Sanford Gold. They both taught this same method. They had sheets, and once you'd done one thing they'd give you the next. I learned this way of harmony they were teaching, and it was very important to me because it really explained a lot. But it didn't explain everything: other things, they were just expecting you to be able to hear and understand."

In addition to the lessons with Aless, Tony rode into New York for any concerts he could go to on his own. When he was about 16, he saw Thelonious Monk playing solo piano in Central Park, opening for the classic Miles Davis Quintet, featuring Wayne Shorter, Herbie Hancock, Ron Carter, and Tony Williams. "I loved it. That was one of the last gigs they did as a group."

In 1968 and again in 1969, while still in high school, Tony went to a summer jazz camp at the University of Connecticut in Storrs, with a first-rate faculty. Jerry Coker taught improvisation, and David Baker arranging. Pepper Adams, one of the great jazz baritone saxophone players, coached an ensemble in which Tony performed. Tony was impressed:

"He was definitely coming out of the bebop school. But he was also very contemporary, and I always thought he played the baritone like a tenor, which I liked. The flexibility and the technique. By the 70s he was influenced by everything that had happened in the 60s: he was playing very chromatically and also using pentatonic scales."

It was at this camp that Tony first met the trombonist Gary Valente, who was soon to become a close colleague.

During that senior year, Tony had his driver's license and access to a family car, in which he would often visit record stores and the Village Vanguard in New York.

"That was an easy hit from New Jersey: go through the tunnel and you're down in the Village there. At the Vanguard I saw all kinds of people. The Thad Jones–Mel Lewis Big Band performed every Monday. Pepper Adams was playing bari in the band. I would visit with him every time I went to the Vanguard. He was very gracious; said hello and sat down at my table. He was somebody I was always thrilled to know, because there he was sitting up with this band that I would have loved to play with. The Village Vanguard is very small, and you can't believe it when you see the whole band squashed together on the stage. It's a tiny space and a big band. The first row of tables was right next to Roland Hanna sitting at the piano. There is no band room; the band just hangs out wherever on a break. As I was going to the men's room, I said hello to Mel Lewis one time: 'I'd love to play in your band someday.' And he goes, 'Yeah, if I live long enough.' If I had lived in New York, I certainly would have tried to get on the gig somehow."

And he would go to other concerts: at Town Hall and Carnegie Hall, among other places, where he recalls hearing Duke Ellington, Jaki Byard, and Joe Farrell. In a concert series at the Museum of Modern Art, he saw Cecil Taylor as well as Sonny Rollins giving a solo saxophone recital in the Garden: "phenomenal stuff."

Tony saw Miles a second time at the Village Gate, taking a date from high school.

"I told her, 'This is Miles Davis; I really like him.' I didn't know anything about what he'd been doing. I didn't have the buzz on what Miles was up to. He came out, and it wasn't the quintet: some configuration of the *Bitches Brew* band. It was electronic, and everything was really long and fusion-oriented. I had never heard anything like that and I didn't know what to think about it. I knew it was really different: not what I was expecting. I had liked the acoustic quintet a lot. I don't think I got into *Bitches Brew* until much later."

Tony feels that he did not yet know enough to pick up much from the musical side of these performances. Rather, he learned about the art of live performance. "At the time, there was a whole other element to consider: how people stand, the attitude they have...." The music he was listening to on records had more influence on his playing.

Boston

In 1970, Tony graduated from high school. That summer, he studied with Billy Byers at an arranging clinic in Las Vegas. In the fall, on a *Down Beat* scholarship,[3] he went to the Berklee School (now College) of Music in Boston, a vast conservatory—it now has more than 4,400 students—that trains undergraduates largely in jazz and other types of popular music. Privately, he studied the saxophone with one of the Berklee instructors, Andy McGhee.

"Andy turned me on to Nicholas Slonimsky's *Thesaurus of Scales and Intervals*: made me play a page out of the book for each lesson. We worked on tunes and read through transcriptions. He also introduced me to some of the essential classical repertoire, such as Paul Creston's Sonata and Alexandr Glazounov's Concerto."

But Tony was actually a composition major at Berklee and thinking of himself more as a composer than a player at that time.

"I really enjoyed writing things for horns and hearing the different textures that could be gotten. So I took all the writing and arranging courses. I actually passed out of a few because I was a little advanced. I studied arranging with Phil Wilson and Herb Pomeroy, who were both very knowledgeable and excellent teachers. And the things that I learned for composition, for arranging, for orchestration were very helpful in my own playing. Because Berklee had a specific system of chord-scales going with different chords and functions, and they carried that through the college globally. You'd go to an improv class and they'd talk about a certain scale, and you'd go to an arranging course and they'd talk about the same scale in a different context. So it started to make sense to me. And in a way it also makes sense compositionally: just picking the note that's going to sound the hippest."

The Berklee approach meshed with his earlier lessons from Aless and Gold, giving him a harmonic foundation that has served him well to the present day.

"I've expanded on it and gotten it to a point where, as I look at certain things that are different harmonically—people are constantly expanding the parameters of things,

> especially in jazz—I can always understand why it works. And you have to add in classical theory to that eventually, because it's all part of the same thing. If you're going to improvise in free jazz, there's no harmonic thing you can add to that: it has to come from more of a compositional approach. Why does this work? OK, because this rhythmic motive is developing, and we're developing this, and harmonically this is working with that."

Tony took part in various combos that were directed at times by two teachers who were celebrated players: the alto saxophonist Charlie Mariano; and the vibraphonist Gary Burton, who eventually moved up to dean of curriculum, then served in the newly created position of vice president of the college from 1996 until his retirement in 2004.[4]

Tony was surprised to find that his studies at Berklee indirectly helped his playing. "All the writing courses, all the composition, all the orchestration: all influenced the way I play, the notes that I choose. And being a horn player, also, it was very important to learn piano." Before long he came to realize that "playing was my first love and writing was only to get me there: the composition was only to set up the playing."

Eager to get out and play the saxophone, Tony left Berklee after two years in 1972, without obtaining a degree, and remained based in Boston for the next five years. He remembers that his father disapproved of him dropping out of school. One of his first "big gigs" was with the soul singer Marvin Gaye.

Soon Tony became involved with The Twentieth Century Limited, a rock 'n' roll band named after a famous train that ran from New York to Chicago for thirty years (1938–1967).[5] The band was led by Roger Hock, whom Tony describes as "not a great musician, more of a conceptualizer. He would hire as good musicians as he could; try to keep a band together." The band was attempting a fusion of rock and jazz, in the manner of Blood, Sweat and Tears, or Chicago. "So I figured that was a direction I should look at or pursue. I wasn't really so adamantly pursuing a career as a jazz artist. I just thought, 'Maybe I have to do these things.'" Besides playing in the band, Tony composed and wrote arrangements for it. The band performed frequently in the Boston area, around Cape Cod, and traveled a little around New England, offering him some experience of playing professionally, day in day out.

> "There's certain things I got together on that gig. The one thing that was nice about it was there were long periods where we played every night, and I needed to do that. A lot of times it was just very bread-and-butter horn-section stuff, and I needed to do that, too. There were solos, definitely, that I played, and certain things that I could work on every night: little things. Short solos, but conceptual things. At that point I was really starting to listen with real understanding for the very first time. I would listen to Joe Henderson and go, 'Oh, wow, listen to that! I understand now.' And I would start to listen to Coltrane and go, 'Oh, yeah, that's really something.' So on the gig I would try to bring that out in my playing. And it did start to come out just then. I think just then is when I really started to be able to play."

But after a couple of years in the band, Tony became disillusioned. He said to himself, "No, I don't have to do this at all. I never want to do it again."

Tony then became more dedicated to jazz: "a period of very meager income." Around 1974, he co-founded and co-led a jazz group, Inner Visions, with the trombonist Gary Valente, a student from the New England Conservatory, and two other NEC students, Ed Schuller on bass and Anton Fig on drums. Fig soon became too busy and left the group. (In 1976, he moved to New York and developed a major career as a session drummer, including working in the house band for the David Letterman Show on ABC TV.) D. Sharpe came in to replace Fig, providing an unexpected bonus: his wife Nancy was a great macrobiotic cook.

> "D. Sharpe had jam sessions at his house, trying to have, say, all-bebop sessions, or ones where he mixed different kinds of musicians to see what would happen. The food was great: always a pot of rice, a pot of chickpea stew, on the stove. They did us a big favor: gave us some real food for a change, for a minute, for a day. They helped me out a lot. I crashed at their house a lot, when I was kind of in between houses."

Tony recalls with a laugh, "D. Sharpe was maybe five years older than me [1947–1987][6] and definitely seemed older and wiser. He was all of 25 or 26, you know." The group performed in the Boston area and gave a few live broadcasts on WGBH, Tony's first experience of radio. "We did some groove things, but that band was more acoustic, more influenced by the avant-garde experiments of the 60s and early 70s."

Tony now found himself hanging out at NEC, doing rehearsals, and playing in recitals (non-paying "friend-gigs") for students graduating from the jazz program there. It proved to be an important formative period for his playing.

> "I was hanging out with people like me who were focused only on music. That was what you did. You practiced, thought about music, went over to somebody's house and did a little jam rehearsal, came home and ate, either went out to listen to music or practiced some more. I think everybody needs to spend some time like that where that's all you're doing.
>
> "I remember reading an interview that Paul Desmond did with Charlie Parker:
>
> PD. Another thing that's been a major factor in your playing is this fantastic technique that nobody's quite equaled. I've always wondered about that ... whether that came behind practicing or whether that was just from playing, whether it evolved gradually.
> CP. ... I can't see where there's anything fantastic about it all. I put quite a bit of study into the horn, that's true. In fact the neighbors threatened to ask my mother to move once when we were living out West. She said I was driving them crazy with the horn. I used to put in at least 11 to 15 hours a day.... I did that for over a period of 3 to 4 years.... That's the facts, anyway (chuckle).[7]
>
> "So that was the period where I got to do that. I woke up and there wasn't anything else to do. I think when you're in school, you don't have time to do that."

Tony was doing what he loved, but the money didn't follow immediately.

> "I guess I was just about getting by. I would do a lot of dumb gigs—certain rock gigs and funk gigs—just to be making a little bit of money. But the difference was in the attitude: 'I'm doing this as a sideman, just making some money: that's not what I do. I'm just a free, contracted musician here.' Whereas before, when I was doing the rock band, I was an integral part, writing the music, doing the arrangements, and taking it seriously. I could never do that again."

Tony also took every opportunity to listen to other bands in the Boston area. His main inspiration for Inner Visions came from the local group Ghetto/Mysticism, directed by the trumpeter Stanton Davis, Jr. (b. 1945), a native of New Orleans who had moved to Boston in 1967 to study at Berklee, then NEC. Tony recalled:

"I saw those guys play and thought, 'Wow, that's really a thing; there's some energy there.' That's when I started taking myself seriously as a jazz artist: 'That's what I want to do. I've learned all this stuff, had these different experiences; I really want to be a jazz artist.' I wasn't thinking economically; didn't really have a financial plan, which would have been helpful. I was just trusting that if I pursued what I wanted to do artistically, other things would fall into place.

"One of the bases of Stanton's vision for that band was the book *The Mysticism of Sound* by Hazrat Inayat Khan.[8] Stanton read that book and learned about the importance of sound, its relevance: how the vibrations work. And his music was very powerful. He was probably one of the most successful people of our age in developing and presenting something in Boston. He had a certain degree of popularity, and it was always a happening when his band played.

"They did one or two records [actually only *Brighter Days* (recorded 1975–76)].[9] I have the first one, and it's very cool. Stanton was highly directed, especially at that time, and the music was uplifting. It was grooves, always electric bass, definitely coming out of the Miles/Herbie Hancock kind of fusion. Killer musicians: some of the best musicians in Boston. That's another reason why it sounded so good. He always picked the right guys, and they always made the music a high experience.

"This group was a big influence on me in putting together a concept that worked, musically and spiritually. I said, 'That's cool: I want to do that, too.'"

By the age of 21 or 22, Tony started hearing the spirituality in John Coltrane's recordings, which had already influenced him musically for several years.

"He was the most important person for me. Not only musically but even spiritually. Of course, all his later music was in that direction. But that was probably the first time something went off in my mind: 'Wow, what is it about spirituality, and how is that connected to music? I like that, so what is that?' So that opened some doors for me to explore."

Beyond Coltrane and Stanton Davis, Tony began to notice the spiritual element in "Sun Ra, all the 'out' avant-garde stuff at the time, Albert Ayler."

"I asked myself, 'Where is this stuff coming from?' With Inner Visions we were trying to play like that, and to me it was very fulfilling and also very enlightening from a learning perspective. It was just sound. You didn't have to deal with chord-scales, you didn't even have to deal with time. Of course, we were also trying to learn how to play with chords. But this one free area just seemed to be very intense and I had an aptitude for it."

Yet Coltrane remained the main influence on his spirituality.

"Coltrane was at the top of the list, no question. The last of his recorded output would definitely be in the 'energy' category. I just loved that: went right to that like a moth to the flame. We were trying to get to that place where we could create that feeling, that uplifting 'energy' feeling. We were young and probably didn't sound that great a lot of times. But we were trying to explore those areas. That was really what sucked me into this idea of spirituality and mysticism—the mysticism of sound. I discovered that Coltrane had been studying each religion, reading books, finding out the metaphysical aspects of each religion. There are Christian mystics, Jewish mystics, mystics in every religion. That is quite different from the surface and the ritual of the religion, so a lot of people don't see that. That's what I wanted to see. I said, 'That's it: that's what the religion is really about. This other stuff is packaged for the masses. That's fine and dandy, and makes everybody have better lives and everything, but I want the direct experience, the real stuff.' Those are the trails I followed. I was looking at different things, going to different meetings. I remember one time Gene Roma, a drummer a little older than I was—Gary Valente and I did some gigs with him—he invited us to an ashram to see a saintly woman from India who was going to lead a meditation, and I went out there.[10] That was really one of my very first experiences of an Indian mystic. It was a guided meditation, where there was a talk first, then chanting. I liked it a lot. So that started me on reading a little bit about different things."

Meeting Joan

In summer 1975, Tony met the young artist and spiritual initiate Joan Lissy (b. 1951): an important catalytic moment for his life, personally and spiritually. Tony had gone to Provincetown on Cape Cod for a summer-long gig with Inner Visions, upstairs at a restaurant called the Café Edwige. Joan was trying to earn a little money before her summer art course began at the Cape School of Art by doing charcoal portraits on the street, just down the road from the cafe. In between portraits, she read in her little library of metaphysical books. She recalls:

"The drummer, D. Sharpe, came over to me one day while I was doing portraits and said: 'This is very nice'; because he liked drawing. He told me, 'We're all playing upstairs Friday night, and you should come and check us out.' So I came up, and had my drawing pad and was drawing them, and D. Sharpe was just real sweet. I saw Tony, but I just thought: 'OK, he plays saxophone, that's nice.' He wasn't friendly at all; didn't talk to me a bit. You know, I really had no feelings about him when I met him the first time. It was just like, 'He plays saxophone, this is a drum, this is a tree.'"

Then Joan began to run into Tony around town.

"We used to have this thing where neither one of us had a phone, but we'd go to the same place at the same time. We did that a lot. A couple of days later, I'm sitting at my spot—and everybody in the whole town would walk by this spot—just sitting in one place and watching the whole world go by, when I wasn't reading."

At that point, the gig at the Café Edwige had fallen through, and Inner Visions managed to find a little work at the Governor Bradford Hotel, right next to Joan's spot on the street.

"And Tony came by. He was handing out posters for the Governor Bradford gig. So he just handed me the poster: take that; and he just walked on. Nothing, nothing, nothing."

At the time of that gig, Joan, sitting outside the hotel, could hear every note.

> "I thought, 'Wow, they sound really great.' About the time that this was going on, a friend of mine named Tony who was in the Bahai faith, I guess he was worried about me, because out of the blue he said: 'You really should meet somebody, and just pray.' He was a nice person; his wife was lovely. I said, 'That's nice, Tony, that's good.' So this particular day, I'd already heard Tony Dagradi playing, and I was sitting in my spot, waiting for the next customer, reading a book about Buddhism, and I remember it was 12 noon. I remember saying, 'OK, Master'—because I was already initiated—I said: 'OK, I'm ready to make the commitment. Just send somebody. I'm ready, I'm ready to make the commitment.' It wasn't ten minutes before Tony Dagradi walked by. I said, 'It really was a great set,' and we just started talking. He started looking at the book I was reading, and we talked about it. I thought, 'Wow, that was quick!' The other Tony was right: just pray and look what happens. Tony Dagradi gave me this little wooden flute, and I went: 'Well, duh,' and that was it. Of course, I'd seen him before, but that was the first time we actually connected. I really felt like I had prayed and made a commitment, and it was answered. I actually liked the fact that he didn't notice me earlier. I liked that, because it said to me, 'He doesn't hit on everybody he sees. He's not like some musicians, you know? He's not 24/7.'"

Tony recalls with a laugh: "Then I had to go back to Boston, because there was no gig and no house or anything. So I went back to Boston, and then Joan came there. But then right when she came to Boston, I had a gig on Cape Cod."

Tony began to read Joan's books and pamphlets about Sant Mat and Kirpal Singh, the Master who had initiated Joan in 1972. Sant Mat means literally "the teachings of the saints." A related term is Surat Shabd Yoga: not a yoga of positions, but a yoga of meditation. To Tony, these writings "seemed like pure gold." He remembers saying to himself, "I can't find any flaw in this: this seems like the way to go." Kirpal Singh had left the body in 1974, after which the line had no living master until three years later in 1977, when Sant Ajaib Singh became the Master. When he visited the United States for the first time that same year, Tony went to see him immediately and received the initiation, on 7 May.

Tony is bound by the tenets of Sant Mat not to reveal any details of his inner spiritual experience. But he made some general statements for public consumption in the liner notes for *Sweet Remembrance*, a recording he made in 1987 (see pp. 75–79):

> "In this esoteric science each initiate is asked for cultivate and develop the five cardinal virtues of non-violence, truthfulness, chastity, love for all, and selfless service. In addition, an aspirant must follow a strict vegetarian diet, earn his or her own living in an honest manner, and keep a close watch over all thoughts, words, and deeds.... At the time of initiation, the Master instructs new seekers in a specific meditation technique and outlines signposts which the *jiva* (soul) will encounter on the inner planes."[11]

In the mid-1970s, Inner Visions continued performing in the Boston area. Tony recalled:

> "I felt that I was really working on music seriously, and it was a great experience for me putting a band together: presenting things, putting out flyers, trying to advertise a little bit. But I wasn't making much money, and I guess I was getting tired of that when I'd do a jazz gig. There are 200,000 students in Boston, and even if they aren't

going to a college of music, a lot of them play music. So most students will play for the door. That was a very normal thing. Book the gig at the Zircon, or Michael's Pub, or 1369, which were all places that would 'hire' musicians (basically you were working for the door)."

So Tony started looking for a band, not necessary a jazz band, with which he could go out on the road. He recalls:

"I almost took a gig with Wayne Cochran, who was the white James Brown. A lot of people have done that gig. Johnny Vidacovich did it, at least for a short time. The word got to me that they needed a saxophone player—one of their guys was leaving. I went and looked at the band. It was toward the end of his career: he was much more popular before, had had a much bigger band. At that point I think he only had about six horns when I saw him. But they were all doing steps; it was a show. I knew immediately I didn't want to do that."

The next band he considered, a well-known soul group called Archie Bell and The Drells, proved to be more appealing. In 1967, while waiting to be sent to the army in Germany, Bell had made a funky single called "Tighten Up," using a Houston soul band called the TSU Tornados for instrumental backup.[12] It became a million-record hit, top of the pop and R&B charts. Bell quickly formed The Drells and went on to make a number of other hits, including "Do the Choo Choo," "Dancing to Your Music," "Girl You're Too Young," "I Can't Stop Dancing," "Let's Groove," and "Showdown." Tony recalls:

"They were playing at the Boston Club, and I went to check them out. I might have sat in with them, I can't remember. They needed somebody, as somebody was leaving the band. So I said, 'OK, let me do this for a while.' I was glad I did it. The rhythm section was really great, really funky. But other than the rhythm section, it was a very ordinary soul group. The horn section was marginal. I remember taking the train down to Philadelphia and doing the first couple of gigs there: Jersey and Philadelphia. And then we did a tour: basically it was a kind of chitlin circuit thing. I did that for several months in 1976–77. One thing I remember: I took rice and beans with me to cook, and the other musicians always wanted them."

The repertoire presumably included the soul-disco hit "Everybody Have a Good Time" and other songs from the album *Where Will You Be when the Party's over*, issued in November 1976: the title song, "Dancin' Man," "Don't Let Love Get You Down," "I Bet I Can Do That Dance You're Doin'," "I Swear You're Beautiful," "Nothing Comes Easy," and "Right Here is Where I Want to Be."[13] (According to Tony, The Drells' recordings from this period were made with studio musicians in Philadelphia, not the touring band.)

James Singleton, shortly to become Tony's colleague in Astral Project, believes that Tony playing with such a band "was not only typical of jazz horn players of the time, but a big part of his subsequent style. This emphasis on the rhythm possibly contributed to Tony's intense rhythmic feel. Tork [David Torkanowsky] used to quote the old timers as saying, 'Every tub must stand on its own bottom,' which means that everyone is responsible for the beat, not just bass players and drummers."

At first, Tony had left Joan behind in their apartment in Boston. Then, for the last couple of weeks of The Drells' long tour, she moved out of the apartment and joined the band on the road. Tony recalls:

"At that point I think we were playing in L.A., and then the band was based out of Houston. Joan and I went to Houston, and the band had a little time off before the next tour would start up. I said, 'Well, no, I think I'm done. I think I've had enough.' So I had to make a decision about what to do now. Should I go to New York? But I was a little scared of New York, and when I'd talk to people there, they'd tell me how slow it was. Going to L.A. and being a studio guy didn't hold any attraction, although I think I would enjoy it now. Should I go back to Boston?...."

Joan had been to New Orleans, was acquainted with some artists on Jackson Square, and knew she could make some money there painting portraits. She told Tony, "Well, there's music in New Orleans." He remembers replying, "Yeah, I don't wanna play Dixieland." At that point in his life, "That's really the only thing I knew about New Orleans." Still, they went to the Crescent City and gave it a shot.

Notes

1. According to Walter Schweikardt, orchestra contractor at the Paper Mill Playhouse, Millburn, NJ, D'Addario played there "off and on for about ten years" before his death in July 1988, serving as contractor for the last year, and also worked as contractor for the Meadowbrook Theatre in Cedar Grove, NJ. E-mail message from Beth Johnson Tucker, Assistant to the CEO, Paper Mill Playhouse, 5 January 2006.

2. http://tonydagradi.com/biography.html; accessed 7 June 2005.

3. http://tonydagradi.com/biography.html; accessed 7 June 2005.

4. See http://www.berklee.edu/news/1749/gary-burton-and-berklee; accessed 25 September 2013.

5. See Richard J. Cook, Sr., *The Twentieth Century Limited, 1938–1967* (Lynchburg, VA: TLC Publishing, 1993).

6. Ernie Santusuosso, "Jazz Drummer D. Sharpe is Mourned," *Boston Globe*, 23 January 1987, section Arts and Film, 55; http://www.discogs.com/artist/D.+Sharpe; accessed 25 September 2013.

7. From a radio interview in early 1954, quoted in Doug Ramsey, *Take Five: The Public and Private Lives of Paul Desmond* (Seattle: Parkside Publications, 2005), 162.

8. For a recent version, see *The Mysticism of Sound and Music: The Sufi Teaching of Hazrat Inayat Khan*, rev. ed. (Boston: Shambhala, 1996).

9. Stanton Davis and Ghetto/Mysticism, *Brighter Days* (Outrageous Records 2, [1977?]). For a

description, see Lasocki, *A Higher Fusion*, 18.

10. Gene Roma has taught percussion at Berklee, the Newton Percussion Academy, and the Milton Academy. As a performer he has worked mostly with Broadway shows and tours, and eventually became a member of the Boston-based jazz trumpeter Johnny Souza's quartet (see http://www.johnnysouza.com/harborjazz.html; accessed 25 September 2013). He remained involved with eastern spirituality enough to play percussion on "The Command of the Lord," a track on *Compassion: Special Message from His Holiness the XIVth Dalai Lama* (Louisville, KY: Millennia Music, 2001).

11. Tony Dagradi, liner notes to his CD *Sweet Remembrance* (1987).

12. See Jeff Jarema, notes to *Tightening Up: The Best of Archie Bell & The Drells* (Rhino R2 71725, c1994).

13. Archie Bell & The Drells, *Where Will You Go When the Party's over* (Philadelphia International Records PZ 34323, 1976).

2. EARLY DAYS IN NEW ORLEANS

Tony and Joan arrived in New Orleans early in 1977 (he believes it was in January, February, or perhaps March). He started visiting clubs and "sitting in," which at that time, he notes, was "a rite of passage in the jazz world." Soon, he was spending a great deal of time at Lu & Charlie's jazz club on Rampart Street.[1] "I was there practically every night. I sat in there with everybody I could: [the pianist] Ellis Marsalis, [the drummer] James Black, whoever was there." Black's trio included Rusty Gilder on bass and David Torkanowsky on Fender Rhodes. Tony remembers liking Tork's playing. "He reminded me of Alan Pasqua, someone I had played with in Boston who was a really good pianist. Tork seemed to be the most contemporary pianist that I heard down here." Tony remembers only too well asking to sit in with this trio.

"James Black looked at me and he didn't think I could play, but he still said, 'OK, go on and play.' They were playing something like 'Impressions.' Tork played a solo, and when it came time for my solo, James Black just stopped playing (laughs). I said to myself, 'OK, I don't need a drummer.' But James actually got to a point where he would call me for gigs, too. He knew that I could play with him, and knew that I wouldn't back off."[2]

Tony's earliest advertised performance in New Orleans that I have been able to trace was with the James Black Ensemble at Jazz Fest on 15 April 1978, along with Black's girlfriend, the singer "Sister Mary" Bonnette; Earl Turbinton, alto sax; Roger Lewis, baritone sax; David Torkanowsky, piano; and James Singleton, bass.

Jazz outside Storyville (*ca.* 1980); from left to right, Tony Dagradi, James Singleton, Earl Turbinton, John Vidacovich

Tony also sat in on Bourbon Street, with Frogman Henry and Gary Brown, among others. "There seemed to be an interesting scene here. And after a bit people were calling me for gigs, and I started doing jazz gigs and meeting different people. I thought, 'OK, there's something here; it seems to be comfortable for me,' and I stayed."

One of the first people to hire Tony, for what was probably his first paid gig at Lu & Charlie's, was the jazz pianist, composer, and educator Willie Metcalf, Jr. (1930–2004), who had been living in New Orleans only a couple of years himself. Metcalf, a recovering heroin addict, had founded an Academy of Black Arts in Detroit in 1972, "a program designed to instill culture values and provide positive role models for Detroit's inner-city youth."[3] On moving to New Orleans in 1975, Metcalf brought the Academy with him, using it as a vehicle to persuade black youngsters away from drugs, crime, and violence, and teaching free summer workshops in music, dance, and chess. Tony remembers:

> "I saw Willie at Lu & Charlie's one night and sat in with him, sat in on a couple of tunes, and got to know him a little bit, and he liked what I was doing. So the next time he had a gig there, he called me for it. And I remember a lot of people were up there, and we didn't make much money individually."

Metcalf immediately involved Tony in his activities.

> "He had me helping with some of his students. I would help coach some of the ensembles. It wasn't far from my house: he was on Dryades,[4] I think, and I was living on Carondolet and 3rd or 4th Street—kind of Uptown, Garden District. At that time the kids who were going to this camp were, like, Wynton and Branford Marsalis and Donald Harrison and Terence Blanchard. They were around 15 or 16 at the time, and I was only 25, so it was pretty funny. They were all great players even then."

The next person to hire Tony was Frank Puzzullo, a jazz pianist who had been working with John Vidacovich in Al Belletto's band since coming to New Orleans in 1970, and had founded the jazz program at Loyola University in 1975. Puzzullo led a band that included two tenor sax players, among them Bob Sheppard. Tony recalls, "That's the gig where I met John and James Singleton for the first time. We did a couple of weekends at Lu & Charlie's." Feeling more settled, he then persuaded Charlie Bering, the music director at the club, to allow him to bring in his colleagues from Boston—James Harvey, Schuller, Sharpe, and Valente—for gigs on a couple of consecutive weekends in May.

> "I was up in Boston, just visiting. I said, 'Man, I got this gig down in New Orleans. Come on down. You can crash at my apartment, and we'll just work these two weekend gigs, and try to get some other gigs maybe.' They were all into it, because we were all young: do anything at that time. So we drove down in a van together. I think we drove straight from Boston to New Orleans without stopping: that's how crazy we were. And by the time I got here—we hadn't really slept or anything—I could hardly remember how to get to my apartment. The gig: the first weekend was really great.
>
> "And then D. Sharpe, who was a great drummer—played with Carla Bley and all these different people—was walking around my neighborhood. I lived around Corondelet and Washington. I remember that Joan was staying in the northeast while these gigs happened. Our landlord was really shocked to see these wild-looking guys crashing at our apartment

and told me that everyone had to leave. D. Sharpe ended up staying a few blocks away on Dryades at Willie Metcalf's studio. While walking back and forth he got mugged: some kids on bicycles came and knocked him down and hurt his hand, so he couldn't play. He was in shock. I called his wife, who was all upset, and I took him to Charity Hospital. Throughout the wait at the hospital he apologized to me for 'atttracting' negative energy. D. Sharpe was a constant source of inspiration to me, musically and spiritually. After he was treated at the hospital, I sent him home on a plane.

"James Black played the second weekend with us. He did a great job: everybody loved playing with him. And James is James: he had a little bit of attitude with him, but he enjoyed playing with everybody. I think everybody was like me: he knew that everybody was pretty serious about playing."

Tony soon discovered that, in order to make a living in New Orleans, you had to play many types of gig and many types of music.

"At Lu & Charlie's you'd hear people doing their jazz gigs, but in New Orleans everybody does a lot of different things. When I said, 'You know, I gotta make some money,' people would point me towards things like society work or big-band work. I did a lot of society work where you'd play for a carnival ball or a wedding, that kind of thing. It was part of what you did."

By February 1978, Tony was established enough in New Orleans to be listed—along with James Singleton and John Vidacovich—among the members of Musicians for Music, a non-profit organization founded by the bassist Ramsey McLean "to provide the musicians with a chance to escape the constraints of commercial bar and nightclub gigs."[5] McLean is quoted as saying, a month after Lu & Charlie's closed, "We don't want to poison the water we drink from, but the club owners aren't doing enough for the jazz musicians in this city. We're not working very much." Ironically, even though the organization was sponsored by the Louisiana Arts Council, the State Department of Culture, Recreation and Tourism, and the National Endowment for the Arts, the musicians were said to be doing a month-long series of concerts "for a minimal fee."

Professor Longhair
Towards the end of 1977, Tony became acquainted with the legendary New Orleans pianist and singer Professor Longhair (1918–1980), real name Henry Roeland Byrd, aka Roy Byrd, aka Fess, one of the fathers of both rhythm-and-blues and rock 'n' roll. It happened this way: Tony had done a gig in Puzzullo's band with the tenor saxophonist Andy Kaslow, the husband of Allison Miner. Miner (1949–1995), a co-founder of the New Orleans Jazz Fest in 1970 and one of its prime movers for the first five years, was one of the people who had rediscovered Longhair in 1971 and put his career on track. After moving away from New Orleans in 1974, Kaslow and Miner returned at the end of 1977, to find that Longhair's management deal had gone sour, so they were trying to kick-start his career once more. Tony, asked by Kaslow whether he had heard of Longhair, replied, "Well, I haven't been here long: I don't know who he is." So Kaslow took him to Tipitina's, the newly opened club named after a Longhair song, where the master was playing with only Alfred "Uganda" Roberts on congas and bongos. Tony recalled: "It was definitely a temple built to Fess, and when he got on the stage, it was like watching the high priest at the altar." Longhair had played with semi-regular groups since 1971. Now,

according to The Radiators' bassist Reggie Scanlan, who had been working with Longhair that year, Miner "was intent on changing the band and, [determination] being a hallmark of hers, did exactly that. With the exception of Uganda, everyone in the band was out."[6] As Tony relates,

> "Miner and Kaslow said, 'We're going to put a band together, a new band, for him to do some work.' So that was it. It was the two tenors, a real New Orleans thing. Fats Domino loved to have about ten tenors and a baritone in his band. Fess had a bunch of records where he had the two tenors and maybe a baritone. So it was a standard kind of thing. The instrumentation of the first band was piano, the tenors, bass, drums, guitar, and Uganda playing percussion."

Tony recalls that *Big Chief*, *The Last Mardi Gras*, and *Rum and Coke*, all albums made from live recordings at Tipitina's on 3–4 February 1978 with Kaslow,[7] represented "some of the first gigs that we did with Professor Longhair. The band wasn't together at all. The horns were scuffling, trying to get the stuff together and be able to tell one tune from another—definitely working by the seat of our pants." Nevertheless, these recordings constitute a remarkable document from the early days of Longhair's last working band: no fewer than twenty-eight songs, seventeen of them in multiple versions, covering the bulk of his repertoire.

The saxes generally play on the heads and add riffs in between. They are also given fifteen solos over the forty-six tracks, or about a third of the time.[8] As far as I can tell by ear, only one sax player takes the solo on a particular song, and it's the same player on each version. For example, Tony always solos on "How Long Has That Train Been Gone" and "Her Mind Is Gone"; Kaslow, on "Doin' it." Sometimes Longhair initiates the solos with a shouted "Blow," once or several times. It's generally easy to tell Tony from Kaslow. Even though Kaslow picked up some of the screaming style from Tony, his tone is less well-developed, he tends to stick to a few rhythmic figures, and the general effect is lumbering. Tony, in contrast, sounds beautiful, as well as screams he adds little runs and passing harmonies, and the general effect is exciting and joyous. Good examples are the three versions of "How Long Has That Train Been Gone" (all three albums) and the two versions of "Her Mind Is Gone" (*Big Chief* and *The Last Mardi Gras 2*) and "I've Got my Mojo Working" (*The Last Mardi Gras 1*). On "Jambalaya" (*The Last Mardi Gras 1*), coming in a little late without a signal, he takes his time to develop the solo, paraphrasing the theme instead of just "blowing," despite the repeated injunctions from Longhair.

Vincent Fumar in the *Times–Picayune*, remarked kindly about *The Last Mardi Gras*: "The music is representative of what Longhair was doing at the time, mainly sorting through different rhythm sections while slowly returning to a classic rhythm-and-blues horn sound via Kaslow. The tandem sax riffs by Kaslow and Dagradi were something of a breakthrough, representing one of the few times in recent years that the once-standard R&B device of using two saxophones— out of favor since about 1960—was faithfully restored.... The sax duo sounds fine, though somewhat under-miked and needing a baritone [sax] sound."[9] Ron Weinstock in *Living Blues* wrote that "The horns never quite make their presence felt ... though occasionally they or the guitarist do solo."[10]

It's worth mentioning that Tony did not go to Munich with Professor Longhair on what is reported to be 19 March 1978, a performance captured on the CD *Live in Germany*, when the two tenor saxophonists were Andy Kaslow and Lon Price.[11] The tour came up too quickly and Tony had a prior commitment: he was taking a few classes at the University of New Orleans.

The two-CD set *Byrd Lives!* is said to have been recorded live at Tipitina's the same year. It includes twenty-four songs (three of them in two versions), among them six not heard in

February.[12] Ice Cube Slim, the Tipitina's employee who preserved the tapes for twenty years before their commercial release, notes an important difference

> "between these recordings and all the others that have been released to date.... whenever Byrd was aware that he was being recorded—he wasn't aware here—he always became uptight and paranoid. What you have on this CD are the sounds of the relaxed and unhurried perpetual-motion Mardi Gras-machine that I inevitably heard spilling out of the club as I walked to the corner of Tchoupitoulas and Napoleon, with an evening of dancing and frolicking to the music of Byrd and his wonderful band ahead."[13]

(Tony comments wrily: "These might be great gig tapes, but nobody in the band was ever contacted for permission to release the tracks and certainly no one was ever paid for the recording.")

The saxes again add great drive and color to most songs, of course on the heads and also punctuating in the background throughout. Surprisingly, only five songs have sax solos: the first "Doin' it," "Whole Lotta Lovin'," "Hey Little Girl," "Fess's Boogie," and "Lucille." The first three solos are somewhat routine. But Tony's presence is felt on "Fess's Boogie," where he plays intensely with a mature tone, honking and squealing to great effect. On "Lucille," there is clearly a switch from the routine Kaslow to the exciting Tony at 1:55, after Fess shouts "Go, go, go!"

Tony found it an "amazing experience" working with Longhair:

> "Whenever we played at Tipitina's, it was packed. And Tipitina's wasn't renovated: it was just one low-ceiling box with no air-conditioning and a thousand people. Tipitina's was his home base, but we would do gigs around town: at the Dream Palace, at the Maple Leaf, and at Jed's; a couple of Jazz Festivals. We also went on a European tour—my first—in April 1979. We played in Stockholm, Oslo, and even above the Arctic Circle. I well remember that Stockholm's harbor was frozen and there was snow piled 12 to 15 feet deep on the sides of the road."

Advertisements in the *Times–Picayune* confirm Tony's recollection of Longhair's gigs. He worked at Tipitina's, generally on a double bill with other blues or funk bands, on 16, 31 December 1978, 3, 24–25 February, 21 April, 4 May, 30 June, 28 July, 25 August, 21–22 September, 6, 27–28 October, 24 November, 15 December 1979; and 1, 6, 25–26 January 1980. He also worked at the Dream Palace (30 December 1979, 19 January 1980), Jimmy's (3 August, 6 November 1979), Ole Man River's (23 February 1979), and Rosy's (1–2 May 1979), as well as three different performances at the Jazz Fest in 1979 (22 and 27 April, 6 May). A video made about Longhair by a well-known New Orleans video artist, Stevenson Palfi, includes a short clip from a concert at the Superdome in 1978, in which Tony and Kaslow can be seen standing in the middle front of the stage, riffing away while rocking back and forth.[14] A surviving private recording of the 1978 New Year's Eve performance at Tipitina's reveals a surprising development: Tony takes long and less riff-based solos on soprano sax on "Every Day I Have the Blues" and "I'm Moving on," although he still plays a funky tenor on "I've Got my Mojo Working" and "How Long."

For this band, Tony wrote a piece called "Mess o' Fess." "It was just a Professor Longhair kind of tune, and it was instrumental. We used to do it as our band tune before Fess would come out. That was fun. It was my first New Orleans-based composition."

Tony Dagradi *ca*. 1979–80

Both Tony and his Astral Project colleague John Vidacovich were part of a North American tour by Longhair's band in May–June 1979.[15] Robert Palmer noted, previewing an appearance by what was advertised as "Professor Longhair's New Orleans Blues Septet" at the Village Gate on 18–20 May[16]:

"He has successfully toured Europe and played engagements in New York and other major United States cities, but this is the first time he has put a band together and hit the American road for an extended period.... The first tour will take Professor Longhair up the Eastern seaboard from Washington to Canada.....

"New Yorkers will be able to hear for the time what Professor Longhair sounds like with a substantial band behind him. 'It's a full force' is how he described it a few days ago. 'I like a full, powerful rhythm section, and ever since I did "Big Chief"'—a classic of New Orleans syncopation, recorded in 1965—'I've been wild for big outfits.'...[17]

"The band includes some excellent young New Orleans musicians. The drummer, John Vidacovich, is generally regarded as the finest young modern-jazz percussionist in the city.... the tenor saxophonists are Andrew Kaslow, whose tight horn arrangements capture the flavor of Professor Longhair's celebrated early records, and Tony Dagradi...."[18]

Palmer, who had lived in New Orleans in the early 1970s and knew Longhair well, wrote later about this New York performance:

"He was fronting the tight, well-rehearsed band heard on *Crawfish Fiesta*; the dark, cavernous Village Gate was packed and jumping. Nobody was just sitting and listening; even the critics were up and dancing.

"I remember pouring sweat on the dance floor, beginning to lose myself in the irresistible rhythmic undertow, when I noticed a florid, flushed face looming up into my face. It was Alan Lomax, the distinguished folklorist who'd recorded Son House and the pre-Chicago Muddy Waters and so many other American masters for the Library of Congress, but he wasn't acting distinguished that night.... 'The music,' he roared. 'This music we're hearing, right here, right now, is at this very moment the best goddamn music that anybody could possibly be making, anywhere on this planet. This music is the center of the whole goddamn universe.'"[19]

The celebrated jazz critic Gary Giddins, who heard the same performances at the Gate, observed that "his five accompanists preceded him with a 45-minute set of their own, divagating between Grover Washington's middlebrow funk and more successfully realized Coltrane swing. When Longhair sat down at the keyboard, all the parts came together."[20]

The name Longhair himself gave to his new group, the Blues Scholars, referred back to a recording he made in November 1953 using the house band for J & M Studios, consisting of two saxophones (Lee Allen, tenor; Alvin "Red" Tyler, baritone), guitar, bass, and drums. Palmer described, as well as anyone ever has, the particular rhythmic appeal of Longhair's music in such a band:

"The music was irresistibly kinetic. Even by himself, Professor Longhair is a master of polyrhythms: his major contribution to New Orleans music has been to combine Caribbean rhythms and the city's rich African rhythmic heritage with the blues. But when he has a band to work with, he apportions the parts so that almost every instrument is playing a different contributing pattern. The horns pull against the steady chopping of the guitar, the drums embroider a syncopated bass part, and the Professor's piano adds another layer of rhythmic tension. Like the playing of an African drum orchestra or the funk of James Brown, this is music capable of setting each part of one's body moving to a different rhythm."[21]

Mike Joyce, reviewing the band's performance on 13 May at The Bayou in Washington DC, wrote: "Making one of his rare appearances away from New Orleans last night, Professor Longhair delighted the crowd at The Bayou with his exuberance, his wit and, of course, his infectious music.... His repertoire hasn't changed much in the last 25 years. He still performs 'Mardi Gras in New Orleans' and follows it with a florid rendition of 'She Ain't Got no Hair,' which is nicely supported by his band, The Blues Scholars."[22]

By the time Longhair recorded *Crawfish Fiesta* in November 1979, the horn arrangements had been well worked out. Although they are credited by Palmer to Kaslow, and on the record to both Tony and Kaslow, Tony remarked with a laugh: "A lot of things we worked out together, but I remember that one person was doing more." (Tony had far more experience in both playing and arranging than Kaslow, who later gave up the music business to work on a doctorate in behavioral science at Columbia University, then went into human relations work.[23]) On the recording, Tony is quite recognizable, although he really goes wild, with lots of honking and squealing. He himself feels that:

"The weakest part is the horn solos on that record, because they're not as correctly 'indigenous' as they should have been. If I did that record now, it would be much more correct. But that might have been the first real record I ever did. I was still thinking of Coltrane a little too much on those Longhair recordings. I should have been thinking about King Curtis. But I was trying. It was a night-to-night thing. Some nights I could do that, and other times I couldn't restrain myself from going a little further out."

One amusing story about the recording session:

"Dagradi recalled that on one song Fess declared, 'I want the tempo somewhere between 9 and 14.' Nobody had a clue to what he meant until he showed them the old metronome he used, with its numbers missing. In their place, Byrd had scratched his own numbers, and sure enough, right between '9' and '14' was the tempo he sought."[24]

Although Joyce and other writers have stated that Longhair recycled his material for his whole career, his recordings—both commercial and live—suggest that late in life he wrote or covered a number of new songs. *Crawfish Fiesta* is a roughly equal mixture of the old ("Bald Head," "Her Mind is Gone," "In the Wee Wee Hours," all first recorded in 1949), the newer ("Something on Your Mind," 1963; "Big Chief," 1964; "Whole Lotta Lovin'," 1971; "Cry to Me," 1972; "Willie Fugal's Blues," 1975), and the new: songs receiving their first recorded performance ("Crawfish Fiesta," "It's my Fault, Darling," "Red Beans," "You're Driving me Crazy").[25]

Crawfish Fiesta is generally recognized as the finest studio recording Longhair ever made, although there are other candidates.[26] Most importantly, he was in fine voice, without having to resort much to yodeling, and his piano playing sounded crisp. As a bonus, John Vidacovich was Longhair's liveliest drummer, and the sax section wails. In general, the band fills in the empty spaces in the music better than previous bands, so there are no longueurs. I even like those saxophone solos that Tony feels were not authentically in style, because they don't simply mimic the early solos of Robert Parker, Allen, Tyler, and others, but combine R&B figures with more sophisticated jazz phrasing and implied harmonies. John reported that Longhair continually taught him how to play certain rhythms, but no one has mentioned Longhair trying to teach Tony how to solo. I suspect that the "further out" quality of his solos tacitly received Longhair's approval, because he told an interviewer in 1978, "I'm a jazz kind of fellow inside and I have to listen to jazz; it helps me develop in the field that I'm in."[27]

Several reviewers made kind remarks about the saxophones on this recording. "The three saxes ... add a very important touch, contributing much to the overall sound" (Thomas J. Cullen III in *Living Blues*).[28] "From down the hall, the LP sounds like 50s R&B—Amos Milburn, say, or Cecil Gant—but that's mainly the three saxes, Fess's powerful boogie-woogie left, and the fact that most of the tunes are blues.... the Blues Scholars are tight, snappy, and perfectly locked into Fess's tricky groove" (Michael Goodwin in *The Village Voice*).[29] "The horn section's playing is equally stunning, ensembles tight, solos hot" (Michael Goldberg in *Down Beat*).[30] Jim Mentel in the *Boston Globe* wrote that "The horn section is tasteful."[31] Noah Shapiro in *Sing Out* singles out one sax moment: "In a wild remake of Fats Domino's 'Whole Lotta Loving,' [Longhair] yodels and scats like no one else, singing a delightful harmony bit with the sax solo."[32] In contrast, Robert Palmer in the *New York Times* noted that "There are plenty of riffing saxophones" in the "rocking band," but felt he "would have liked to hear more of Mr. [Mac] Rebennack's stinging guitar and perhaps a bit less of the saxophonists."[33]

On 30 January 1980, the night before *Crawfish Fiesta* was released, Professor Longhair died unexpectedly as his career was finally taking off. Tony and Andy Kaslow were among the pallbearers at Longhair's funeral on 2 February, along with another member of the Blues Scholars (Tony doesn't remember who), the soul singer Ernie K-Doe, and Quint Davis, director of Jazz Fest.[34]

Lagniappe

At the 1979 Jazz Fest, Tony played in two groups besides Longhair's (and Astral Project), one fusion and the other latin. Apart from the pianist–leader and Tony, the Archer Dunn Salsa Sextet featured his Astral Project colleague Mark Sanders on percussion (21 April). In Victor Sirker & The Circuit Breakers, Tony appeared in distinguished company with a couple of ex-Longhair sidemen—David Lee Watson, bass; and Earl Gordon, drums—as well as Sirker, guitar; Coco York, vocals; and Larry Sieberth, keyboards (22 April).

On 21 April, Tony started playing weekly through June at Tyler's Beer Garden, which had quickly become the most important jazz venue in the city under music manager Jonathan Rome, with the Alvin Young Quartet, including Michael Pellera, piano; Young, bass; and James Black, drums. Tony also played there with Astral Project, as we will explore in chapter 4.

Tony took part in another commercial recording in 1979: *Long Walk on a Short Pier*, a jazz-rock album by Sea Level, a band made up of former Allman Brothers Band sidemen.[35] But he wasn't present in person, as Dave Lynch explains:

"*Long Walk on a Short Pier* begins with [the keyboardist] Chuck Leavell's slick R&B/dance track 'Tear Down This Wall,' recorded by the band at Capricorn's studio in Macon but punched up with a horn section recorded at [Randall] Bramblett's old stamping ground of Sea Saint Studio in New Orleans, where he had recorded *Light of the Night*, his stellar—and far less slick—sophomore solo album released by Polydor in 1976. The horn section enlivens 'My Love,' another uptempo track written and sung by Leavell."[36]

Tony's tenor sound can be distinctly heard in the rocking ensemble riffs.

In 1980, Tony participated in another recording as a sideman, released the following year: Ron Cuccia's *Music from the Big Tomato*.[37] As usual, Vincent Fumar had insight into the album:

"Ron Cuccia stands alone in a field of performance—reciting poetry to jazz accompaniment—that is generally regarded as a defunct novelty.... Cuccia's imagery is terrifyingly vivid in 'When the Heat Comes Down,' a number about a New Orleans heat wave which is done in a classically intense beatnik style, with bass and drums (James Singleton and John Vidacovich) and saxophone obbligatos by Tony Dagradi.... 'Waterfall Me' ... is essentially a [John] Magnie-devised gospel vehicle with Dagradi's obbligatos a bit heavy on the commercial funk side. (Dagradi's recent *Oasis* album offers a much more complete picture of his talents.)"[38]

Tony supplies monkey-like squeals in the background on his tenor sax on the opening 'Monkey Jaw/Monkey Gras." The gospel-tinged "Bignonia" and "Water Rise: Well Within" both bring out Tony's best wailing rhythm-and-blues style on tenor. On the funky "Ain't it Just Like me" he takes out his soprano and swings just as hard, switching to tenor for the out head. He turns in a kind of sax-player's flute at the end of "Create Yourself," fluid but undeveloped in tone. The "darkened entrances" referred to in "Enter: The Dream" inspire apposite soprano sax punctuations. His screaming tenor well depicts the riotous "Riot Act." And on the concluding

"Trying' to Sing," which starts like "Hand Jive" then goes back to the prevailing gospel tone of the album, Tony's tenor squeals complete the revival-meeting atmosphere.

Notes

1. On the club, see "Interlude: Jazz at Lu & Charlie's: An Interview with Lula Lowe Lewis (2004)," in Lasocki, *A Higher Fusion*, 29–41.

2. Tony Dagradi, interview with Lula Lowe Lewis, 4 April 2004, for the Lu & Charlie's Preservation Society.

3. Keith Spera, "Willie Metcalf Jr., 74, Pianist, Jazz Mentor," *Times–Picayune*, 11 December 2004, section Metro, 04.

4. In the 1980s, Dryades Street was renamed Oretha Castle Haley Boulevard.

5. Alan Citron, "Musicians Help Themselves," *Times–Picayune*, 19 February 1978, section 2, 5.

6. Reported in Matthew Haggman, "Reggie's Apprenticeship"; posted on www.georgeporterjr.com/Chat/messages/3013.html; accessed 4 September 2005.

7. *Big Chief* (Santa Monica, CA: Rhino R2 71446 [1993]); *The Last Mardi Gras* (New York: Atlantic Deluxe SD 2–4001, pc1982); *Rum and Coke* (Santa Monica, CA: Rhino R2 71447, 1993; New York: Tomato TOM–2041, pc2002). *Ball the Wall*, also recorded at Tipitina's, probably on 10 March 1978, does not include the saxophones.

8. *Big Chief*: 'How Long Has That Train Been Gone," "I'm Movin' on," "She Walks Right in," "Her Mind Is Gone," "I've Got my Mojo Working," and "Doin' it"; *Rum and Coke*: "Whole Lotta Lovin'," "Doing it," and "How Long"; *The Last Mardi Gras 1*: "Jambalaya," "Got my Mojo Working," and "Doin' it"; *The Last Mardi Gras 2*: "Shake, Rattle & Roll," "Her Mind Is Gone," and "How Long."

9. Vincent Fumar, "Memories of a Mardi Gras Past," *Times–Picayune*, 25 June 1982, section Lagniappe, 8. According to Scanlan, Longhair had already been using two tenors in 1977: David Lastie and Lon Price. (See Haggman, "Reggie's Apprenticeship.") But Price left New Orleans that year. See Skip Spratt, "Lon Price," *Saxophone Journal* 30, no. 3 (January/February 2006): 30.

10. Ron Weinstock, review in *Living Blues*, no. 56 (spring 1983): 28–29.

11. Le Kremlin-Bicêtre, France: Fan Club Records FCD 97 (422273), cp1992. *The Taper's Almanac Professor Longhair Discography*, compiled by Bill DeBlonk, http://www.geocities.com/tapersalmanac/fess.html, accessed 14 October 2005, is the source of the date of 19 March 1978 for an "audience tape." Price confirms in Spratt, "Lon Price," 27, that he did one European tour with Longhair. A video of Professor Longhair's group on youtube labeled "Nice Jazz Festival 1979," showing Kaslow and Price, is in fact dated 7 July 1978 in the opening credits; see http://www.youtube.com/watch?v=PX1vwDe9Z94; accessed 28 September

2013. Is the Munich CD therefore from the same tour as Nice, the summer tour that Tony missed?

12. The title is a pun on "Bird Lives!," the phrase that Charlie "Bird" Parker's fans wrote on walls after his early death in 1955.

13. Ice Cube Slim, liner notes to *Byrd Lives!* (1998).

14. *Piano Players Rarely ever Play together*, produced and directed by Stevenson J. Palfi (New Orleans: Stevenson Productions, 1982); videocassette.

15. The tour included two nights at Jonathan Swift's in Boston, and one night (9 June) at the John Harms Englewood Plaza, Englewood, NJ. See Ernie Santosuosso, "Weekend: Two Clubs Revive Big-Band Nights," *Boston Globe*, 8 February 1980, section Arts/Films; advertisement in *New York Times*, 8 June 1979, C4.

16. See "Arts and Leisure Guide," *New York Times*, 13 May 1979, D35.

17. The original recording of "Big Chief" in 1964 (released on both sides of a 45 rpm record, Watch 45-1900), featured a fifteen-piece horn section; Longhair only played the piano, the singing and whistling being provided by the song's composer, Earl King.

18. Robert Palmer, "Prof. Longhair is Swinging at the Gate," *New York Times*, 18 May 1979, C13.

19. Robert Palmer, "Professor Longhair: Deep South Piano and the Barrelhouse Blues," in Pete Welding and Toby Byron, ed., *Bluesland: Portraits of Twelve Major American Blues Masters* (New York: Dutton, 1991), 175.

20. Gary Giddins, *Riding on a Blue Note: American Jazz and Pop* (New York: Oxford University Press, 1981), 110 (originally published in the *Village Voice*, June 1979).

21. Palmer, "Prof. Longhair is Swinging at the Gate."

22. Mike Joyce, "Professor Longhair," *Washington Post*, 14 May 1979, section Performing Arts, B13.

23. See http://www.college.columbia.edu/cct/spr99/46a.html; accessed 1 July 2005.

24. Grace Lichtenstein and Laura Dankner, *Musical Gumbo: The Music of New Orleans* (New York: W. W. Norton, 1993), 87–88, citing an interview that Tony gave to Lichtenstein, February 1992. For an account of the recording session, see Jason Berry, Jonathan Foose, and Tad Jones, *Up from the Cradle of Jazz: New Orleans Music since World War II* (Athens, GA: University of Georgia Press, 1986; reprinted, New York: Da Capo Press, 1992), 22–24.

25. Michael Goodwin, "Goodbye Professor, Goodbye Professor," *The Village Voice* 25 (3 March 1980): 59, does describe "Red Beans" as "a Bend City retread of two Muddy Waters tunes,

'Got My Mojo Working' and 'Louisiana Blues.'" And Noah Shapiro, review in *Sing Out!* 28, no. 1 (1980): 41, notes that "Crawfish Fiesta" is "an eccentric, delicate medley of 'A Tisket, A Tasket,' the Andrews Sisters' 'Drinking Rum and Coca Cola,' and, believe it or not, the 'Looney Toons' cartoon theme."

26. Palmer ("Professor Longhair: Deep South Piano," 174–75) votes for *House Party New Orleans Style: The Lost Sessions, 1971–72* (Rounder CD-2057, 1987). "In addition to its exuberance and intensity, and Longhair's rapport with both drummers [Edward "Shiba" Kimbrough and Zig Modeliste], on this record he leans more toward 'straight' blues.... *Crawfish Fiesta* ... is a fitting memorial, but *House Party* is the Longhair collection I'd take along to that desert island."

27. Max Jones, "I'm a Little Rowdy with my Playing: Professor Longhair Talks to Max Jones," *Melody Maker*, 1 April 1978, 44. Longhair also wrote some "oo-bop-sha-bam" type of scat singing into "Whole Lotta Loving" (e.g., on *Crawfish Fiesta*).

28. Thomas J. Cullen III, review in *Living Blues*, no. 47 (summer 1980): 24.

29. Goodwin, "Goodbye Professor."

30. Michael Goldberg, review in *Down Beat* 47, no. 6 (June 1980): 36.

31. Jim Mentel, review in *Boston Globe*, 28 February 1980, section Calendar.

32. Noah Shapiro, review in *Sing Out!* 28, no. 1 (1980): 41.

33. Robert Palmer, review in *New York Times*, 8 February 1980, C28.

34. Goodwin, "Goodbye Professor."

35. Sea Level, *Long Walk on a Short Pier* (Macon, GA: Capricorn Records CPN 0227, 1979).

36. Dave Lynch, review on allmusic.com; accessed 9 October 2013. Lynch claims that, because of Capricorn's bankruptcy, this album wasn't issued in the United States until 1998. But through gemm.com I picked up a cut-out LP of the album with a copyright date of 1979.

37. Ron Cuccia, *Music from the Big Tomato* (New Orleans: Armageddon Record ARM 10, cp1981).

38. Vincent Fumar, review in *Times–Picayune*, 15 May 1981, section Lagniappe, 10.

3. *OASIS* AND NOSE

Gramavision Label Signs Up Saxophonist Dagradi by Wanda Freeman
Billboard, 18 April 1981

NEW ORLEANS—"I'm unknown and they're unknown, so we'll grow together," says jazz saxophonist Tony Dagradi, who, after 15 years of playing professionally, has signed on with his first record label, the 1½-year-old Gramavision Inc.

His album *Oasis* also features trombonist Gary Valente and drummer D. Sharpe, both of Carla Bley's band, with whom Dagradi tours regularly. It's the first LP on which Dagradi stars, but the musician has participated on other records, including Professor Longhair's *Crawfish Fiesta* (Alligator Records).

Dagradi leads a band called Astral Project, and has performed often with Gatemouth Brown and Nat Adderley. He was literally discovered, Hollywood-style, by Gramavision president Jonathan F. P. Rose when Rose was visiting New Orleans in 1979.

Rose produced *The Europeans* movie soundtrack, which he says got him off the ground, and reports that Gramavision now has Ralph Simon's *Time Being* and pianist Earl Rose's *Solo*.

Dagradi says he has a three-year, three-record contract with Gramavision. "This was the first opportunity that seemed comfortable to me. The deal was very nice. I could call the tunes; there's no interference musically. I trusted them with the mix."

He recently recorded *Social Studies* for Watt Records with Carla Bley's band, and hopes his next Gramavision record will be with Astral Project, which was formed three years ago and plays three to six nights a week here.

The group is billed with Nancy Wilson and Ramsey Lewis at the Saenger [Theater] for the New Orleans Jazz and Heritage Festival, and will also perform outdoors at the Fest. "I hope to pick up some management then," Dagradi says.

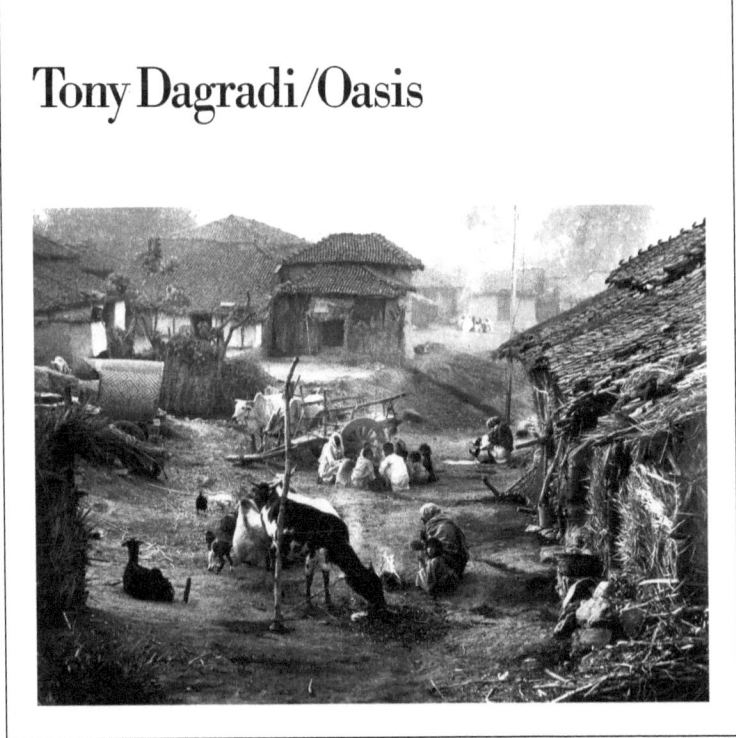

Oasis

Oasis. TD, ss (3), ts (1–2, 4–7); Gary Valente, trombone; James Harvey aka Snake, p (4, 7); Kenny Werner, p (1–3, 5–6); Ed Schuller, b; D. Sharpe, d. Recorded at Grog Kill Studios, Woodstock, NY, March 1980. Gramavision GR 8001, 1980.
1. Urban Disturbance (TD) (5:18)
2. Oasis (TD) (5:23)
3. Juanita (TD) (5:54)
4. Ghana Folk Song (James Harvey) (4:33)
5. Radiation (TD) (8:31)
6. Esther (D. Sharpe) (7:06)
7. Green Jacket (James Harvey) (5:40)

To work with him on his first Gramavision record, *Oasis*, recorded in March 1980, Tony chose three of his Inner Visions colleagues—Gary Valente on trombone, Ed Schuller on bass, and D. Sharpe on drums—and alternated the piano chair between two New York pianists: Kenny Werner, whom he had met at Berklee, and James Harvey aka Snake aka JJ, a prodigy who attended the New England Conservatory. Valente and Sharpe had become members of the Carla Bley Band by this time, but they were not, as we might expect, the ones who arranged for *Oasis* to be recorded in Bley's own recording studio, Grog Kill Studios, in Woodstock, NY. Tony noted: "That was strictly a deal between Jonathan Rose at Gramavision and Carla and her then-husband Mike Mantler. It was a real studio in the basement of her house in Woodstock: a very comfortable space away from the city. All of Carla's records from that period were recorded there." Of the seven compositions on *Oasis*, four are by Tony, two by Harvey, and one by Sharpe. (Tony's "Urban Disturbance" was to remain in the repertoire of Astral Project until at least 2001.) At this early stage in the development of all the musicians, the compositions generally make a stronger impression than the solos.

The introduction to the opening "Urban Disturbance," over a C pedal, has a Jazz Messengers feel. The tune, in AA' form, with the 16 + 22 measure structure creating a sense of urban disease, develops the opening motive, melodically or rhythmically. In the short solos, curiously, everyone's sense of swing has virtually no rhythmic inequality. Valente plays fast and blurred, intermixed with slower phrases. Tony plays in a more linear fashion, but also employs contrasting phrases, soon squeezing into the high register with squealing and wailing—a sense of non-melody as melody. His tone is coarser than it became by the mid-80s. Werner, too, plays in a linear style. His solo is followed by a wild joint improvisation between Valente and Tony. On the out chorus, the melody of the eight measures of C pedal is replaced with a jagged motive that further develops the material. Tony's cadenza on the final held chord anticipates his later style.

The A section of the title song, "Oasis," written in 7/4 time, also has a Jazz Messengers feel, because the melody is in parallel fourths. But the B section is funkier, if only because it has a single, syncopated line. The whole piece (intro, AB, coda) is built on a two-measure bass ostinato and a two-chord vamp (Am7, G7sus4). Werner plays a nice introduction, with syncopated "floating" chords. Valente and Tony manage to sound like more than a duo. Tony takes a funky solo, leading into Coltrane-like runs, then back to funk. Werner's solo emphasizes the syncopations from his intro, mixing McCoy Tyner with Bobby Timmons. After one chorus of the head, Valente and Tony trade fours with more continuity of line than usual on such occasions.

The head of "Juanita," a lyrical lady, has some structural features in common with "Oasis," despite being in AABA form. It's built on a two-measure bass ostinato featuring leaps of a fifth and a minor seventh or sixth. The A section alternates Ebmaj7/C and Dbmaj7/C chords; the B section simply moves up a fourth to Abmaj7/F and Gbmaj7/F. Tony's soprano sax sounds a little thin in the high register, but perhaps that was the result of the recording. He solos in a Coltrane-like manner over a static accompaniment dominated by Werner's Tyner-like chords. Werner's solo features busy chords, then a fast melodic arc.

Harvey's "Ghana Folk Song" opens with Tony (doing a good imitation of Ornette Coleman's dirge style) and Valente unaccompanied in unison. Then the rhythm section enters to create an atmosphere of jubilation—Ornette feted in Ghana. As two critics pointed out, the tune appeared on the album *Old and New Dreams* with Don Cherry, Dewey Redman, Charlie Haden, and Ed Blackwell the previous year under the title "Togo" and attributed to Blackwell, "based on a Ghanese traditional."[1] Tony told me that "Harvey learned the piece from Don Cherry before anybody recorded it; at the time he knew it only as a Ghana folk song." The solos are on a highly rhythmic vamp. Tony wails in his solo. A riffy refrain then leads to a variation on the head, followed by the head proper, and a short, chaotic solo from Harvey. The refrain and head return. Tony comes in with a second solo, with Valente underneath him plus what seems to be his own overdub, more forward in the balance. The track fades out.

Because of its prominent minor seconds, imparting a Middle Eastern flavor, Tony's "Radiation" could with more justice have been called "Oasis." Once more the piece is built on a two-measure bass ostinato containing leaps. The first eight measures (A) set out a syncopated melody over a D Phrygian chord. The next eight measures (B) have a variant of this melody over C7(b9, b13). A returns with the melody an octave higher. And finally C presents a stretched-out variant of the melody over a chord sequence. But the "blowing form"—that is, the structure for the solos—only alternates A and B. The best part of Werner's short solo is the fully chorded version of the theme. Valente proves busy again, with some nicely judged slower phrases. Tony's solo opens with low growling, then moves on to "free" runs and squeals. The head comes to an end, then there's an unexpected four-note bass ostinato that serves as backdrop for a conga-sounding drum solo. The head returns again, with shrieks on the last note.

Sharpe's "Esther" has the flavor of an Ornette dirge, with Valente taking the role of Don Cherry, modified by Werner's fills. As the rhythm section creates a busy background, Tony plays his best solo on the disc, with high repeated notes, leading to a passage that's lyrical but intermixed with growls and controlled use of the altissimo register without squeals. Valente is all blustery bursts. The dirge returns, moving to a peaceful end.

Harvey's second tune, "Green Jacket," begins like a slow, "walking" version of Monk's "Crepuscule with Nellie," with the composer doing a good Thelonious imitation behind. The piece then picks up tempo and takes on a Charles Mingus character, with a humorous eruption at the end. Harvey's short arc of a solo is reminiscent not of Monk but of Cecil Taylor. He then plays at times wildly active dissonances under the two horn solos: Valente all staccato bursts and smears; Tony more linear than usual. The final head is followed by the Monkish introduction.

Oasis received positive reviews from *Cadence* and *Jazz Journal International*, two magazines who don't pull any punches, although both reviewers were preoccupied with tracing the influences on both the playing and the composing. The longest and most detailed was by Kevin Whitehead in *Cadence*:

> "Those who delight in such matters can have a field day spotting the stylistic allusions that crop up intermittently on Tony Dagradi's *Oasis*—allusions to: Carla Bley's big band (and related units: Charlie Haden's Liberation Music Orchestra and Robert Wyatt's

'Ruth' band; and related soloists: Haden, Roswell Rudd, Gary Windo, Terry Adams), the composing and arranging of Charles Mingus (James Harvey's 'Green Jacket'), Coltrane the sopranoist, Dave Holland's intro to *Conference of the Birds*.... On first listening I was put off some by these stylistic derivations, though the musicians never wear out a single mask, and do reveal themselves. But the quality of this impeccably played (and recorded) music won me over. There are a lot of reasons for *Oasis*' success: energy and good humor; a nosegay of pretty, catchy melodies (of which D. Sharpe's rapturous 'Esther' may be the prettiest), some unshowy arranging that turns blowing vehicles into something a bit more elaborate and texturally satisfying (Dagradi makes very efficient use of only two horns, occasionally overdubbing them for added richness), [and] the rhythm section.... Dagradi's rough-edged, throaty tenor (judiciously vibratoed) varies in tone from stridency to bassoon-like thickness.... *Oasis* is like an old Blue Note date with another fifteen years of jazz history and sophistication under its belt. Not 'important' or 'historically significant' (except as all good music is), but extremely enjoyable listening."[2]

The distinguished British critic Chris Sheridan also wrote perceptively in *Jazz Journal International*:

"The use of two Carla Bley alumni (Valente, Sharpe) is not the only reason why this music reflects her contemporary influence, nor is hers the only influence explored by the musicians on this bustling, good-humored album. There are the omnipresent Coltrane, spots of Mingus and Coleman, contemporary impressionism à la ECM, and even a hint of Jazz Crusaders funk.... Dagradi has absorbed much Coltrane—also much Coleman. But he is full of ideas, and his vigorous lines swing infectiously. Valente has drawn on Roswell Rudd, clearly—but he, too, solos strongly throughout. Both are men to watch, for this album, for all its influences, is a most promising and enjoyable debut."[3]

Giving the album four and a half stars, Michael G. Nastos remarked tersely on allmusic.com: "An all-original, creative jazz program with Kenny Werner (p) and Gary Valente (tb); this was a hard-blowing date. A nice cross-section between improvisational and ethnic ideals."

New Orleans Saxophone Ensemble

The New New Orleans Music: New Music Jazz. The New Orleans Saxophone Ensemble: TD, ts, leader; Earl Turbinton, Jr., ss, as; Fred Kemp, ts; Roger Lewis, bs. Recorded at Ultrasonic Studios, New Orleans, Louisiana, 21 October 1985. UPC 011661206625. Rounder CD 2066, cp1988.
1. NOSE Blues (TD) (5:12)
2. In a Sentimental Mood (lyrics, Manny Kurtz; music, Duke Ellington) (4:28)
3. Amazing Grace (trad.) (5:55)
4. Gemini Rising (TD) (4:25)
5. Radiation (TD) (7:30)
Coupled with: The Improvisational Arts Quintet (Edward "Kidd" Jordan, ss, ts; Kent Jordan, fl, piccolo; Clyde Kerr, Jr., tpt; Darryl Levine [i.e., Darrell Lavigne], p; Elton Heron, b; Alvin Fielder, d; Johnathan Bloom, perc [6]): 6. River Niger; 7. New Found Love; 8. Blues for A.T.
  "Gemini Rising" reissued on *Modern New Orleans Masters* (Rounder 2072, 1990) and *City of Dreams: A Collection of New Orleans Music* (Rounder 11661-2197-2, 2007).
  "NOSE Blues" reissued on *That's Core Jazz*, Vol. 2 (Line COCD 9.01125, 1991).

The liner notes identify Tony as the leader of the New Orleans Saxophone Ensemble, and although they don't say so, he also did all the arrangements: of his own three pieces as well as the two standards. He told me: "The music recorded accurately represents what we were doing at the time. Roger Lewis liked 'Gemini Rising' so much he had me write an arrangement for the Dirty Dozen.[4] And, because of the Dozen's recording, 'Gemini' has become a New Orleans brass-band standard."

"NOSE Blues" is a study in riffs, solo punctuations, walking bass, and composed interludes like big-band solis. Turbinton's solo style on alto emphasizes fast scales in a discursive manner; Kemp, Tony, and Lewis later show him how to make scales interesting (and Lewis vies for the title of fastest baritone on earth).

On Ellington's seductive "In a Sentimental Mood," Turbinton plays the melody in a Johnny Hodges-like fashion on alto, followed by effective countermelodies and big-band soli-style close harmonies. Turbinton takes a scale-based solo over a walking bass in the baritone, and also has the coda after an abbreviated out chorus.

The arrangement and performance of "Amazing Grace" turn the famous hymn, with its message of forgiveness and redemption, into a gospel of funk. A funky statement of the head leads to a funky riff and a solo by Kemp based on fast bursts of sound. After a harmonized riff is punctuated by a further riff, Lewis enters with a riffy solo, turning more Coltrane-like, and finally the others enter against it in free fashion, culminating in wild chaos. The head returns in a different harmonization (see p. 150), and Tony takes the funky coda against sustained chords.

The arrangement of "Gemini Rising" that Lewis liked so much is a compilation of funky riffs, made even more effective by having Turbinton on soprano to create a beautiful soundscape. The varied solo segments have the opening riff as a constant background. The head returns and terminates abruptly and effectively.

My favorite arrangement, contrasting beautifully with the original version on *Oasis*, is the concluding "Radiation." Tony begins with the opening motive of the original bass ostinato, then overlaps it in the four voices. That leads into his passionate free solo, at once Eastern and bluesy, and he continues by playing the melody at the same level of intensity in the head, during which the harmonizing brings out the Eastern influence. Turbinton's soprano solo is more effective this time because he uses Eastern scales. It leads straight into a varied statement of the head, beginning with half of the *a* phrase, then the *d* phrase, and on to the overlapping opening motive. Tony takes the coda as another passionate free solo.

The reviews were mixed. Milo Fine in *Cadence* sniffed: "The New Orleans answer to sax-quartet mania is pleasant-sounding and clearly rooted in the jazz tradition. However, with their rather standard arrangements of standard material and generic originals, they add little creative substance to the genre."[5] More positive was Lloyd Sachs, later a strong supporter of Astral Project, in the *Chicago Sun-Times*: "Drawing a joyous bead on 'In a Sentimental Mood,' 'Amazing Grace,' and three Dagradi originals, the quartet applies a buoyant light touch to both its harmonizing and independent investigations."[6] Mike Joyce in the *Washington Post*, while noting the group's inspiration, also saw its originality: "The influence of the World Saxophone Quartet has become so pervasive that it's impossible to listen to this group and not be struck by the resemblance, both in terms of material ('In a Sentimental Mood') and execution. But because the arrangements are often propelled by a strutting New Orleans pulse, and the horns coalesce and play off one another in such colorful and inventive fashion, the music soon develops a thrust and personality all its own."[7] The most perceptive critic was Vincent Fumar in the *Times–Picayune*, who noted: "The four saxophonists don't just settle on playing riffs while each takes a solo turn. There are gingerly harmonized figures as well as riffs, and the harmony also is gorgeous. 'In a Sentimental Mood' is splendid in its ensemble smoothness, while 'Amazing Grace' is powered by rugged solos and dissonant interludes."[8]

Notes

1. ECM 1154, 1979. For the critics, see the reviews cited below.

2. Kevin Whitehead, review in *Cadence* 7, no. 3 (March 1981): 78–79.

3. Chris Sheridan, review in *Jazz Journal International* 34, no. 8 (August 1981): 30.

4. "Gemini Rising" is included on Dirty Dozen Brass Band, *Voodoo* (New York: CBS Records, 1989); re-released on *The Dirty Dozen Brass Band* (New York: Columbia/Legacy, 1997).

5. Milo Fine, review in *Cadence* 15, no. 5 (May 1989): 81–82.

6. Lloyd Sachs, review in *Chicago Sun–Times*, 5 January 1989, section 2, Features, 40.

7. Mike Joyce, review in *Washington Post*, 22 January 1989, g.

8. Vincent Fumar, review in *Times–Picayune*, 2 December 1988, section Lagniappe, 14.

4. ASTRAL PROJECT, 1978–85

Within a year of his arrival in New Orleans, Tony had heard all the modern jazz players in town and was drawn to three of his own generation: David Torkanowsky (b. 1956) on keyboards, James Singleton (b. 1955) on bass, and John Vidacovich (b. 1949) on drums. "I looked at everyone as potential band members and I put together the best." James had recently arrived in New Orleans himself, on New Year's Eve 1976, after dropping out of North Texas State University (now University of North Texas) to work with the blues artist Clarence "Gatemouth" Brown. Tork had grown up in the Crescent City. Both Tork and James, like Tony, had briefly attended Berklee. John, a native of New Orleans, had studied music at Loyola University, with many philosophy and religion courses on the side. Already a seasoned professional, he had started to make recordings at the age of 13, worked steadily with Al Belletto's groups, spent the best part of a year gigging in Italy, and founded three groups of his own.

Tony's mind went back to Inner Visions:

"When I got to New Orleans, I really wanted to put something together that would continue that: offer me a forum to compose and to play what I wanted to play. Because I knew that I would be playing as a sideman with other people, to get over and get by, and I wanted to have something that I was doing for myself. I had that in the back of my mind all along. As soon as I got here, and as I met more people, I got excited about the idea. And finally, I played with John and James and David in different situations, so I knew that I wanted to play with them."

With these compatible musicians, Tony put together a fusion-oriented group, similar to Ghetto/Mysticism.

"I had James mostly playing electric bass, which I don't even think he owns anymore. David was playing electric keyboards, and we didn't have guitar at the time. We did a lot of things that were very groove-oriented. Of course, we still do that today, but then they were more funk–groove-oriented. Johnny once characterized it as 'James Brown on acid.' It was very funk, locked-in grooves, where we would just blow over the grooves."

Tony remembered that Ghetto/Mysticism "had a full rhythm section: guitar, bass, drums, keyboards, a killer percussionist (Les Lumley). It was so glorious that I wanted to have a percussionist, too." James had worked with Mark Sanders (b. 1953) and recommended him, so Tony agreed to give him a try. Tony appreciated the addition:

"Mark was great. Mark and Johnny had to work to develop a certain partnership. And they did. Mark had real strong Cuban influences, and he brought that to the band. So we would go there with him. A percussionist is out of his element when you're just playing straight-ahead swing. There's not really an essential place for that, but there is a little zone in which you can play. Which he found: he did that. And not only was he in the tradition of what was going on at the time, he was also a very nice colorist. He would pick up a little thing and go 'whissh, purr.' So he would accentuate things; not necessarily be locked into a time-keeping role. He was very flexible. That was also a nice part of the band."

The new group needed a name. After the success of The Blues Project in the 1960s, "Project" had become a fashionable appendage. "Astral" referred to the notion that, as Tony put it, "the astral plane is a spiritual plane where everything's more refined, more beautiful than on the physical plane. So Astral Project was an attempt to create in music what was a little beyond the physical plane."

James confirmed the mixed nature of the style:

"Tony was the leader of the band. He started the band. He had a profound and very mature compositional style. He had already composed in different styles. He had clearly matched his compositional style to his playing style. But when he started the band, he wanted to get into groove-oriented music. I was playing electric bass a lot of the time. The fusion thing in jazz was still very strong. Bands like Weather Report and Return to Forever were touring. Tony had had a deep background in rhythm-and-blues himself. He had definitely come up in what was called the Energy Music School, where the emphasis was on high energy and intensity, perhaps less on lyric quality."

No one in the group can remember the exact time and place of its first gig. There's little chance that it took place at Lu & Charlie's, where Tony had been sitting in, because the group does not appear in the surviving records from July–December 1977 and the club closed on 1 January 1978. But Tony remembered the group's first Jazz Fest (the New Orleans Jazz and Heritage Festival) on 7 April 1978: "It was on a little stage, and the Jazz Fest was really small. I remember the whole fairgrounds was open, and anyone could walk right up to the stage on any stage." John added: "Yes, pull your car right up to the stage. Pull your drums out there. Girls pouring out of the cars, drinking beers, hiding momma under the blanket. Kicks."

The group told me it has played at every Jazz Fest from 1978 through the time of writing, 2014. I say "told me" because it does not appear in the official listings for 1979. But Tony believes that the listing for the "David Torkanowsky Quintet featuring Bobby McFerrin" that year "probably" referred to Astral Project. John has certainly participated every year since the festival's inception in 1970.

Tony mentioned to the New Orleans journalist Geraldine Wyckoff that this first configuration of Astral Project covered Grover Washington material.[1] He said the same thing to me, adding:

"We were also doing a few covers, like some funky covers. One of the things that was the most interesting was we'd do a tune by Dewey Redman ['Qow']. That one stayed with us a long time. We did a Gato Barbieri arrangement of 'Ruby, Ruby' and probably some Headhunters kind of stuff. Also there was one record [*Hear & Now*] that Don Cherry had that was sort of fusion-y: the whole record was sort of a fusion thing that he did based on some oriental-sounding scales. So we did a little bit of that as well."

Astral Project alone could not provide a steady living, so its members had to take a variety of other gigs: jazz whenever possible, but also blues, rhythm-and-blues, and other popular genres, in which they also put their heart and soul. As the pianist Henry Butler put it at the time: "John Vidacovich and Tony Dagradi are excellent jazz musicians, but they're also excellent musicians from an eclectic standpoint. It's a way of life."[2] As we will see in chapters 5 and 6, Tony played regularly with Ramsey McLean and also toured with the Carla Bley Band.

The celebrated vocalist Bobby McFerrin spent seven months in New Orleans in 1979, before moving on to San Francisco and fame. He reminisced:

Astral Project, *ca.* 1980; from left to right, David Torkanowsky, John Vidacovich, Tony Dagradi, James Singleton, Mark Sanders

"I had the most wonderful time of my life in New Orleans—I stayed out all night and slept all day. The first time I heard Astral Project was when they were with Luther Kent. Then I heard Tony, David, James, and Johnny play separately. I was really taken by them and everything they were doing. I had just driven into town from Baton Rouge and I asked if I could sit in. They said, 'Sure, just wait until the last number.' I can't remember what we did, but it was really up tempo. They just kicked it off, but I kept up with them. For about six weeks I just kept sitting in with them here and there. They asked me to do some regular gigs with them, which I did until I left."[3]

McFerrin added: "That group offered me a chance to get away from the piano and be a singer—concentrate on one thing. So that was a really good experience. Those cats are monsters: stellar musicians."[4] He also credits the members of the group with being his first teachers in jazz. "We'd start a tune in one place and end up in a whole other room. They were constantly playing with the tunes, playing with the changes, playing with the keys, playing with the feel. It was like going to school because, until that point, I never fronted a band before. They taught me that. So when I left them and went to another situation, I sort of knew what to do."[5] James returned the compliment: "We worked a lot around New Orleans, including many, many nights on Bourbon Street, and we learned a lot about collective improvisation with him." The group invited McFerrin back for gigs at Jazz Fest in 1980–83.

Astral Project's main gig in 1979 took place at the Old Absinthe Bar, 400 Bourbon Street, in the French Quarter, three or four nights a week.[6] The group would play from 10:00 pm until 2:00 am. Then—and this is what McFerrin was referring to—the members would leave their instruments in place and, after a brief break, perform in a celebrated New Orleans blues big band, Luther Kent and Trick Bag, until 6:00 am. Going far beyond the blues, the band presented a wide range of styles, from city and jump blues to big-band jazz fusion, jazz pop, funk, and fervent ballads, including instrumentals.

James Singleton has written about his experience with Trick Bag:

"Being on the bandstand with Charlie [Brent] (and Luther) was an education and a revelation. It was about being a troubleshooter, swingin' at any tempo, and getting to the bottom of the basics. Oftentimes tunes would be repeated. This aspect of Bourbon Street really annoyed me, but Charlie and Luther (and of course Johnny V) showed me that 'it ain't the tune, it's the man playin' it.' They played every note like it was the last chance for romance and the first, fresh scent of seduction. The band always seemed to be on."[7]

The well-known cornet player Nat Adderley (1931–2000), younger brother of the alto saxophonist Julian "Cannonball" Adderley, made an extended visit to New Orleans in 1980. He played at Tyler's Beer Garden, located Uptown on Magazine Street, fourteen times with the house rhythm section of Tork, James, and John and various horn players between 24 March and 17 April. Four of the gigs were advertised as being with this rhythm section plus Tony and Mark Sanders, or in other words, the full personnel of Astral Project.

As a side-benefit of the Adderley sessions in 1980, Astral Project continued to play a weekly gig at Tyler's for the remainder of that year (advertised 24 April–4 November). Tony remembers that "The gigs were very loose and a lot of fun." At the same time, the Old Absinthe Bar gig continued weekly until 12 June, when the bar changed owners and instituted a different music policy. Then the group switched to the newly opened Faubourg (advertised 4 July–17 October), and in the New Year to the Blues Saloon (advertised 18 January–14 March 1981).

Recall that after Tony signed a contract with Gramavision in 1980 to make three albums, he recorded the first one, *Oasis*, immediately, using his colleagues from Inner Visions and two New York pianists. The second album, *Lunar Eclipse*, was recorded a year later, this time using his Astral Project colleagues: Tork, James, John, and Mark, and released in June 1982. He announced it at Jazz Fest on 1 May that year as "our newest album," so he could certainly view it as the group's rather than his own, even though it came out under his name. He composed all the pieces: "Les deux couleurs," "Duplicity ," "Heart to Heart," "Lunar Eclipse," and "Whirl." (For a description of this recording, see Lasocki, *A Higher Fusion*, chapter 2.)

Tony summed up Astral Project's experience in its first few years:

"Initially, I had a big push and I got a lot of gigs around town, and that was the end of my vision at that point. We would do things that would come up, but not too much. After a couple of years, I said to myself: 'Must be time to do something else.' But no, it just retained an identity, and people kept calling for gigs. At different points, when I was thinking at the back of my mind that we must be done, this must be over, David picked up the ball and booked the band—locally, anyway."

James confirmed Tork's role in the booking: "There was a period where he was very proactive. And he was coming up with a lot of these gigs that we did before it really changed, before the

World's Fair. He was very aggressive about the band for a while."

As we will see in chapter 5, an abrupt turn in Tony's own career made the continuation of Astral Project more difficult. In 1980, soon after he signed the contract with Gramavision, he also joined the Carla Bley Band and toured with it until 1985. That gig took him out of New Orleans, and mostly to Europe, a few times a year for several weeks at a time. In 1982, Astral Project gave only seven advertised performances, and the number of advertised performances increased to only nine in 1983. Then it dropped abruptly to four in 1984, the year of the World Exposition, which drew musicians (and audiences) away from the bars and clubs. After that, many venues folded, and the wealth of gigs in oil-boom New Orleans abruptly dried up.

Musically, during the early 1980s Astral Project went through a series of parallel evolutions, as James noted:

"Tony definitely formed the band, and when he formed the band he had a vision and he had compositions and he was the strongest player in the band, to my ear. Gradually, through time, it evolved into more of a cooperative thing. And he tangled a bit with Tork, because Tork is the son of a conductor and a great leader. Tork was such a strong personality and such a strong musical presence that what people talk about as 'shifting gears' would often happen during his solo. And then how do you get back to the place where Tony wants you to be?

"After the band had been together for a few years, everyone's influence became pervasive. We had group compositions. We had compositions that we improvised in rehearsal and that we would do on the gig, that Tony hadn't written any more than anybody else. It just evolved. We had this piece called the 'Monkey Parade'—I remember that. It became a kind of soprano saxophone and *quica* duet—Mark Sanders' *quica*, the

Brazilian *quica*—and a detuned electric bass—kind of a slapped bass—combined with Johnny's ratty parade snare drum. That's when we started really getting a group organic awareness that probably went beyond Tony's original idea."

Above all, as Jonathan Tabak put it, Astral Project "became an artistic haven where, free from the restrictions of specific genres or a leader's requirements, they could experiment with new ideas and influences in a totally supportive, comfortable environment."[8]

Notes

1. Geraldine Wyckoff, "Astral Project Blasts off Jazz Month," *Gambit Weekly*, 29 September 1992.

2. Quoted in Vincent Fumar, "Henry Butler Shows off a New Sound," *Times–Picayune*, 21 July 1989, section Lagniappe, L7.

3. Quoted in Vincent Fumar, "Bobby McFerrin Solos with Unusual Jazz Style," *Times–Picayune*, 20 May 1988, section Lagniappe, 6.

4. Quoted in Robin Tolleson, "Stroke of Genius: Artist Wears Many Hats—All Well," *Mountain Xpress* (Asheville, NC) 8, no. 6 (18 September 2001): 34.

5. Quoted in Carlo Wolff, "McFerrin Happy to be Playing with Friends Again," *The Plain Dealer* (Cleveland, Ohio), Final/All Edition, 30 June 1999, Section: Entertainment, 1E. See also Theodore P. Mahne, "Singer Crosses Musical Boundaries," *Times–Picayune*, 6 April 1995, section Living, E1.

6. Confusingly, The Old Absinthe House at 240 Bourbon Street and The Old Absinthe Bar at 400 Bourbon Street both bore the sign "The Old Absinthe House Bar." The origins of the two establishments are disputed. The bartenders at the House believe that the Bar was once located there and moved to its present location in the early twentieth century. But the manager of the Bar, Larry Geer, claimed in 1989 that his researches showed the Bar was opened in 1806, half a century before the House. "This is the original bar, the one that was [the pirate] Jean Lafitte's hangout, and the one that Andrew Jackson leaned on." See Jill T. Anding, "A Tale of Two Houses," *Times–Picayune*, 11 August 1989, section Lagniappe, 7.

7. James Singleton, "Obituary: Charlie Brent, 1948–2006," *OffBeat*, January 2007, 44.

8. Jonathan Tabak, "Astral Project at 20," *OffBeat* 12, no. 6 (June 1999). Available from http://www.offbeat.com/ob9906/astral_project.html; accessed 23 March 2004.

5. THE CARLA BLEY BAND

Tony with the Carla Bley Band, early 1980s; from left to right, Arturo O'Farrill, Carla Bley, Tony Dagradi, Steve Swallow

At the end of 1980, the gap in Tony's performing schedule resulting from Professor Longhair's death was filled when, through two of his Inner Visions colleagues, he became involved with the Carla Bley Band.

> "Both D. Sharpe and Gary Valente were working with Carla before me. They were in the version of the band before the one that I joined. Gary had come to replace Roswell Rudd, and he was in the band with a tenor player from England, Gary Windo. We recorded *Oasis* in Carla's studio in Woodstock in March, and I met her at that time; and when Gary Windo left the band, they recommended me and she goes 'Oh, I remember him; I liked him,' and that was it. That was cool. It happened very quickly.
>
> "Carla would work two or maybe three times a year. And it was very nice; I really enjoyed it a lot. Basically what we would do was rehearse for two or three days, in Manhattan usually, then go out on tour for two or three or four weeks."

Playing with Bley gave Tony "his first international exposure in a topnotch working ensemble."[1] He had certainly joined the band by 6 November, when he is listed among the personnel for a concert in Paris.[2]

Tony took part in four recordings by The Carla Bley Band between 1980 and 1984. The first was *Social Studies*, recorded between September and December 1980, and released the following year jointly with ECM.[3] Tony told me:

> "When I joined the band, they had actually recorded most of the tracks for *Social Studies*.

When I began this session, all of the rhythm tracks, horn section parts and solos were done. I think that someone else may have attempted some of the solos that Carla asked me to do. But she wasn't satisfied with what she had on tape. On the first tour that I did with Carla I was often featured on 'Útviklingssang.' When we returned she really wanted to capture my version of that piece. I went up to her studio at Christmas time, right after the first tour, and overdubbed all my parts on the existing tracks."

Of "Copyright Royalties," Barry Kernfeld wrote perceptively, "Selecting the title ... is presumably Bley's way of asking the question: 'If I create a highly original, almost unrecognizable recomposition of 'Mood Indigo,' why shouldn't the copyright royalties come to me rather than the estates of Duke Ellington, Irving Mills and Barney Bigard?' Borrowing existing structures, revising themes, retitling and then claiming composer credit is of course common practice in jazz, but no one has ever put it so bluntly."[4] Tony takes a beautiful clarinet solo, with a gorgeous tone, paying tribute to his illustrious predecessor Bigard. In the first chorus he is accompanied only by tuba and drums, then the remaining winds join in on the second.

Tony was given a wonderful feature in the dirge-like "Útviklingssang" (Norwegian for "evolving song"). Kernfeld observed: "This ballad is a study in orchestration, harmonization, and style, as Bley places a simple but majestic minor-key melody in varied jazz-rock settings, and then hands the piece over to Dagradi, whose improvisations add a jazz-soul flavor." In Bob Blumenthal's opinion, Tony's solo "carried the blue-edged grit of Stanley Turrentine, an unexpected yet thoroughly compatible touch."[5] Lynden Barber considered "the achingly remorseful 'Útviklingssang'" the outstanding moment of the album, and the exception to the band "meekly producing when they should be cutting loose."[6]

On the jazz-rock "Floater," Tony has a short "wailing" solo in the ensemble. The *Down Beat* critic John Diliberto complained: "Bley sabotages any movement by her sidemen beyond the constricting borders of her song forms. As soon as a head of steam builds, such as Tony Dagradi's solo on 'Floater,' Bley's arrangement chokes it off."[7]

On the concluding "Walking Batteriewoman," which Kernfeld dubs "a completely wacked-out parody of formulaic soul-jazz organ combos" in which "odd-metered and irregularly metered free-jazz themes alternate with passages of conventional soul jazz," Tony inexplicably produces an imitation of Coleman Hawkins.

On *Live!*, recorded in August 1981 and released the following year, Tony is given precious little solo space. When the bass and piano introduction on "Still in the Room" morphs into a double-time section, he celebrates with a couple of brisk tenor choruses that sound as if they had been taken from *Lunar Eclipse*. He sounds right at home on the jazz-funk "Song Sung Long," entering honking, then mixing danceable licks with some "out" phrases.

Youtube has videos of seven performances from a concert that the Carla Bley Band gave at the Jazz Jamboree in Warsaw, Poland on 24 October 1981.[8] In addition to another version of "Still in the Room," which has a solo by Tony that mixes a linear approach with screams, he is given solos on "King Korn" (Lester Young plus wails), "Egyptian" (linear plus lots of wails and screams), and "Blind and Crippled" (fluent on the flute, nicely mixing single and double time).[9] Tony recalls:

"I have a few very specific memories about that Warsaw gig and subsequent tour. First, Warsaw was having a food shortage. People were hungry. One of the big events of the festival was when the borscht booth opened up. We stayed at a four-star hotel, but the choices for vegetarian food were very slim. I ended up with some sautéed mushrooms that turned out to be very, very bad! We flew to London the next day with three days off before our UK tour began. I spent the whole three days between my bed and the bathroom. When I was well enough to venture out, I am fairly certain that it was Guy Fawkes Day [5 November]."

You can see how Tony did on "Útviklingssang" when fully integrated into the band, on a video on youtube said to be taken from French TV around 1982—a long, mature, soulful solo, over sustained harmonies, that becomes almost unbearable in its intensity.[10]

The third recording that Tony made with the Carla Bley Band, again in her Woodstock basement studio, was the soundtrack for *Mortelle randonnée* (roughly, "Deadly Drive") (1983), a rather silly French movie directed by Claude Miller, part film noir, part *Bonnie and Clyde*.[11] I was able to see it only on the DVD, which unfortunately cuts out 20–30 minutes of the action.[12]

The movie's main redeeming feature is the charismatic acting of Michel Serrault as Beauvoir, known as "The Eye" (L'Œil), a hard-bitten detective obsessed with finding his daughter, from whom he was separated when she was 1 year old and his wife left him. When he is hired by the parents of a college student to identify the student's new girlfriend, he gets more than he bargained for. Catherine Latriis (many aliases), played by a blank-expressioned Isabelle Adjani, immediately kills the student, after he has turned his savings over to her. Instead of going to the police, Beauvoir, who now has the notion that she may be his long-lost daughter, begins to trail her all over France, as she kills one rich suitor after another. When she falls in love with a blind Swiss architect (!), who sets her up in a gallery, the jealous Beauvoir pushes him under a bus. Catherine picks up a woman hitchhiker, the two of them rob a bank, and the woman is shot by the police during the robbery. Blanker than ever, wherever she goes, Catherine orders several pears (a symbol of female fertility?) and Players Senior Service cigarettes (British, so perhaps a symbol of her international sophistication?), and reads *Hamlet* in English (a preoccupation with death?). She also loves the song "La Paloma," which of course crops up throughout the movie. Catherine is eventually cornered by the police, then commits suicide by driving through the upper windows of a multi-storey parking ramp.

Tony remarked: "Carla used 'La Paloma,' which is an Italian kind of tango, as the underlying theme. We did that in many different ways on this record, not only as a tango: the tempo changes, the key changes from major to minor...." Clearly, the music is movie music and was intended as such. But it can also be listened to almost like a modern classical piece: a set of variations with interludes. In that respect I find it highly successful as well as full of beautiful combinations of sound color. Tony's mahogany tone on tenor is recognizable in the combinations, especially during the atmospheric fragmentation of the theme in "Los palominos." He has a rather Hodges-like solo in "Musique mécanique" (4:15–4:53) and a brief impassioned one in "La Paloma" (7:18–7:33).

Tony also took part in *I Hate to Sing*, compiled from both live and studio recordings made between August 1981 and January 1983, and released in 1984. Stacia Proefrock wrote of this album:

"Elements of vaudevillian silliness show up on many Carla Bley albums, but usually as grace notes within compositions that are known for their musical strength and density. *I Hate to Sing* is a notable exception: here the airy, goofy tone seems to be the only thing holding the album together. Fans of The Carla Bley Band will appreciate the group's jovial performance and loose, swinging style, but this is little more than a novelty album. Not until the final track, 'Battleship,' does the band really stretch itself musically; by then the preceding jokey, toneless vocals and open, pendular riffs have set the mood to such an extent that the listener is almost stunned by the contrasting non-fluffiness."[13]

In Don Palmer's vivid description:

"'Battleship' is a work of genius, as Mrs. Bley introduces it with the sounds of a telegraph transmitter, explosions, and shouts of battle. Following with one of her all-too-short calliope-like organ solos that recalls Ellington's 'It Don't Mean a Thing' or the more zany 'East St. Louis Toodle-doo,' Mrs. Bley charts the piece through several tempos, accentuating the shifts with sustained harmonies and concentric melodic phrases which hover around ominous bass and tuba lines. The pace also fluctuates as Mrs. Bley's horn section—the altoist Steve Slagle, tenorist Tony Dagradi, tubist Bob Stewart, French hornist Vincent Chancy, trombonist Gary Valente, and trumpeter Michael Mantler—stagger and share phrases in a conversational vein, until reveille signals a descent into the maelstrom. Mr. Mantler's tightly coiled, skittery trumpet takes the lead over a host of blips, bleeps, and shrieks which hark back to the telegraphic introduction. The collective solo ends as the ensemble incrementally coalesces into a striking, melodic crescendo, followed by a revoiced 'My Country 'Tis of Thee' and 'Taps.'"[14]

On the opening jokey "Internationale," a Bley-esque celebration of "surmounting language barriers," Tony has to say the lines "I'm an Eskimo. I would like a drink right here. Garçon?" Exactly.

A performance of the Monkish "Ups and Downs" by the band, recorded live by NDR in Hamburg, Germany on 14 March 1984, appeared commercially on the album *For Taylor Storer*.[15] The album was released in a limited edition in tribute to the recently deceased general manager of the New Music Distribution Service, which had grown to be one of the most important musical service organizations in the country, carrying more than 4,000 privately produced albums on 300 independently owned labels. Tony has to follow an excellent alto solo by Steve Slagle that includes some trademark Dagradi screams. Tony's linear-plus-screams approach comes off less effectively than usual, but the trading of solo fragments between the two sax players afterwards and in the coda is exhilarating.

There is a surviving video—apparently removed from youtube for a copyright violation but still available elsewhere on the Web—of a version of Henry Mancini's "Pink Panther" by the Carla Bley Band, made in 1984, to judge by the personnel.[16] Tony states the famous cartoon theme beautifully, some musical horseplay ensues, and then the mood turns to jazz-rock for Tony to take a wailing solo.

Still based on New Orleans, Tony flew back and forth to work with Carla until 1985.[17] Yet Tony's participation in the Bley band attracted little critical attention, and the band's recordings strongly suggest that he played third fiddle to the star wind player, his old colleague Gary Valente on trombone, and the man who soon became the other saxophonist, Steve Slagle. This impression is backed up by the critic John S. Wilson in the *New York Times*. Of a performance at Seventh Avenue South in July 1981, Wilson wrote: "The principal contrast to Mr. Valente and Miss Bley's heavy ensemble masses comes from Steve Slagle, an agile, bop-influenced alto saxophonist who builds the band up to some wildly swinging passages with the help of a tenor saxophonist, Tony Dagradi, in whose playing there are some echoes of Sonny Rollins."[18] Eighteen months later, Wilson could still say: "And [the] two saxophonists, Steve Slagle and Tony Dagradi, are in the process of establishing an interrelationship that seems to be giving her another coloristic source."[19]

The reviewer of the band's performance at Jazz City in Edmonton, Alberta on 21 August 1982 had mixed feelings about Tony: "As gifted an orchestrator as any in jazz, [Bley] can create an amazing variety of moods from just six horns and two keyboards; sombre is her best [mood], with its gorgeous legato horn lines and slow, sliding trombone figures—one such ballad piece [presumably "Útviklingssang"] for tenorman Tony Dagradi (this year's Gato Barbieri [who played as a guest on Bley's *Tropic Appetites*, 1974]) was an early showstopper.... Her soloists, Dagradi, Steve Stagle ... are gifted players but not quite original ones. Yet they may never sound any better than they do in this most original band."[20]

Tony Dagradi, 1984

Years later, Tony reminisced approvingly about Bley's compositions, making it clear that this was the aspect of the band that had appealed to him the most.

"'Carla's music can only be played by improvisers, but she also demands that you be able to read and interpret the music and work in the context she's set up,' Dagradi said. 'She'll never say "Here's a head, let's blow for 20 minutes."'

"Dagradi praised the 'witty eclecticism' of Bley's compositions and the quirky taste that sometimes led her to arrange the work of others. 'Some nights we'd play rock 'n' roll, tangos, straight-ahead jazz, and the score to Fellini's *8½*. She even had us do the theme from the Pink Panther movies, because she'd been watching them all morning on the tour bus.'

"Bley's signature compositions 'stand up to anything,' Dagradi said. 'You can't compare her to anyone. She's in a class by herself, the way Ellington is in a class by himself, too.'"[21]

Meanwhile Back in New Orleans

The Jazz & Heritage Festival Crossword[22]
8 May 1981

DOWN
50. ---- Dagradi

Working with The Carla Bley Band also came at a price for Tony's work in New Orleans. He told a *Down Beat* interviewer, the New Orleans pianist Joel Simpson, in spring 1982:

"'I love Carla. People think of her as avant garde, but she writes some very beautiful ballads.' This misperception of Carla is unfortunately typical of American audiences, though not of European ones. 'They love her over in Europe,' says Tony, 'and we make more money over there than here. We only tour in the U.S. several weeks, but we spend two or three months out of the year in Europe.'

"But he no longer makes five or six gigs a week when he's home. 'Ever since I started working with Carla, people won't give me a steady gig.' So he lines up as much work as he can before he goes off on tour, usually for about four weeks, then comes home and works sporadically for six. 'The money comes to about the same thing. I just have more spare time.'"[23]

Tony's decreased performance opportunities in New Orleans are more than confirmed by the advertisements in the *Times–Picayune* in 1981 and 82. He is not mentioned in a single ad, besides Astral Project, for 1981. The following year, apart from the large-group performances mentioned below, Tony is listed only during Jazz Fest: in a duet with Larry Sieberth at the Faubourg (3 May); in a large jam session at Prout's Club Alhambra (6 May); as a member of Ramsey McLean and The Lifers (7 May); and in a performance with local horns (Earl Turbinton, Jr., Clyde Kerr, Jr.) and a nationally ranked rhythm section of Cedar Walton, piano, Buster Williams, bass, and Billy Higgins, drums, at the Faubourg (9 May). An ad for one of Astral Project's seven advertised performances, on 30 October at the Contemporary Arts Center, notes that Tony had "been spending a lot of time lately touring Europe with jazz pianist Carla

Bley."

After working with Willie Metcalf, Tony continued to be involved in jazz education. The *Times–Picayune* announced that on 16 March 1981 the Contemporary Arts Center would host a ten-week "New Orleans Jazz Workshop," with classes in "beginning, intermediate, and advanced composition, jazz piano and drumming, blues, improvisation, and jazz rhythm, taught by a faculty including Joel Simpson, Tony Dagradi, Al Belletto, Jonathan Bloom [percussion], and Connor Shaw [drums]." Belletto was one of the fathers of modern jazz in New Orleans and a mentor to John Vidacovich.

In 1981, Tony acquired the main tenor saxophone he used as his main horn until 2007; it has now lost so much of its lacquer that it appears to be an antique.

"When I got it, it was a prize. A local repairman found this saxophone, and it was in beautiful condition: the lacquer was all very nice. But it's been played hard and often, which is its function in life, so it looks a little sad now in the lacquerware. It was made in 1958, a desirable vintage for a Selmer Mark VI. It's what they call five-digit, which means that the serial number on it is above 75,000. I have another instrument from 1937 [see p. 141], which is actually the first modern saxophone, and it really set the stage and standard for all the instruments that came after it. I really like it a lot: it has a great sound. It's definitely my back-up horn. And sometimes I'll just pick it up and get focused into where it's at. But I always go back to the VI, saying, 'Yes, it's really comfortable.'"

Also in 1981, Tony obtained a grant from the National Endowment for the Arts to write a suite entitled *Portraits and Sketches*, which was performed on 19 February the following year at the Contemporary Arts Center, funded by a further grant from the Louisiana State Arts Council. The performers, according to an advertisement in the *Times–Picayune*, were "eleven of New Orleans' finest musicians." Another ad names six of them: Clyde Kerr, Jr. (trumpet), Kidd Jordan (saxophone), David Torkanowsky (piano), Walter Payton (bass), and John Vidacovich (drums). Tony's feature article in *Down Beat* described the suite as follows: "it was conceived as a tribute to his major musical influences, including among others, Charles Mingus, Miles Davis, and Sun Ra. Each composition dedicated to a particular person captured something essential of their style while providing a vehicle for some very moving soloing by Dagradi and his sidemen."[24]

"Tony Dagradi and an 11-piece ensemble" performed again in a Brown Bag Concert in Duncan Plaza, adjacent to City Hall, on 11 May, during Jazz Fest. A surviving photograph of what was to be called the Astral Orchestra eight years later finds Astral Project augmented by Walter Payton (tuba), Kidd Jordan (saxophone), Kent Jordan (flute and piccolo), Wendell Brunious (trumpet) rather than Kerr, and Art Baron (trombone) (see p. 48).

Gradually, New Orleans came to have an influence on Tony's playing:

"When I first got here and people listened to me, they would say, 'Oh, you're not from here.' And at the same time, when I used to go back to New York and play with some people, they'd say, 'Oh, where are you from?' So some of that New Orleans stuff was definitely coming in. I think that I always liked trying to find some kind of personal approach to whatever I was doing. My M.O. is trying to digest what's happened before and to regurgitate it in some other way, some way that hopefully is somewhat original."

An expanded Astral Project, assembled for Tony Dagradi's suite *Portraits and Sketches*, 1982: from left to right, John Vidacovich holding daughter Laura, Walter Payton, Kidd Jordan, Kent Jordan, David Torkanowsky, Tony Dagradi, James Singleton, Mark Sanders, Wendell Brunious, Art Baron.

Notes

1. http://tonydagradi.com/biography.html; accessed 7 June 2005.

2. Concert available from EzTorrent; accessed 28 September 2013.

3. Carla Bley, *Social Studies* (ECM WATT/11 78118–23111–2, c1981).

4. Barry Kernfeld, *The Blackwell Guide to Recorded Jazz*, 2nd ed. (Oxford and Cambridge, MA: Blackwell, 1995), 512.

5. Bob Blumenthal, review in *Musician, Player & Listener*, no. 36 (September–October 1981): 102, 104.

6. Lynden Barber, review in *Melody Maker* 56 (22 August 1981): 14.

7. John Diliberto, review in *Down Beat* 48, no. 12 (December 1981): 52–53.

8. The only piece missing is "Time and Us." See the set-list on EzTorrent.

9. "Blind and Crippled" (http://www.youtube.com/watch?v=lMlkBgHFTKE), "Blunt Object" (http://www.youtube.com/watch?v=6Vj9Kml51yM), "Egyptian" (http://www.youtube.com/watch?v=xYqALYWfKyE), "The Internationale" (http://www.youtube.com/watch?v=Cau2uZrFjmQ), "King Korn" (http://www.youtube.com/watch?v=r9lMWaGCwj0), "Reactionary Tango" (http://www.youtube.com/watch?v=0uOw3EpGDMQ and http://www.youtube.com/watch?v=GbcG_mlXRNA), and "Still in the Room" (http://www.youtube.cm/watch?v=J_LWsX_k-jo); all accessed 27 September 2013.

10. http://www.youtube.com/watch?v=8qH1tqkElvI. Tony can also be seen in the band, although he doesn't solo, on "The Piano Lesson" (http://www.youtube.com/watch?v=6OJlu5yy8tg) and "Real Life Hits" (http://www.youtube.com/watch?v=Cau2uZrFjmQ); all accessed 27 September 2013.

11. Carla Bley, *Extraits de la bande originale du film* Mortelle randonnée (Watt Works 812 097–1, 1983).

12. *Mortelle randonnée*, DVD (New York: Wellspring FLV–5395, 2003).

13. Stacia Proefrock, review on allmusic.com; accessed 28 September 2013.

14. Don Palmer, "Carla Bley Returns to Form," *New York Times*, 10 February 1985, 97.

15. *For Taylor Storer* ([New York:]: TS 001; TS Records, 1988).

16. http://www.dailymotion.com/video/x4yaiz_carla-bley-big-band-pink-panther_music; personnel listed on http://www.tunesbaby.com/dm/?x=x4yaiz; both accessed 28 September 2013. The band played "Pink Panther" with similar personnel on 7 July 1984 at the Bracknell Jazz Festival in England, according to the information given on http://www.bootsdaily.

com/?nav=details&id=353613; accessed 28 September 2013.

17. He had left by *Night-Glo*, recorded June–August 1985, when Paul McCandless is the only sax player listed.

18. John S. Wilson, "Carla Bley's Band at Seventh Avenue South," *New York Times*, 1 August 1981, section 1, 8.

19. John S. Wilson, "Carla Bley's Jazz Style Taps Many Roots," *New York Times*, 9 January 1983, section 2, 21.

20. M[ark] M[iller], "Carla Bley's Many Faces: Mistress of Deception," *Globe and Mail* (Edmonton, Alberta), 23 August 1982, P14.

21. Chris Waddington, "Jazz Bandleader Carla Bley is Full of Musical Surprises," *Star Tribune* (Minneapolis), 28 June 2003, section Variety, 1E.

22. The Jazz & Heritage Festival Crossword, *Times–Picayune*, 8 May 1981, section Lagniappe, 4–5.

23. Joel Simpson, "Tony Dagradi: From the Crescent City to the Crowned Heads of Europe, Saxist Tony Dagradi has Moved from Second Line to Front Line," *Down Beat* 49, no. 7 (July 1982): 54.

24. Simpson, "Tony Dagradi."

6. THE LONG VIEW OF RAMSEY

From at least 1980 to 1985, Tony played regularly with the bassist and cellist Ramsey McLean.

"I'm not sure where I met Ramsey: it might have been Tipitina's or Lu & Charlie's. We were about the same age [Ramsey b. 1951, Tony 1952], and he was actively trying to lead a group. His bands were always changing, depending on the availability of people. He had a group called The Lifers. Later it was called The Survivors. He had all these names like that. He was working a lot. When Snug Harbor first opened—and it was called The Faubourg—every Friday was Ramsey McLean and The Lifers, and every Saturday it was Astral Project. I played with both bands, so I was there every Friday and Saturday night. I did a lot of different gigs with Ramsey."

Tony's memory of the gigs is both confirmed and corrected by an ad in the *Times-Picayune* for 4 July 1980:

"FOR LATE-NIGHTERS ONLY. The Faubourg Restaurant, 626 Frenchmen St., is becoming a haven for those yearning for music in the wee hours of the morning. Each Friday and Saturday, the restaurant's bar features local acts from 1 to 5 a.m. Performing tonight [Friday] is Astral Project, and taking the stage Saturday night are regulars Ramsey McLean and The Lifers. Sanka, anyone?"

When I interviewed Ramsey, who's a riot, he told me the following story about meeting Tony:

RM. I had a band that was two saxophones, an incredibly volatile drummer, and I played bass. I wrote everything. They refused to play other people's tunes. I let them play their songs, too, but it was all original music.
And we go to play at Tipitina's, and I realize that night, I can't stand the fact that everybody plays ten-minute, twenty-minute solos. I'm finished with it. I'm trying to get out of long form, and they're all thinking, "Here's my man: here's the guy that's going to let me figure out my stuff live on the stage, and he's got a job and will pay me money." I'm trying to get out of this: I don't want to do this anymore. I want to do three- or four-minute songs and, like, have a life. But I couldn't get out of the gig. So we're playing and it's miserable. And then this white guy comes up—'cause I was the only white guy in the band; everybody else was these crazy black people—and he says, "Hey, man, could I sit in?" I asked the other people if it was OK, to get an Amen. And one of the guys says, "This kid's good; he's all right; let him play." And it was Tony. That was how we met: that was the first meeting.
Tony's a very good diplomat. He knows: back off; let them choke on their own stuff. He's good at that. So he doesn't play at first; he lets the other people play. And so, of course, they play these ten-minute fucking solos. And I'm being driven mad by this stuff. And so then Tony goes to play, and as soon as he takes his first breath, I know he's ready for ten minutes. He's heavily gone; he's ready to go. He has good ammo, he has good range, and he knows what's going to happen. And I think, "I can't take this any more, but I got to put on a good face for the audience." And he sounds really great, you know
Then we get to the end of it, and this other guy comes to the bandstand and he goes, "Hey, could I do a song with you?" And I don't know who this guy was. And Tony says,

"Hey, man, this guy's really good: you should let him do a song with you." And I thought, "OK, well, it's a song, and that's like three or four minutes. I'll feel better about that, because I don't want these extended solos. Enough of that shit." The guy comes up and guess who it is? Bobby McFerrin. I've never heard his name, never met him. So he comes up, he sings this song, and he's going "poop-oop-oop-boo-woop-boop-boop." And he does a ten-minute solo! OK, machine guns for everybody. I want slaughter here; kill everybody. No, you'd never heard vocals like this; you'd never heard anything like it. This guy was so good, you wanted him to do thirty minutes. Like, whoa, keep going, man, I'm liking this. I've never heard this before. Wow! And the next thing you know, he's Bobby McFerrin. That was the first time I ever met Bobby: I met Bobby through Tony. And Bobby's the sweetheart of the world, you know.

  DL. So this was on the very same occasion. You met them both.

  RM. Yeah, right. Like, what?!

  DL. These long solos must be wearing on the bass player: you have to play repetitive patterns over and over.

  RM. Don't forget: I was the band leader. I paid everybody. I didn't have to do nothing I didn't want to do. If I didn't like what was going on, I just changed or stopped it.

  DL. So after that night you fired the guys who were playing ten-minute solos?

  RM. That was it. Good night, goodbye, see you later: that was it.

Ramsey McLean and The Lifers played at Jazz Fest in 1980 and 1981, and were still together under a third name in February 1984, when the Contemporary Arts Center's New Jazz/New Music series featured "Ramsey McLean and the Refugees" with the saxophonist Dickie Landry, Roger Lewis, Kirk Joseph, and Tony. Soon afterwards, McLean left New Orleans and went to live in New York, later developing a career as a writer of lyrics for popular songs. The early work of The Lifers is well documented on the group's album *History's Made Every Moment: New Orleans Now*, released and at least partly recorded in 1981.[1]

I asked McLean to comment on this album:

  DL. Some of it was live at the Faubourg, and some of it was made in the studio.

  RM. "The Painter" song we did in the studio. But that was all [actually also "E.T. All"]. We didn't know what a studio was. Nowadays we control everything in our studio. Back then it was just completely live. So everything was live. And there was no rehearsal. We were what you call waltzers (?). We thought we could do anything. And that was the first night we found out, whoa, we'd better rehearse a little bit. 'Cause it really wasn't very good.

  DL. So you did rehearse a little before you went on?

  RM. Yeah. But I mean, we'd never done that. It was just like: everybody could read music, except me, because I wrote the music, so I didn't need to read it. And it would be swell. But when you went to record, the level of "cleanliness" that was required for recording was so much more than that of a live performance. None of us had ever been there—we didn't know. We thought we'd just record what we play. And when we heard what we played, it was so sloppy it was ridiculous; it was pathetic. So then we rehearsed, and the next night was a good night.

  If you think about recording, from the conception, and you're talking about Dixieland music, ragtime music: these are all live events; it just happens. And if you take the evolution of recording, then you get Benny Goodman, which is live but very heady live, like where you can tell the audience, "We may have to do this song more than once." That was an evolution of recording. And when you get in the 50s and 60s, you get into multi-tracking, where you can make it better. And when you get into the 80s and 90s and it's digital, you can redo anything you want; it doesn't matter whether you're any good or not. But the way everybody else came through it, you had to be good.

With that group everything was completely spontaneous. We did our best to plan and be on time and be professional, but we all knew that it was all spontaneity. It was just: either go this way or that. It really didn't matter who showed up. And we would do the best we could.

History's Made Every Moment earned a long rave review from Vincent Fumar that is worth quoting at length:

Bassist Ramsey McLean and his group, the Lifers, have for several years been performing in a number of jazz styles in local clubs. Now they have released their first recorded work, a self-produced effort recorded locally in both a club setting and a studio.

History's Made Every Moment: New Orleans Now! may be said to represent an act of self-determination for the group, since they controlled the product from start to finish, without the aid of an established record label, even a small jazz one. Certainly part of the record's strength is derived from this decision, and the results are promising for similar stylists who might be considering taking the same step.

All of the group's members ... are individually accomplished. McLean plays bass with a wide tone and a nimble pulse that are balanced handsomely by a formidable bowing technique. Dagradi, who plays tenor and soprano saxophones, reveals a chameleon-like adaptability in his music-making. As a pianist, [Larry] Sieberth switches from a recognizable post-bebop style to a more contemporary, Keith Jarrett-like rhapsodizing. And [Alvin] Fielder is a galvanic drum force who pushes each piece with firm snare accents and concise cymbal work.

Five of the compositions were recorded live at Faubourg, the Frenchmen Street club where the group has been in residence for several months. The rest was cut at the Rosemont Studio. McLean and Fielder are credited as the producers.

The numbers range from conventionally styled bebop to avant-garde outings. Dagradi handles most of the solos, starting with the first number, "Go for the Throat," which opens with a Horace Silver-like theme that gives way to the saxophonist's shifting styles. Dagradi runs the gamut from a ponderous bass-clarinet obbligato to straightforward John Coltrane accents, with an occasional jaunt into the commercial funk sound of a Stanley Turrentine. Fielder maintains a busy profile throughout, and Sieberth's piano solo covers everything from post-bop to wildly impressionistic arpeggios. There are moments when the ensemble resorts to discord for its own sake, but a reprise of the theme puts the whole thing in perspective.

McLean shows more than just his classical string training with "The Painter," wherein he plays cello to Dagradi's tenor saxophone. It's a well-composed duo with stern tonal contrasts that somehow intersect despite the darkly meditative mood of the piece. Its effect is to create a mood of urgency and melancholy in less than three minutes.

"Bwe-bop" is exactly the kind of up-tempo excursion that suits the group best. Dagradi's tenor courses ruggedly, with a touch of hard swing. Sieberth's piano virtually dances throughout, and Fielder remains on top of it all. The fast pace is invigorating, and the number is one of the finest examples of a true bop style that any local group has pulled off in years.

Two of the more free-form pieces, "(Everybody Needs) a Little Rest" and "Burning Instructions for Angel Wings," are contributions to the school of formalized dissonance. The former features Dagradi on soprano and McLean on cello, but mostly Sieberth on synthesizer. The latter is for the most part an exchange between Fielder and Sieberth, with lots of room for Dagradi's breathless phrases. Whether the dissonances are calculated or improvised, they don't quite show off the group's skills as well as the more conventionally composed pieces.

Drummer Ricky Sebastian and percussionist Mark Sanders make guest appearances on "E. T. All," a studio cut that has Dagradi playing both tenor and soprano saxes. The bigger attraction on the second side, though, is the well-crafted "Still (There's a Mingus Among Us)." As a tribute to the late bassist Charles Mingus, the number is very much on target, being a balance of blues and ballad pomp. The piece opens with a pretty, blues-tinged Sieberth solo, after which the rest join in with a straight blues theme, thus establishing a familiar Mingus trademark, before Dagradi's tenor eases in with one of the best ballad statements he's ever put on record. The blues motif returns, and McLean pumps darkly as they again switch between the two styles. The form is not an easy one, but it works to showcase each player in the best possible way.

McLean and company have been heard only in brief snatches on previous recordings. With this album they are captured in their element, and with a minimum of cosmetic aid. It is no exaggeration to say that *History's Made Every Moment: New Orleans Now!* is one of the best modern jazz albums the city has produced in years. Knowing that they did it on their own somehow makes it just a bit better.[2]

The album even received a surprisingly positive review in *Down Beat*;

"It is apparent that the music of the 80s is, to borrow Jack DeJohnnette's term, multidirectional, denoting a process of inclusion rather than specialization. Bassist Ramsey McLean and The Lifers ... support the assertion emphatically on *New Orleans Now!*, a spunky, well-proportioned album. The issue here is not simply one of diversity—though any album that taps the down-home soul and the urbane elegance of Mingus, the spiritual lyricism of Coltrane and his descendants, the far-reaching implications of synthesized sound and overdubbing, and more, cannot be cited for narrow-mindedness—but the ability to make source material sing as one's own creation. McLean and The Lifers demonstrate their ability to do so on each of the album's seven compositions. Each of the musicians approach every stylistic proposition with fluency and conviction, giving such varied settings as 'A Little Rest,' a Shoreresque ballad replete with tranquil Moog washes, the labyrinthine 'Bwe-Bop' (good bop still comes in three-minute packages), and the shifting colors of the free-form 'Burning Instructions for Angel Wings,' a vitality and a durability. Recommended."[3]

I don't believe the reviewers got across just how varied Tony's solos are on this album. On "Go for the Throat," the funky and jaunty tune, a little like Charles Mingus's "Fables of Faubus," including a Mingus-like change of pace, prompts an appropriate solo from Tony on bass clarinet, incorporating some mannerisms from Eric Dolphy, who played both that instrument and alto sax on Mingus's recordings of the early 1960s. "The Painter"—which Patrice Fisher told me McLean wrote to describe John Vidacovich's playing—ironically has no drums: it's a slow, meditative duet for tenor sax and cello, ending with an interesting not-quite-unison. The crazy bebop "Bwe-Bop" brings out Tony's hard bop style, with a few nods to Coltrane. On "(Everybody Needs) A Little Rest," after the "barnyard noises" from the added percussion die down, Tony creates overlapping tenor and soprano sax parts by virtue of overdubbing. "Still (There's a Mingus Among Us)" is by turns bluesy, like a Coltrane ballad, and like a Tony ballad. And the final free-jazz "Burning Instructions for Angel Wings" inspires some cackles and fragmented runs in the manner of wild late Coltrane.

The Long View
Ramsey McLean and Tony Dagradi, *The Long View*. McLean, cello, b, mburu [i.e., mbira] (5), Tibetan bells; TD, ss (1), ts (3, 6–7), fl (2), bclar (4). Recorded in the Playhouse of Longue Vue Gardens, New Orleans, Lousiana, January 1983. Prescription Records Pres. 4, c1983.
1. Swan Song (McLean) (7:20)
2. The Dark Horse (McLean) (4:47)
3. Without (McLean) (7:55)
4. Resurrection (For the Living) (McLean) (6:43)
5. Say "Good Night" (McLean) (0:36)
6. Purloin (McLean) (4:52)
7. High Pressure Zone (McLean, TD) (4:55)

From back of cover of *The Long View*: Ramsey McLean (left) and Tony Dagradi

I asked Ramsey McLean what he did after he fired the musicians who were playing ten-minute solos:

> RM. I ended up with Charles Neville from the Neville Brothers.
> DL. I heard him playing with you on the *Jump Jazz* record.[4]
> RM. That's good. That's a good record. Charles and I fell in, and things really changed, because we started playing, just the two of us. We didn't want anybody else. For financial reasons, but also artistically, because we didn't really need a piano player; we didn't really need a drummer. We were like Ornette Coleman and Charlie Haden without Ed Blackwell and Don Cherry, because we didn't need them. And then everybody else started doing that. Because it was a viable way to make a living on a Sunday through a Wednesday, when you didn't need a band.

McLean may have started playing duets with Neville, but by December 1981 he was working with Tony, as implied by a laudatory review from Vincent Fumar for their performance at the first anniversary party for radio station WWOZ at Tipitina's: "saxophonist Tony Dagradi and bassist Ramsey McLean dashed through a set with a couple of guests ([Kirk] Joseph of the Dirty Dozen and Roger Lewis). As usual, McLean's tone was wide and resilient, his attack steady and brave. Dagradi's big, gulping tone buzzed and wailed over the few numbers they performed, and the two of them proved that they are still progressing in big steps."[5] The duo were still working together on 22 April 1983, when the "Ramsey McLean Duo with Tony Dagradi" had a gig at Snug Harbor.

    DL. How did *The Long View* come about?

    RM. It was just a way to make a record quickly, intelligently, simply. Hit the high points: just the high points. Don't bother with everybody else's neuroses. Do it. 'Cause we had all that stuff worked out.

    DL. It's really a beautiful record.

    RM. Thank you.

    DL. And I don't think Tony's ever played better.

    RM. It was totally spontaneous. There was some rehearsal, but it was so minimal. And what's on the tape, really, has nothing to do with the rehearsals. The format. We kept the format. But what transpired was at the moment. It was always understood that you would defer. Tony was always good at that. Never attempt to take charge of a situation: defer to the person that came in with the message. I wasn't that way with him. But he was literate and I was illiterate. So that was a big difference. I was always trying to communicate like a storyteller: there was no book to read. Whereas he could communicate with other people in terms of literature, writing: he could read the book. So if you were a good writer, and you gave the writing to him, he was one hell of a relayer. He didn't make up the story. He retold the story. But when you tell a story, as you know, if they only publish one volume of the book, we're not looking too good here. We need to be published in general. Tony was excellent at communicating a singular story to a graphic (?) mass. He could get it across.

    DL. Yeah, he is a really beautiful storyteller. He can play a melody spontaneously in such a beautiful and natural way.

    RM. Yeah. And if you could describe it in words, you certainly wouldn't have to read it. And if you could describe it in words, you wouldn't have to hear it. And if you could describe it in words, you wouldn't have to see it. Like, what are you going to do with a Picasso? Take Picasso. It's like Cubism: kind of like this, kind of like that. But you see the thing and you go, "Oh, yeah, yeah, I get that." Tony is like that: you gotta hear him. He tells an interesting story.

    DL. What about the circumstances of recording *The Long View*?

    RM. I wanted to do something completely different. And so we ended up at Longue Vue Gardens, which was the domain of people that had founded the Sears Corporation. I'd been there for years, and it was all very hoity toity, very high-end—extreme wealth. And I ended up being the music director there. I would bring in people to play. As I learned about the compound—the sundry buildings and grounds—there was a playhouse. The floor was made out of a hard wood, oak, and the walls and ceilings were made out of soft wood, cypress, which was the equivalent to how Stradivari would make a violin: hard wood for the back and sides, and soft wood for the soundboard and sides. The action was taking place on the soft wood, and the reaction was taking place on the hard wood. So that was this room, and I decided we'd record there, and we did.

    The guy that was the engineer [John DuBois] had invented a board that was, I'd say, 12 inches across by 12 inches wide by maybe 16 inches tall. And it was a 16-channel board with two lights that looked like the Jetsons. And that was yet to be invented in this world.

In other words, the guy brought in the prototype of all reduction. He brought in the first version of taking 48 feet and making it into 16 inches, and nobody had ever seen this. I'd never seen it in Manhattan, never seen it in London, never seen it anywhere. The guy was a genius. And to be on a recording like that stepped everybody up: you had to be better than you ever thought you could be. Because the engineer just changed the world. So, why don't we go with him? And that was what we did.

DL. Quite a story.

RM. It's the plain truth. And all it was, was three people, just having a good time, on a given night.

When I went to mix the record, my girlfriend had been so harsh on me, that by the time I got to the mix, I had left the tape at the house. I was so upset. I had to go back and get the tape. And Tony had to sit there and wait for me.

DL. Did you come into that recording session with written compositions, or did you play something from memory, or what?

RM. It's what you call "worked out." They were written, but I didn't want them to be played as they were notated—I wanted them in his interpretation. That's what jazz is: jazz is improvisation, interpretation, collaboration, compensation, expectation, and realization: all end in ION. That's what you do in the jazz world. You come in strong with your own ideas, and you leave with a huge appreciation and love for other human beings. And I think that's what jazz in the end really is. It's not some sort of music: that's the outgrowth of it. Because without humans, we got nothing.

Once again, Fumar raved about the album:

There are few jazz musicians who don't yearn to create music outside the context in which they are usually known. The demands of the nightclub circuit and record companies being what they are, however, such opportunities are rare, so anything beyond the conventional usually remains unheard outside the rehearsal hall or the private tape collection. The display of striking originality, then, becomes a small, secretive business.

The colony of musicians producing unconventional works in New Orleans is very small, and is heard from infrequently. Bassist Ramsey McLean and reed man Tony Dagradi have been working the local scene for several years, generally doing what is expected of them as accompanists, but occasionally stepping out into relatively uncharted ground. With the album *The Long View* ... McLean and Dagradi not only tread new ground, but also stretch the limits of jazz in a way that most record companies would consider taboo.

The Long View is a collection of duets recorded last year in the Playhouse at Longue View Gardens.... The music—not "free" jazz and only tenuously linked to the avant-garde—is completely unlike anything that is apt to be heard in a jazz club.

From a compositional standpoint, *The Long View* represents the most original music now emanating from the local jazz community (a community which, on the basis of the duo's present offering, must now be expanded to include part of the chamber-music crowd).

With one exception, the compositions are credited to McLean. His works eschew orthodox structures for the most part, while engaging two instruments in involved dialogues that respect both jazz and classical-music forms. The album is more than just an attempt to dispel doubts about the ability of two instruments, especially a reed and a string instrument, to sustain musical interest beyond novelty effects.

The opener, "Swan Song," introduces a pattern often repeated in the other works: a gradual movement from a meditative motif to a bluesy one. McLean has developed a formidable pizzicato style. He picks in what is almost a guitar style [note that he also plays the guitar], occasionally even strumming, and varying the tempo from a tango to a waltz. Dagradi, playing soprano saxophone, strikes an Oriental groove, but soon works his way to an impressive array of blues licks. The waltz figure under his soaring blues lines is a striking effect.

McLean bows the cello nimbly on "Without," which features tenor saxophone and cello in close elegiac harmonizing. In mood and texture the piece actually combines the serene plaintiveness of a Shostakovich string quartet with the contorted blues phrasing of John Coltrane.

Another lament is "Resurrection (for the Living)," which is similar in pattern to "Without," but with Dagradi's bass clarinet providing a weightier blues feeling. "Purloin" is also somewhat on the morose side, but with a tinge of optimism.

The sole work on the album credited to both musicians is "High Pressure Zone," which comes the closest of all the pieces to being a standard uptempo jazz romp. McLean's playing, both plucked and bowed, suggests the tonal breadth of that master Charlie Haden, and the piece comes off as part ominous, part playful.

The Long View can loosely be described as bluesy Orientalism in a chamber-music context. McLean and Dagradi have both recorded in the past, but those discs don't compare to this one in cleverness and virtuosity. The two players simply have never sounded better on records.

It would have been easy for McLean and Dagradi to enlist a band, play standard-length solos with expected rhythms, and hold the results out to whatever jazz label might bite. Prescription Records is a fledgling outfit. While most labels of the sort are used by artists seeking a showcase to boost them to more lucrative deals, the music of *The Long View* suggests that McLean and Dagradi have no such concern.[6]

Two other critics, one national and one local, also heartily approved:

"... while it is an extremely difficult task to sustain a program entirely of ballad material, McLean and Dagradi do it successfully through their seamless execution of McLean's imaginative material. They perform these pieces flawlessly, letting the music unfold at its own pace, letting go gradually to an emotional climax, then reining themselves back to the melody. They blend the sounds of their instruments in the unified way that [Eric] Dolphy and [Art] Davis did—the timbre of one instrument reflects in the timbre of the other until it is sometimes hard to distinguish string from reed. The tunes sound simpler than they are because of the assured performance they get."[7]

"Dagradi is a superb soloist on all horns, with his stately gliding song on 'Swan' getting my vote for one of the most lyrical reed solos ever to come out of the Crescent City—a paragon of jazz lyrical reed tradition: [Alphonse] Picou, [Johnny] Dodds, [Irving] Fazola, [Omer] Simeon, [George] Lewis, [Albert] Burbank, [Al] Belletto, [Nat] Perrilliat, [Alvin "Red"] Tyler, et al. On 'Resurrection' on bass clarinet he does as much to resuscitate that horn as did [Harry] Carney and [Eric] Dolphy. On flute he haunts 'The Dark Horse' with overdubs. On tenor he is fittingly angular on 'Purloin' and 'Zone.' As he has demonstrated with the Bley band that takes no prisoners, Dagradi is an interesting, thoroughly contemporary reed soloist."[8]

These reviews almost say it all, except ... On "The Dark Horse," there was no overdubbing. What sounds like a slightly out-of-sync folk flute accompanying Tony's flute was actually McLean's cello playing high harmonics. Tony plays the flute with a beautiful tone, by the way, despite the difficulty of doing so for saxophonists, in a style that sounds like some twentieth-century classical piece, descended from Claude Debussy's *Syrinx* or Olivier Messiaen's *Le merle noir* and akin to Henri Dutilleux or André Jolivet.[9] In fact much of the album sounds like modern classical chamber music, with impressive improvised counterpoint. The changes of instrumentation (soprano sax and bass, flute and cello, tenor sax and cello, bass clarinet and bass, tenor sax and bass), with McLean alternating among plucking, bowing, and strumming, relieve what could have been a sense of sameness about the pieces. Even McLean's brief mbira solo ("Say 'Good Night'") is cute. It's well worth finding a used copy of the LP of this album, long out of print and never re-released on CD.

Tony Dagradi, late 1980s

Notes

1. Ramsey McLean & The Lifers, *History's Made Every Moment: New Orleans Now!* (New Orleans: Prescription Records RM–1981, c1981).

2. Vincent Fumar, "The Do-it-yourself Way to Discs," *Times–Picayune*, 12 June 1982, section Lagniappe, 9.

3. Bill Shoemaker, review in *Down Beat* 49, no. 11 (November 1982): 44.

4. *The New New Orleans Music: Jump Jazz* (Cambridge, MA: Rounder CD 2065, 1988), including five tracks by Ramsey McLean and The Survivors recorded in New Orleans in October 1985 and February 1986; the members include Charles Neville and Steve Masakowski.

5. Vincent Fumar, "'Happy Birthday' Sung to WWOZ with N.O. Accent," *Times–Picayune*, 18 December 1981, section Lagniappe, 13.

6. Vincent Fumar, review in *Times–Picayune*, 6 April 1984, section Lagniappe, 15

7. Ed Hazell, review in *Coda*, no. 204 (October–November 1985): 27.

8. Rhodes Spedale, review in *Jazz Times* 15, no. 2 (February 1985): 17.

9. I owe this insight to Harvey Sollberger.

7. BACK TO SCHOOL; SIDEMAN, 1984–90

Back to School

The feature article about Tony in *Down Beat* in 1982 considered him poised for stardom:

> "Why do some very good musicians remain fixtures of their local scene all their lives, while others move into the national spotlight? Is it talent, strategy, or luck? For an answer you might look at the career of Tony Dagradi. With the April release of his second album as leader (*Lunar Eclipse* on Gramavision[1]) and with his regular overseas and national tours in Carla Bley's 10-piece band, the saxophonist, based in New Orleans, seems to be in dead center of making that transition.... It's a safe bet that Tony Dagradi will become more widely known. He has both the talent and the drive, neither of which gets in the way of his basic warmth as a human being."[2]

But three years later, he talked to the *Times–Picayune*'s Vincent Fumar about the difficulties of becoming established outside New Orleans and the lack of work at home:

> "'The cost of living is so high in New York. And there's so much competition, so many good musicians who aren't doing anything. There's not enough good, creative work to hand out to everyone. Here, at least I'm presenting my music, which is more important to me than being in New York. And being in New Orleans and in Louisiana you can get grants easier than you can in New York or Los Angeles because not as many people apply.'
>
> "But Dagradi claims that working locally certainly isn't everything. 'What I'm trying to do is use New Orleans as a base,' he says. 'I travel from here rather than from New York or L.A. So far it's been slow. The scene in New Orleans is starting to be kind of disappointing, the jazz scene especially. I was fortunate to hook up with Carla Bley, since most of my income is from traveling and recording, and not so much from being in New Orleans and doing gigs here.
>
> "'Right now most of my energy is put into making contacts so that I can perform out of town, especially in Europe. Because there's no future playing in town, for anybody in any town. Even if you live in New York or L.A., if you want to be a creative musician you have to travel to other cities. There are a good number of clubs in New York, but not enough for the number of musicians.'"[3]

Soon after that interview, however, Bley stopped using her ten-piece band and switched to smaller ensembles, necessitating a change of tack for Tony in his career.

> "I said to myself: 'I'm doing a lot of gigs, working all the time, taking every single gig that I get a phone call about, if I can possibly take it.' That started to not be very enjoyable or rewarding musically, because I would take anything. I could take the money, and I could do it. But I said: 'I don't want to go play a wedding, play a bunch of stupid stuff. That doesn't make me feel good.' I would come home and say, 'This sucks.' So I said, 'OK, let me work on this teaching thing: I'll get my academic credentials.'"

During the 1985–86 academic year he completed a bachelor's degree at Loyola University of New Orleans. That went rapidly, as he wasn't required to take any saxophone lessons and he could apply credits from his courses at Berklee and The University of New Orleans.

At the end of that academic year, in May 1986, Fumar reported that Tony

"now wants to expand his music by working with a string quartet and electronic music. But the act of improvising always remains uppermost in his mind. 'As a jazz musician I think people don't realize that the longer you improvise, the more conscious the act of composition becomes,' he said. 'It's very spontaneous, but it's also very deliberate. People don't realize it—they think that jazz is just freedom and expressing your soul and heart. But it's also technique. It's getting your fingers to do what your mind and the inspiration of the moment tell you. And it's a lot of years of trying to understand what makes great music great. It all comes out in a flash.'"[4]

After nine years in New Orleans, Tony still remarked about his musical identity: "I don't know if I can say that I feel like a New Orleanian.... I don't know if I'll ever feel bold enough to say that I'm from New Orleans."[5]

During the 1987–88 academic year, Tony was hired as the sabbatical replacement for the saxophone teacher at Loyola, Paul McGinley, a full-time job with "part-time money," as he recalls. He taught saxophone, improvisation, and ensembles.

That same academic year, Tony began a master's degree (MFA) at Tulane University, finishing it in December 1989. He had a tuition waver and was a Teaching Assistant, teaching "a theory course to non-music majors: very lightweight stuff," through spring 1990. He notes: "That worked out pretty easily, but at the same time I was performing as hard as I was normally, and running between Loyola and Tulane. So it was a stressful time for a couple of years." His saxophone teacher at Tulane was Edward "Kidd" Jordan, best known in New Orleans as an exponent of free jazz, but Tony studied almost entirely classical repertoire with him.

Tony told Fumar that after graduating, "What I'd like to do is be part of a progressive jazz department during the school year and travel the rest of the time in Europe or Japan.... [Jazz is] an exotic art form in those places, and they respect it as [much] a[s] classical music. They understand that it's a high art form, and in this country it's not."[6]

To Tony's surprise and good fortune, immediately after he finished his master's degree, McGinley retired from Loyola. Starting in fall 1990, Tony was hired to replace him permanently: a tenure-track position involving instructing both jazz and classical saxophone, directing the top jazz combo, and teaching an improvisation course. He reflected: "I think my goals in doing that were mainly that I would have teaching as a source of income, and I would not have to be prostituting myself musically on all these other gigs. And that's definitely come to pass."

Sideman, 1984–90

Between 1984 and 1990, Tony appeared on several recordings as a sideman. The first was by the fusion band Woodenhead, featuring the outstanding guitarist Jimmy Robinson. Fumar set the scene well: "... it wasn't until the 1970s that the mixture of electric guitars and keyboards became a dominant formula for certain 'fusion' starts. And by that time Woodenhead was well under way. Woodenhead has carried the banner of jazz-rock in New Orleans for years, and has won fans from both sides of the musical fence.... Woodenhead rarely deals in the soporific treacle that other jazz-rock often amounts to. Much of the group's rhythmic sensibility has been influenced by the fast, aggressive 'progressive rock' (now a largely defunct term) that flourished in the early 1970s.... Overall, Woodenhead tends to sound less formula-ridden than many critically praised jazz and rock groups that come to mind. In some respects its sound can be considered heavy metal without the posturing, fusion jazz without the sleepiness."[7]

Fumar went on to encapsulate Tony's appearance on *Woodenhead Live!* (1984)[8]: "Guest appearances are made by saxophonist Tony Dagradi and percussionist Mark Sanders. The album was recorded at Jimmy's [Music Club].... Dagradi first appears on Fran Comiskey's 'Morse Code,' playing soprano saxophone. Sanders is heard on conga drums, and Comiskey and Dagradi get most of the solo time. On 'Sifted through Silk,' Dagradi is at his John Coltrane-influenced best. [Jimmy] Robinson smoothly provides the bridge between Dagradi's first solo and a gentle Fran Comiskey acoustic-piano solo. It's a jazz number and proves that when Dagradi builds up a head of steam he can sound ferocious...."

On "Morse Code," Tony is first heard on the head with synthesizer. After a piano solo and a composed interlude he re-enters and lets loose with great urgency, also taking a similar brief solo towards the end of the piece. He plays soprano again on the following short "Drum," showing off his gorgeous tone, and engages in an all-too-brief exchange of tremolos and staccato fragments with Robinson. "Sifted through Silk" is smooth jazz with attitude, and Tony on tenor, in his usual manner of the time, combines Coltrane influence with bluesy licks in both his solos, the first brief and the second building to a big climax, then easing off on the gas pedal.

On his short album *Shadowlove* (1985), the keyboard player Larry Sieberth, later an occasional substitute in Astral Project, uses his synthesizer to create four distinct types of effect.[9] On "God Gave me this Way," the instrument's background schmoozing makes for the smoothest of what would soon be called smooth jazz, but for my taste, it deadens the energy and only Tony's spiritual level raises the track above the level of elevator music. In sharp contrast, on the boppy "Twozies," Sieberth's realistic-sounding big-band riffs power an exciting solo from Tony, and at the end the two men profitably trade twos, then ones. The title track, "Shadow Love," is a nice ballad for Tony, on which Sieberth in his solo creates the astonishingly lifelike sound of a harmonica, sounding for all the world like Toots Thielemans. Finally, on "Bwe Bop" (without Tony), the drummer Ricky Sebastian along with Astral Project's then-percussionist Mark Sanders create an exciting fast groove while Sieberth plays racing lines.

The harpist Patrice Fisher told me that Tony played with her group Jasmine regularly between about 1984 and 1988. "He played flute with us, because I would rather have a flute player than a sax player. So I would always hire flute players, and Tony played flute as well as sax. But after I heard him play sax, of course, I wanted him to play sax." On *Singers* (1985), Tony plays a unison line on the flute with Fisher's harp on the intro and head of "Summer Rain," contributes effective counterpoint behind the singer, then takes a medium-tempo solo in a similar style to his normal saxophone work.[10] Tony appears on four songs on Fisher's *Foreign Affairs* (1986), made in conjunction with Jasmine and Sounds of Brazil.[11] On "Where Did You Go Last Night?," intensifying the tormented mood of the singer, Laverne Butler, whose boyfriend stayed out all night, he screams and wails in a bluesy style on tenor sax on the intro, his own solo, some counterpoint on the reprise of the head, and the outro. He continues to wail on the fast latin-style "Ponteio." He raises the temperature of the otherwise turgid "Sunday in Rio" with some fast licks in his solo, bluesy inserts, and a "scream" at the end of the song. Finally, on the surprisingly joyful plea of the singer to "Love Me," he brings out his soprano sax and show us what love is all about. I haven't heard Fisher's *Softly Strong* (1987).[12] Fumar's review mentions, "There's more than just a bit of Brazil in 'A toda samba,' which is pleasantly uptempo, and features assertive playing from tenor saxophonist Tony Dagradi and the tune's composer, guitarist Byron Sosa."[13]

In the Nick of Time (1987) by the guitarist Scott Goudeau,[14] at that time a resident of New Orleans, was reviewed with great insight by Fumar:

"Goudeau ... has surrounded himself with players known in both the jazz and fusion fields.... The result is jazz-rock with a sharp edge, and with more tonal variety than would probably have been allowed had the record been made under the auspices of a major label....

"The title track is built upon an appealing riff. Goudeau's guitar has enough of an early-70s tinge (in the manner of fleet-fingered John McLaughlin), and Dagradi's tenor enough brashness, to keep the whole affair from suffering the fate of much fusion—lapsing into dreamland.

"Dagradi, in fact, provides a good deal of the fire. Playing in his commercial style (as opposed to the extended solo work of his jazz gigs), he's heard mostly in the choruses on 'Stereo Lounge,' and elsewhere his brief solos are fluid and robust.

"But the album does dip into the moodier, more austere side of fusion. 'Ash' is heavily atmospheric, with an ominous tom-tom beat and dreamily fragmented piano from [Michael] Pellera. Dagradi harmonizes with Goudeau, and manages to sound gritty and wailing despite the slower tempo....

"With Goudeau's guitar skills and recording savvy, and Dagradi's ruggedly commercial side, *In the Nick of Time* comes off as fusion with hair on its chest, and quite unashamed of its rock element."[15]

Tony plays tenor throughout. He doesn't take a solo on the title track. On "Ash," "Charity," and "Stereo Lounge" his "ruggedly commercial side" sounds to me straight out of his rhythm-and-blues period with a few "out" flurries. On "Family" he brings out his "smooth" side, then becomes freer. On Goudeau's *The Promise* (1988), even Tony's vibrant tenor sax cannot redeem the elevator-music mood of "Hazlehurst," with its heavy synthesizer background, rock-style drumming, and fleet but empty playing by the leader.[16]

The Chicago drummer and composer Damon Short lived in New Orleans from 1983 to 1987. In 1986, he recorded *Penguin Shuffle*, half in New Orleans and half in Dekalb, Illinois.[17] The three New Orleans tracks feature three current and future members of Astral Project—Tony, Steve Masakowski, and James Singleton—as well as the saxophonist Victor Goines, who later achieved fame as a member of the Wynton Marsalis Septet and Jazz at Lincoln Center Orchestra. In 2001, the *Chicago Reader* reported that Short had released the recording in 1988 "in an edition of 1,000—and the 500 copies still sitting in the back of his basement provide a constant reminder of how well that went."[18]

On the opening "S. O. L.," perhaps a portent of the recording's fate, Tony and Goines are both on soprano sax. Goines is discursive and dull; Tony, coming in as the tempo doubles, matches accents well with Short, despite the deadening synthesizer-like comping of Masakowski (on keytar?). "The Penguin," sounding as if it had been composed by Ornette Coleman in a funky mood, pits Goines in the same vein on soprano again against Tony Ornettely funky on bass clarinet. The cutely staccato and dissonant "Circumstantial (Punkbop)" features an energetic tenor "chase" between Tony and Goines, which culminates in an exciting triple solo with Masakowski. One reviewer, Paul Reynolds in *Coda*, singled out Tony as the "notable" soloist on the recording.[19]

In October–December 1987, the now-famous jazz pianist Ellis Marsalis, father of the Marsalis dynasty, hosted a 13-part radio series devoted to New Orleans jazz, "Jazztown," which originated at WWNO and was syndicated on more than 200 public radio stations nationwide.[20] Both Tony and the New Orleans Saxophone Quartet (an alternative name for NOSE) were featured. He recalls that his show was based on the material for the *Dreams of Love* album, with Astral Project, being recorded at that time (see Lasocki, *A Higher Fusion*, chapter 4).

At Snug Harbor on 30 April 1989, during Jazz Fest, Tony was involved in a "jam session" led by Marsalis. The session, recorded for Blue Note Records of Japan, has a number of curious aspects.[21] For a start, no fewer than three saxophonists were advertised—Tony, Rick Margitza, and Earl Turbinton, Jr.—and two bassists—Bill Huntington and James Singleton. But the record bears no trace of Turbinton or James; perhaps they were not available on the day. Instead, the saxophonist Donald Harrison appears on three numbers, playing tenor rather than his usual alto, including a warm solo feature on "I Can't Get Started." He's the only sax player on his own "Jitterbug," for which the great New Orleans drummer David Lee, Jr. is replaced by no less a figure than Art Blakey (he and his Jazz Messengers had played in a concert as part of Jazz Fest the night before), not to mention that the 15-year-old Nicholas Payton sits in on trumpet. Furthermore, you have to pay close attention to tell Tony from Margitza when they are at their most Coltrane-like; and especially on "Some Monk Funk" Tony even picks up some of Margitza's oblique, fragmented way of phrasing, perhaps though jam-session osmosis?

For the record, Tony solos second on "Nothin' but the Blues," first on his own "The Call" (from *Dreams of Love*), second (on soprano) on "After," second on "Some Monk Funk," and between Harrison and Margitza on "A Night in Tunisia." Tony's best solo comes on "The Call": well-developed, relaxed, and intense. Jack Sohmer in *Jazz Times* dubbed the piece a "bright modal blues" among the "swinging originals."[22] Richard Cook and Brian Morton found Tony "all muscle and intensity," and Norman Weinstein declared that "Tony Dagradi, whose playing with Carla Bley was consistently inspired, shines."[23]

My Backyard (1990) by the Mississippi singer and pianist Mose Allison contains some of Tony's best work from this period,[24] and he told me that Allison agrees:

"Whenever I see Mose on a tour, he goes, 'Hey, man: I love that record we did together. Man, there was some things you did that were just perfect.' They just happened to happen on the recording: I was just trying to find a part. I got called up at the last minute for that, so I didn't have any time to prepare. I said, 'You're in the studio? OK, I'll be right over.'

"He had maybe two or three tunes that had little harmonic progressions. And I didn't know the songs yet; I didn't know what his vocal parts were. Whenever I accompany somebody I try to find a line that will accompany the harmony—that will accentuate whatever else is happening. And, you know, it was interesting because just the happenstance of the line that I chose was the perfect counterpoint to the line that he was singing. If I had made any other choice, I would have stepped right on his line."

Allison's NOLA accompanists were John Vidacovich on drums, the veteran New Orleans bass player Bill Huntington, and Steve Masakowski's bluesy guitar (but only on the five songs on which Tony doesn't play).

In "Big Brother," against John's parade rhythm, Tony's cackling entry, developing into a howling climax, personifies Big Brother himself watching you, and the growls in the coda seal your fate. The bluesy "Sentimental Fool" brings out Tony's best powerhouse rhythm-and-blues style on the head. In his solo, he enters like Coltrane, makes the most of the harmonic progression, throws in a few honks, then rounds off beautifully. Ah! On the slow-tempo "Was," Tony comes in after the head, turns up the "luscious" setting on his horn, and creates a perfect chorus. But beautiful! Tony creates considerable rhythmic interest by toying with phrases in four against the 3/4 time of "The Gettin' Paid Waltz." In "Long Song," Allison's ironic speculation on what kind of love song he should write, there are more Big Easy rhythms from John and bluesy interjections from Tony. In his solo Tony melodically takes both tacks: "A line or two about how I just can't go on without you, or maybe that old standby, I'm gonna love you till the day that I die" and "I might just forget about all that stuff and tell 'em how you did me wrong." On the head of "Sleepy Lagoon," Tony employs his best solo ballad style, then, when the tempo doubles, lets loose on his solo in, well, a double-tempo version of the ballad style. And finally, on the title track, Allison wittily describes his sanctuary, commenting on "trees in the wind" and "no need to pretend." Tony then unfurls his ballad style once more, soulful, unpretentious, touching, and never windy.

Critical comment was generally favorable. The most eminent critic, Scott Yanow, noted: "Mose traveled down to New Orleans and used some of the city's best talent. Tony Dagradi often reminds me of Stanley Turrentine (with touches of Coltrane), the versatile drummer John Vidacovich occasionally contributes parade rhythms, and guitarist Steve Masakowski also takes some excellent solos. This quintet [sic] could easily record a fine instrumental album, but then one would miss Mose's stories.... "[25] Elsewhere Yanow dubbed Mose's collaborators "local but world-class musicians."[26] Richard Cook and Brian Morton shrewdly observe that "the New Orleans team that supports him on *My Backyard* has its own agenda as well as following the leader."[27] Furthermore, Clive Davis saw how the NOLA instrumentalists raised Allison's game: "After a gap of almost three years, the singer-pianist is back with a modern New Orleans band and more deadpan reflections on the loser's life. Saxophonist Tony Dagradi and guitarist Steve Masakowski stir a soulful brew, taking some of the pressure off Allison's highly personalized voice."[28] All in all, as Tom Lackner put it, "the Crescent City groove is the perfect foil for Allison. John Vidacovich's drumming and Tony Dagradi's gritty yet lyrical tenor sax playing set the music in its proper light. The groove is unmistakable, yet the music is relaxed, with plenty of supportive dialogue."[29]

Tony continued to perform with Allison when he came to Louisiana over the next few years: for example, at Tipitina's on 26 December 1990 and at Rick's Café Américain in Baton Rouge on 17 April 1992 (both with Huntington and John Vidacovich).[30]

Notes

1. For *Lunar Eclipse*, see David Lasocki, *A Higher Fusion*, chapter 2.

2. Simpson, "Tony Dagradi."

3. Vincent Fumar, "A Summit of the Saxes," *Times–Picayune*, 19 April 1985, section Lagniappe, 12.

4. Vincent Fumar, "N.O.'s Musical Roots Run Deep," *Times–Picayune*, 4 May 1986, section A, 25.

5. Ibid.

6. Vincent Fumar, "In Search of Modern Jazz," *Times–Picayune*, 13 October 1989, section Lagniappe, L6.

7. Vincent Fumar, "Woodenhead Fuses its Sound on Record," *Times–Picayune*, 24 May 1985, section Lagniappe, 20.

8. Woodenhead, *Woodenhead Live!* (New Orleans: Broken Records JR 3685, 1984).

9. Lawrence Sieberth, *Shadowlove* (New Orleans: Broken Records JR–3885, 1985).

10. Patrice Fisher, *Singers* (New Orleans: Broken Records JR–3585, 1985).

11. Jasmine, Sounds of Brazil, Patrice Fisher, *Foreign Affairs* (Broken Records JR–1086, 1986).

12. Patrice Fisher, *Softly Strong* (Broken Records JT1087, 1987).

13. Vincent Fumar, "Listening to Albums by Two Local Trios," *Times–Picayune*, 15 May 1987, section Lagniappe, 10.

14. Scott Goudeau, *In the Nick of Time* (New Orleans: Broken Records BR–1186, 1987).

15. Vincent Fumar, "N.O. Guitarist Makes a Record His Way," *Times–Picayune*, 3 April 1987, section Lagniappe, 9.

16. Scott Goudeau, *The Promise* (New Orleans: Broken Records BR–1288, 1988).

17. Damon Short, *Penguin Shuffle* (Northridge, CA: Blue Room 004, 1987).

18. Peter Margasak, "Post No Bills: Damon Short Tries it at Home," *Chicago Reader* 31, no. 9 (30 November 2001): 1, S.

19. Paul Reynolds, "In the Tradition," *Coda: The Journal of Jazz & Improvised Music*, no. 221 (August–September 1988): 12–14.

20. See Vincent Fumar, "Variety in Pop Music," *Times–Picayune*, 11 September 1987, section Lagniappe, 9; Fumar, "Making Radio More Aware of Jazz," *Times–Picayune*, 25 September 1987, section Lagniappe, 21.

21. Ellis Marsalis, *A Night at Snug Harbor, New Orleans* (Evidence Music ECD 22129, p1989, c1995).

22. Jack Sohmer, review in *Jazz Times* 26, no. 5 (May 1996): 85.

23. Richard Cook and Brian Morton, *The Penguin Guide to Jazz*, 9th ed., 949; Norman Weinstein, review in *Boston Phoenix*; 23–30 November 1995; available from http://www.boston.phoenix.com/alt1/archive/music/reviews/11-23-95/ELLIS_MARSALIS.html; accessed 14 December 2004.

24. Mose Allison, *My Backyard* (Hollywood: Blue Note CDP 7 93840 2, 1990).

25. Scott Yanow, review in *Cadence* 17, no. 4 (April 1991): 83.

26. Scott Yanow, review on www.allmusic.com.

27. Richard Cook and Brian Morton, *The Penguin Guide to Jazz on CD*, 7th ed. (London:

Penguin Books, 2004), 30.

28. Clive Davis, review in *The Times* (London), 19 May 1990, section Features.

29. Tom Lackner, review in *Santa Barbara Independent*, no. 203, 18 October 1990, 27.

30. For the concert at Rick's Café, see Rod Dreher, "After 10 Years, Mose Returns," *The Advocate* (Baton Rouge, LA), 17 April 1992, section Fun, 10–Fun.

8. *IMAGES FROM THE FLOATING WORLD* AND *SWEET REMEMBRANCE*

Images from the Floating World

Images from the Floating World. The Tony Dagradi Trio: TD, ss (4), ts (1–3, 5–7); JS, b; JV, d, p. Recorded at Composers Recording Studio, New Orleans, Louisiana. UPC 4036290072768. Line/Core Records COCD 9.00727 0, c1986.
1. Parading (TD) (5:15)
2. A Flower is a Lovesome Thing (Billy Strayhorn) (7:12)
3. O. F. O. (TD) (6:08)
4. Images from the Floating World (TD) (8:40)
5. Code Blue (TD) (3:58)
6. When Your Own Heart Asks (TD) (9:32)
7. Guru Kirpal Ji Tera Saharah (TD) (6:00)

   Re-released under the title *Parading* (Mirliton 0203, 2002).

   "Guru Kirpal Ji Tera Saharah" reissued on *That's Core Jazz*, Vol. 2 (Line COCD 9.01125, 1991). "Code Blue," "Guru Kirpal Ji Tera Saharah," and "Parading" reissued on *JazzSouth Program 6* (Southern Arts Federation SAF #6, 1993).

The first recording by the Tony Dagradi Trio (Tony, James Singleton, and John Vidacovich), made in 1986 at Steve Masakowski's Composers Recording Studio, had a limited release in Germany in 1990 under the exotic title *Images from the Floating World*. Twelve years later it was issued in the United States under the simpler name of the opening track, *Parading*. It shows off Tony, especially, to good effect: his wonderful sonority on both tenor and soprano saxophones and a high level of improvisational creativity. At times, the group reminds me of the Ornette Coleman Trio, and James agreed: "We were very much influenced by that." Tony's compositions display a pleasing variety of moods, tempos, and approaches. In all, the album is a splendid record of a group of musicians who had already been playing together for nine years.

The title of the album, also of one of its compositions, was actually taken from the standard art book on the Japanese wood-block print by Richard Lane (1978).[1] Tony's wife Joan, an artist, had the book lying around the house. In the Middle Ages, the Japanese term *ukiyo* ("floating world") had the Buddhist sense of the unreliable, transient world we live in; thus "floating" was equivalent to "fleeting." By the seventeenth century the expression had evolved to signify "the stylish world of pleasure, the world of easy women and handsome actors, all the varied pleasures of the flesh."[2] *Ukiyo-e* (floating-world pictures) depicted this newly fashionable hedonistic life. The title of another track on the album, "When Your Own Heart Asks," was taken from a medieval Samurai poem:

To tell others that
It is a rumor
Will not do.
When your own heart asks,
How will you respond?[3]

Tony told me, "I let the spirit of what I knew about Japanese art and shakuhachi music into those particular pieces." The shakuhachi is an end-blown notched flute, tuned to the pentatonic scale, and capable of playing pitch-bends, ornaments, and glissandi with ease over a large compass and dynamic range.

"Parading" began life in this trio format, then was taken up by Astral Project and appeared on *Dreams of Love* the following year (see Lasocki, *A Higher Fusion*, chapter 4). James plays a constant six-note ostinato on the F7 chord throughout Tony's free-ranging solo. The trio format without a chordal instrument, even on a vamp, offers the saxophonist a relaxed space and time to explore. He throws in some "out" playing—a little Ornette-like, a few Albert Ayler-like growls—over the full range of the tenor. John, a sensitive partner, takes a solo that departs from the Second-Line style, then returns to it.

Tony's first recorded performance of Billy Strayhorn's ballad "A Flower is a Lovesome Thing," predating the version on *Astral Project New Orleans LA* by eight years, finds the trio in excellent form. (The composition had already been in his repertory for at least five years, as it's found on a recording of a live performance by Astral Project at Tipitina's on 22 November 1981.) Here Tony states the plaintive theme in a Johnny Hodges-like manner, replete with glissandi and going down to some really resonant low notes, with John supportive on brushes. James provides a slow accompaniment including some double stops, not trying to fill in the musical space, but varying the note-placement around the beat. Tony's solo, a well of invention, takes us on a beautiful process of discovery, with occasional references to the theme, as well as to Hodges and Coleman Hawkins, and a wide range of articulation, perhaps wider than any other jazz sax player around. He moves smoothly back into an abbreviated head, leading to a cadenza over bowed bass and a beautiful tone on the final note.

Tony's avowed tribute, "O. F. O. (One for Ornette)," doesn't sound much like Coleman's music to me, or to some reviewers—"it must be a different Ornette than the one I know"[4]— although Tony affirmed that it does to him. It forms part of a group of three compositions, along with "Fall Out" and "Nose Dive" that "I wrote probably the same week when I was in Provincetown [1982] in between gigs with Carla. And they were all the same kind of tune: harmonically 'out,' somewhat indicative of a tonal center, but 'out.'" The tune of "O. F. O," marked *Rubato* in 3/4 time, is written without barlines in a free rhapsodic style. The basic rhythms constitute variants on a short–long pattern, like some latterday *folia*.[5] The mood is saved from sentimentality by the chromatic sequences in the harmonies. In this performance, the head features very active drums and an unusual bassline from James, employing note placement almost independent of the theme, alternating with "walking." Tony's solo begins in a linear fashion, then quickly turns to "spazzing out" in a Coltrane-like manner. James takes a fast, inventive solo, including some double stops, close to his recent style. John's solo picks up on the same mood, then subtly varies the theme. Tony's restatement of the head leads to a resonant final note once more.

On the title tune, "Images from the Floating World," Tony displays a haunting, oboe-like sound on soprano saxophone. After an intro in long notes embellished by turns, sax and bass play an angular melody, largely in unison. *Group Improvisation—Drummer moves to piano using mallets on strings*. Tony expands the material of the intro against active counterpoint from James. John comes in, as instructed, on the piano strings, playing atonally. Tony responds by also playing in an atonal manner, rather like a modern classical piece. James begins bowing and John makes the strings sound like a funky electronic ostinato, returning to a beat. After a short bowed solo by James, Tony re-enters against James's high bowed bass and John on piano strings plus bellstick. Tony cadences gently—and that would have been a good ending for the piece. *Da capo al fine*. Why do we always have to go back to the head? To me it sounds superfluous here.

"Code Blue" is largely an improvised duet between Tony and John. It opens with a solo by John in a Tony Williams-like style, first on drums, then adding a little cymbal color and finally a fast cymbal beat. Tony on tenor sax enters with repeated-note motives, fast Coltrane licks, flutter-tonguing, wails, staccatissimo articulation, shrieks, and several rhythmic patterns hit simultaneously with John. James enters only on the head—or "tag," as Tony prefers to call it here—which has three short sections of fast repeated motives, separated by two written-out lines for the sax in free rhythm.

According to Tony, "When Your Own Heart Asks" was influenced by a modern classical composition, *Music for Tenor Saxophone and Piano* by M. William Karlins (1972), which he played in a recital "years ago." He explained:

> "Karlin's piece has long sections of improvisation. Usually he gives you a series of notes to use, or sometimes it's not a row but a grouping of notes to improvise on, and then as you play with the accompanist there are cues to get out and get in to the different sections—sometimes rhythmic cues, sometimes melodic cues. It was very interesting, very fun. 'When Your Own Heart Asks' is organized in a similar way to this classical piece, in that it has written music—material that you have to play exactly; and then it has sections of improvisations, although much looser, much more freedom; and then it has very specific cues to get in and out of the sections. So it's very hard to hear the difference between the written music and the improvised music. I thought that was very successful. I should do more of that."

A. *Rubato*. The composition begins with James bowing and John on tom toms. Tony states a majestic theme made up of three-note motives, moving down then up, in a variety of intervals from perfect fifth to minor seventh. Tony disguises the starkness of the intervals with glissandi and scoops. The last phrase comprises faster-moving ascending and descending fourths. B. *(Da capo)*. When James begins a medium-paced ostinato reminiscent of Jimmy Garrison's work with John Coltrane, the A section of the composition feels in retrospect like an introduction. The ostinato leads surprisingly to an angular, Monkish theme, stated in mostly parallel rhythms by sax and bass, and harmonically emphasizing the interval of a ninth. John, instructed to "play 'melody,'" employs brushes. C. *Unaccompanied Bass Solo gradually joined by the Drums then Tenor*. James takes an active solo, developing the ostinato, while John punctuates with cymbals. When Tony enters, the pace picks up, and he trades fierce figures with James before the solo blends seamlessly into ... D. *Cue*. ... a sax–bass duet in free counterpoint, leading into an expansion of the Monkish theme. E. *Tenor Sax Solo 4/4 time, then Drum Solo*. James switches to a walking bass, over which Tony takes a Rollins-esque solo, full of rhythmic variety and alternating motivic development with linear passage work. John's long solo emphasizes tom toms and developing several rhythmic motives. F. *Drums set up original tempo then Da capo al Coda*. The entire B section returns, leading to a lyrical two-measure coda with a bluesy embellishment by Tony on the final note.

The album concludes with "Guru Kirpal Ji Tera Saharah," a rousing piece dedicated to Joan Dagradi's Master, Kirpal Singh. Astral Project had been playing it since 1982. Tony's soprano sax takes on an appropriately Eastern, rasping, shawm-like tone quality. During the first chorus, James plays a repeated note; during the second, a calypso-like eight-note ostinato. John goes to town on toms. Tony knows how to tell a story with this simple material, going in and "out" of the chords, creating ever bigger arcs, and repeating and varying several motives. James maintains his ostinato during John's solo, which plays with the rhythm of the ostinato. Then we're back to the head.

The Penguin Guide to Jazz gave the album high marks: "Slimming the group down to a trio affords Dagradi the space and freedom to turn this into a terrific blowing session. 'Parading' ... becomes a boastful New Orleans march, 'O. F. O.' is a convincing tribute to Ornette Coleman, and there's nothing wasted in the long and impassioned exchanges between the leader and his partners on the other pieces."[6] On the recording's re-release in 2002, Keith Spera wrote in the *Times–Picayune*: "With Dagradi, Vidacovich, and Singleton still members of Astral Project and still performing occasionally as a trio, it is as if the material time-traveled to the present day. With no chordal instrument, the players are given tremendous freedom to roam."[7]

Sweet Remembrance

Sweet Remembrance. TD, ss, ts; Fred Hersch, p; Harvie Swartz, b; Bob Moses, d; Lee Torchia, tambourine [i.e., tanpura]; Ray Spiegel, tabla. Recorded at Sorcerer Sound, New York, 7–8 March 1987. UPC 051518870722. Gramavision 18–8707–2, p1987.
1. Sat Guru Sawan Sha (Invocation) (arr. TD) (4:21)
2. Chelo Ni Saiyo Sirsa (The Journey) (arr. TD) (6:58)
3. Sohana Sha Kirpal Pyara (Ocean of Love) (arr. TD) (5:21)
4. Tu Mera Pita (Our Father) (arr. TD) (4:31)
5. Mayro Mana Kyon Na Su Nay Dhuna Nama (Unstruck Sound) (arr. TD) (1:34)
6. Sweet Remembrance (TD) (7:20)
7. Tati Vao Na Laga Di Ji (The Protecting Circle) (arr. TD) (5:03)
8. Ute Jag Musaphir Bhor Bhai (Awakening) (arr. TD) (5:19)
9. Sant Satguru Satta Swaroopa (O Transcendental Lord) (arr. TD) (6:01)

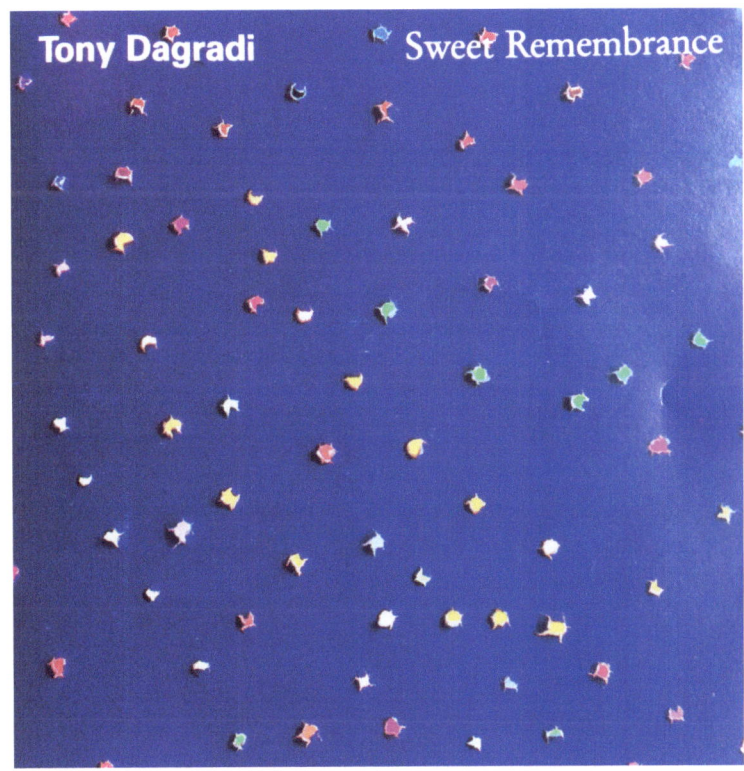

Sweet Remembrance, recorded in March 1987 at Sorcerer Sound in the Soho area of New York City, remains Tony's spiritual masterpiece. He also feels it's probably his best recording, "if for no other reason than it's got this strong concept holding it together."

"But I also felt like I was on a mission from God, when I did that one. I felt that I was being guided and blessed. It was an honor for me to be able to play it, to produce the record. It was very easy for me to do it. The circumstances for the record came together very easily. We were just with Sanji [Sant Ajaib Singh] at a retreat in California for a week, probably longer. And at that point I said, these bhajans are very nice: I wonder what would happen if I put them into a jazz context; maybe that would be helpful to me. Certainly the melodies are very interesting."

In his liner notes, Tony explained the origins of the music and the album in more detail:

"Like many mystic traditions, Sant Mat utilizes music as a means of increasing devotional ardor and remembrance of God within the devotee. As a prelude to each Satsang (meeting), where disciples study the teachings of past and present realized souls, devotional hymns called *bhajans* are sung. The text[s] of these hymns, eloquent poetry written by various masters of this path, offer praise of God as well as exhortations for the initiate to be faithful to his meditation and strong in day-to-day life. When sung with love and devotion, this mystical poetry helps to concentrate the attention of the singers in preparation for meditation.

"While listening to these hauntingly beautiful songs at the feet of my Master, I felt it would be a personally rewarding experience to [arrange] and perform several of them [for] Western instruments in a contemporary setting. From the vast repertoire of *bhajans*, I chose several which seemed exceptionally poignant. To some of these I added a harmonic structure only; on others I took greater liberties with rhythm and form. My main concern in arranging these songs was to preserve the devotional quality of the melodies and, at the same time, create interesting and meaningful vehicles for improvisation.

"I have also included my own composition 'Sweet Remembrance.' The melody of this piece is based on the rhythm of a secret, charged mantra. For me this gives it special significance. Moreover, the title sums up the feeling which I wish to convey with this record.

"It is my hope that this music, arranged and performed with a spirit of love and devotion, will be a source of inspiration and upliftment for the listener. I am grateful that my physical form could be used as a channel for this work, and I feel blessed to be able to use my God-given talents as a composer and improvisor in the sweet remembrance of God and my Guru."

The composition "Sweet Remembrance" had been written by 1982, when it was performed live by Astral Project, and the group also played it at Jazz Fest in 1984.

Tony told me more about circumstances of making the recording:

"So I came home to New Orleans with that idea. And the very first call that I got was my record producer at Gramavision, Jonathan Rose, and he goes, 'You know, I was thinking about it: why don't you make a New Age record next?' So I said, 'OK,' and I ran down what I'd been thinking about. And he said: 'That's perfect.' There was no waiting.

"Actually, it took me a little time to get the arrangements the way I wanted, but basically I had it all plotted out. I made a demo for Rose, actually with Astral Project. And I think I sat on it for a little while, kept it in my pocket at it were. And I remember playing it for some other initiate: 'Listen to this.' And he's a jazz fan, good friend of mine; he said: 'Oh, man, you should send it right off to the record company.' And they said, 'This is perfect.'

"The whole thing, everything fell into place at every point. That recording was done direct to two-track. There was no mixing. When I got done recording it, it was done. No mixing, no overdubs. Kind of nerve-wracking in that respect, because you couldn't go back and repair anything. That was it: bang. You would have to do another take. We were in the studio two days, and most of the first day was just getting the sound of the instruments, getting a decent balance on everything, and we had a great engineer, Jim Anderson. That's what you have to do when you do two-track. You have to make sure it's really what you want, because you can't change it after the fact. If you do multi-track, you can change anything after the fact. We did half one night; half the next day. And then at the end of the day we decided what takes we were going to use, cut the tape together. I walked out with a completed record. It was amazing."

I asked Tony why he hadn't made the recording with his Astral Project colleagues, especially as they did the demo. "I guess because Astral Project had just done the last record for Gramavision, and they were trying to do something different each time. Initially I talked to Charlie Haden and Paul Motian. When it came down to it, we just didn't have the budget." When Tony got together with Fred Hersch (piano), Harvie Swartz (bass), and Bob Moses (drums),

"I explained the whole concept to them and they understood it: these guys were great. They went for the concept. And we talked about how we wanted the music to sound and how we wanted them to play. One thing I told them, I remember: I didn't want it to sound like bebop. They understood what I meant straight away—that it was supposed to be uplifting, have a certain vibe to it. And I think for me in my own mind, I was thinking that I wanted to play very melodically. By telling them not to play bebop I was telling them that I didn't want a lot of notes, a lot of pyrotechnics. Everything simple, beautiful, focused. And they really helped me play a lot better."

A collection of devotional hymns sounds as if it would be monotonous, but Tony's conception of them creates a surprising amount of variety: relaxed on "Sat Guru Sawan Sha," impassioned turning to calypso-like on "Chelo Ni Saiyo Sirsa," soaring on "Sohana Sha Kirpal Pyara," jubilantly rocking on "Tu Mera Pita," sweet on the unaccompanied "Mayro Mana Kyon Na Su Nay Dhuna Nama" with his oboe-like soprano sax, joyously loose on "Sweet Remembrance," Gospel-like on "Tati Vao Na Laga Di Ji," Indian on "Ute Jag Musaphir Bhor Bhai" replete with tabla and tanpura, and back to quietly impassioned on "Sant Satguru Satta Swaroopa." His solos are mature and beautifully developed, placing wails and screams judiciously at strategic moments, varying the rhythm, occasionally playing slightly "out" of the harmony, and always, always with the most exquisite tone. Hersch has a beautiful touch on the piano as well as accompanimental techniques that are always apposite, and his solos are completely absorbing. He's an excellent foil for Tony because, as he said in a recent interview, "I consider myself a very rhythmic player; certainly I've earned my stripes in terms of playing rhythm and doing interesting things with time, but I'm also a melodist."[8] Swartz and Moses know when to be active and when to lay back, and the bassist takes an appropriately jubilant solo on "Tu Mera Pita" and a Gospel-ish one on "Tati Vao Na Laga Di Ji." The order and choice of solos disguise the usual head–solos–head form of jazz, and on "Ute Jag Musaphir Bhor Bhai," instead of an out chorus Tony and Hersch play imitative figures against the drone, getting faster and ending abruptly.

Tony also recorded "Tati Vao Na Laga Di Ji" as "The Protecting Circle" with Astral Project on *Voodoobop*, where it's slower, less bouncy, and more wistful (see Lasocki, *A Higher Fusion*, 131).

Sweet Remembrance received four reviews: one mixed; three sympathetic and highly positive. Puzzlingly, Will Smith saw the album as "a spiritually linked collection somewhat clouded by the ghost of the late John Coltrane.... The music is like Keith Jarrett's combo, with saxist Jan Garbarek, also a Coltrane devotee."[9] Fortunately, the other critics were able to see Tony as influenced by Coltrane but able to communicate his own spiritual message. The best-known critic, Scott Yanow, wrote in *Cadence*:

"*Sweet Remembrance* is Tony Dagradi's *Love Supreme*. The saxophonist has been involved in a mystical Indian religion since 1977, so on his new album he takes eight devotional hymns (which he has updated harmonically and chordally) and adapts them to jazz. Dagradi, whose Coltrane-influenced tone also utilizes the soulful sound of Michael Brecker, plays with an assured inner peace that translates into respectful passion rather than New Age monotony. Pianist Hersch is masterful (at times recalling early Alice Coltrane) and the performances do not necessarily sound religious; in fact some of the music has standard chord changes. Overall, *Sweet Remembrance* is in the vein of Coltrane's 'Welcome' and 'Dear Lord': relaxed and spiritual but never superficial."[10]

Russ Summers in *Option Magazine* also couldn't help making reference to Coltrane:

"... since John Coltrane's death, many jazz artists have tried to capture the master's power, glory, and majesty on vinyl, but have often failed. However, without consciously trying, saxophonist Tony Dagradi has achieved much of the fire thought to be forever lost. With the exception of uptempo tracks such as 'Tu mera dita (Our Father),' which are more soulfully urgent, the tunes rely on swelling, surging ensemble interaction over a few chord changes, a device known to Coltrane fans as 'the sweep.' Instead of basing the music on Coltrane's *Meditations* or *A Love Supreme*, Dagradi draws the spiritual base of his music from devotional hymns of the Sant Mat religion. Although the quartet isn't up to Coltrane's (and few are), it's difficult to believe that the musicians were assembled solely for this session. Pianist Fred Hersch, bassist Harvey Swartz, and drummer Bob Moses all contribute deep and thoughtful playing throughout, helping make the record one that should not be ignored."[11]

Norman Provizer in *Jazziz* even went so far as to see Tony's "spiritual strength" as equal to Coltrane's:

"On *Sweet Remembrance* ... the aggressive tenor pays homage to his spiritual journey with eight devotional hymns (bhajans) and with his own mantra-based composition which furnishes the album's title. Because the hymns are constructed from Hindi folk tunes, to which Dagradi has added the written harmonic structure, this 'remembrance of God through music' is extremely accessible in every sense.

"With the support of fellow Gramavisionaries drummer Bob Moses, bassist Harvie

Swartz, and pianist Fred Hersch, Dagradi's musical offering is lyrical, attractive, and devoid of pretension. His technique on soprano and especially tenor is evocative and exultant. Like so many tenor players, Dagradi speaks of a period when he was 'totally immersed in Trane.' To his credit, the thirty-five-year old saxophonist manages to capture the spiritual strength Coltrane so elegantly epitomized.

"Unlike most recordings in this genre, the songs on *Sweet Remembrance* do not follow the well-worn path of Indo-jazz fusion. Ray Spiegel's tabla and Lee Torchia's [*tanpura*] make brief and modest appearances, but the quartet essentially resists exotica in favor of simple and direct communication."[12]

In *Sweet Remembrance*, Tony dug deep into his spiritual practice as well as his 15-year experience of performing on the jazz scene and his mastery of both soprano and tenor saxophones to create a transcendent and inspiring collection, an authentic celebration of his love and devotion. And he did it in a New York studio with a pick-up group....

Notes

1. Richard Lane, *Images from the Floating World: The Japanese Print; Including an Illustrated Dictionary of Ukiyo-e* (Old Saybrook, CT: Konecky & Konecky, 1978).

2. Lane, *Images from the Floating World*, 11.

3. From the *Gosen waka shu*; translated and cited in Yamamoto Tsunetomo, *Hagakure: The Book of the Samurai*, trans. William Scott Wilson (Tokyo & New York: Kodansha International, 1979), 170 (in n. 4).

4. Steven A. Loewy, review of Astral Project's *Elevado* in *Cadence* 24, no. 8 (August 1998): 136–37.

5. The *folia* was a musical theme and chord sequence used for sets of variations in the seventeenth and eighteenth centuries (and even occasionally in the nineteenth and twentieth centuries): in G minor, i V i VII III VII i V :||: i V i VII III VII i V i.

6. Richard Cook and Brian Morton, *The Penguin Guide to Jazz on CD, LP and Cassette* (Harmondsworth, Middlesex: Penguin Books, 1992), 253–54; also in *The Penguin Guide to Jazz on Compact Disc*, 3rd ed. (London: Penguin Books, 1996), 313.

7. Keith Spera, review in *Times-Picayune*, 18 July 2003, section Lagniappe, 27.

8. Ethan Iverson, interview with Fred Hersch, http://dothemath.typepad.com/dtm/interview-with-fred-hersch.html; accessed 1 October 2013.

9. Will Smith, review in *Omaha World–Herald*, 13 December 1987.

10. Scott Yanow, review in *Cadence* 14, no. 2 (February 1988): 79.

11. Russ Summers, review in *Option Magazine* (details unknown).

12. Norman Provizer, review in *Jazziz*, February/March 1988.

9. ASTRAL PROJECT, 1986–95

In 1986, Mark Sanders returned to his native New York to devote himself to Latin bands. Astral Project must then have played as a quartet for about a year. Around New Orleans, the four remaining musicians in Astral Project often gigged with a guitarist of their own age, Steve Masakowski (b. 1954), who, like Tony, Tork, and James, had attended Berklee. Performing on a seven-string guitar and the keytar, a guitar-synthesizer of his own invention, Steve led an experimental group called Mars, with James on bass, Larry Sieberth on keyboards and electronics, and the legendary New Orleans drummer and composer James Black, as well as the well-known New York saxophonist Dave Liebman whenever he visited New Orleans. Steve, like Tony, also sometimes played with Mark's Afro-Cuban jazz-fusion band, Caliente, of which James was a founding member. Steve had even been advertised as performing with the Astral Project of the day as far back as 25 September 1980, at the opening night of a bar named Smokey's. After Mark had been gone for about a year, Steve replaced him in the group. That must have transpired in summer 1987, as he was not present at JazzFest on 3 May, but did take part in the album *Dreams of Love*, which the group began recording in September.

Dreams of Love, billed as by "Tony Dagradi with Astral Project," reflects the group at the beginning of its new configuration (September 1987 and January 1988). At this point the compositions were still all Tony's—"The Call," "Child's Play," "Dreams of Love," "Morning Star," "Parading," and "Prayer"—except for one standard, "I Cover the Waterfront." (For a discussion of this album, see Lasocki, *A Higher Fusion*, chapter 4.) The image on the cover is a bas-relief sculpture of Tony by his wife Joan.

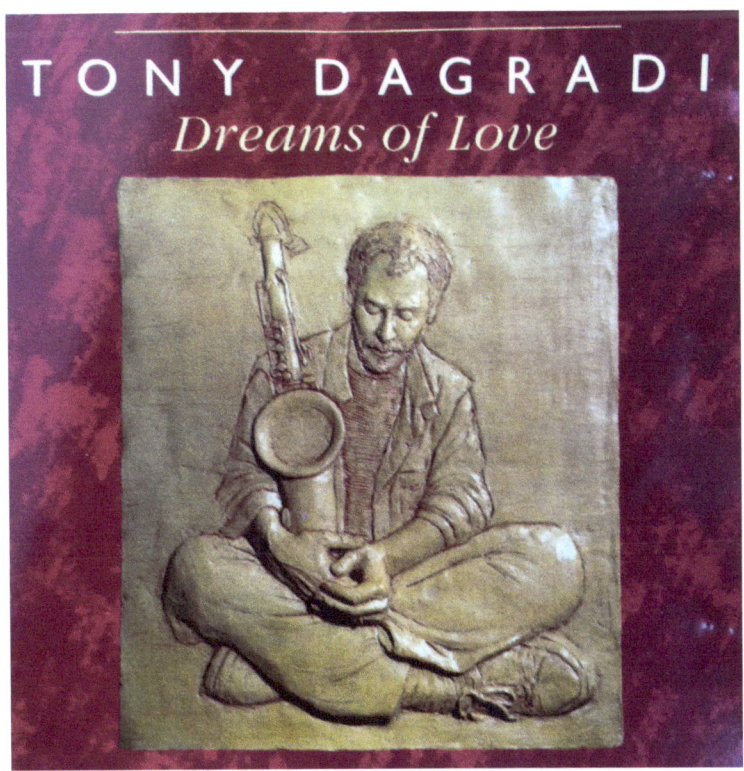

Tony recalls about the late 1970s and 1980 generally, "We played together in a lot of different configurations. But it seemed that the Astral Project thing won over just on the basis of longevity. Since we were all together consistently in the band, it became the thing we did together." Nevertheless, during that period, the members of Astral Project collectively made recordings as sidemen with more than thirty other leaders or groups, in a variety of styles from blues, rock, rock–fusion, and folk to traditional and modern jazz (although modern jazz and blues were in the majority).

The existence of Astral Project itself remained tenuous for the remainder of the 1980s. The group had advertised performances less than once a month, mostly at Snug Harbor, in 1985–86, and the beginning of 1987 was worse. In October 1987, the group snagged a weekly gig at the recently reopened Tyler's,[1] but had lost it by the following April and the dog years returned. And Astral Project's low profile on the New Orleans scene in the 1980s inevitably led to a lack of recognition, even in the local press.

The balance of compositions in Astral Project soon changed, as James recalls, when Steve brought in his own. "It was a huge vision that went very well with Tony's, but was very complete and really broadened the palette and made it a more wide-ranging thing." Adding a new compositional voice also had a hand in the group becoming more democratic. The announcement of a gig at Tulane University on 27 February 1989, which Tony curated as part of his assistantship there, shows how much the balance could swing away from him on one particular night: "Tony Dagradi and Astral Project perform works by James Singleton and David Torkanowsky."

Astral Project remained close to home throughout the 1980s, while its members were in "freelance mode," as Tony dubbed it. "We would do very occasional things out on the road, but mostly it was in New Orleans." In November 1989, the group had its first major gig abroad, at the Berlin Jazz Festival, as part of an all-New Orleans night that also featured Wynton Marsalis and Kent Jordan.[2] But Astral Project had been playing together so little that—as Tony, Tork, and James all told me—it gave a weak performance, although James remembers that "Johnny was great."

Once he started teaching full-time the following year, Tony found Astral Project difficult to maintain.

> "I was really doing way too much stuff. I had to develop some lecture courses, putting in long days, and I was forgetting to call people and remind them about gigs. I was losing it. We had a couple of gigs where people said, 'What do you mean, we have a gig tonight?' Or, 'I didn't know about that gig.' And I'd think, 'I could have sworn I called everybody about the gigs before I locked them in, but I don't know.'
>
> "I'm not even clear if I was really forgetting or whether they were just messing with me, you know. 'Cause usually I'm pretty conscientious. But at that point I just started to have too many things on my plate."

James then took the reins and, as Tony observed, "put a lot of time and energy into booking tours."

In 1990, Steve and John were among the six "contemporary" jazz musicians to be listed on the first Jazz All Stars Honor Roll of *New Orleans Magazine*, along with Clyde Kerr Jr., Red Tyler, Ellis Marsalis, and Bill Huntington.[3] The following year, Tony, Tork, and James received the same honor.

In 1991, Astral Project undertook its first tour of Europe—an extensive one with a couple of dozen gigs in Austria, Germany, Italy, and Switzerland. Tork pulled out at the last minute and Michael Pellera substituted for him on the tour. By this stage, Astral Project's musical style had become malleable. Tony told an interviewer in 1990: "I like the flexibility of this group a great deal. We can sort of work around these questions like Electric vs. Acoustic. I mean, as far as that goes, I probably like an acoustic setting the absolute best, but electric music can be very exciting, and this band has the capacity to do all of it."[4]

In 1992, Tony told Geraldine Wyckoff: "We all agree that we would like to play more as a group, and so more of our energy has been placed in that direction.... I think the identity of the band has become so strong that it is a very viable commercial product now."[5] After playing at Snug Harbor on and off since the club began under the name The Faubourg in 1980, Astral Project secured a regular monthly gig there that lasted almost twenty years.

Reviewing the group's performance at the WWOZ Labor Day celebration on 7 September in Armstrong Park, New Orleans, Kevin Patton put forward the idea that creativity stems from an understanding that jazz is change (as is life). "We can never catch ourselves, much less our music, and this understanding moves the constant restructuring of any 'oneness' or reality or truth. This is the understanding evident in Astral Project's music, and why they are arguably the best quintet in New Orleans, if not the United States."[6]

Astral Project's position as the leading modern-jazz group in New Orleans was confirmed on 17 November 1992, when it won first prize in the Cognac Hennessy Jazz Search, against twenty-five other groups.

After the competition, Scott Aiges wrote:

"Jazz group Astral Project is $10,000 richer after winning the Cognac Hennessy Best of New Orleans Jazz Search at Charlie B's Tuesday night. Last year's winner, the Victor Goines Group, was joined by singer Germaine Bazzle for a set of sultry swing that brought the band second place and a prize of $2,500. Trombonist Rick Trolsen's band Neslort took third place and a $1,000 prize with a set of funky grooves and moody atmospherics. But it was Astral Project's mix of gently explosive bebop, demure Latin jazz, balladry, and Miles Davis-inspired funk—with quick trips into reggae, cha-cha, and rhumba—that most impressed the four judges (Dave Bartholomew, Vincent Fumar, Mike Gourrier, and Geraldine Wyckoff). Goines' group was cool and retro, while synthesizer gave Neslort a modern touch, but Astral Project combined a palette of styles with heaps of soul. Band leader/saxophonist Tony Dagradi said the quintet would split the prize money evenly."[7]

A surviving video of the television broadcast of Astral Project's performance on Cox Cable shows all its members relaxed and taking musical risks. Even on such a big occasion, you feel the soloists biding their time and letting the material develop organically.

Tony introduced the television broadcast with a speech about the group's performance philosophy:

"The strength and impact of the band lie in the individual and collective strengths of the players. These involve personal experiences, musical tastes, and the ability to react sympathetically to musical stimuli provided by other members of the band. We each have a deep and abiding respect for the traditions of jazz and a thorough knowledge of the history of our individual instruments' role in the music. At times, we may emulate the styles of past masters of the idiom, but we never attempt to only mimic what has been done before. Rather, we try to produce music which will stand on its own merits and endure the test of time. A key ingredient in the success of what we do is a kind of unspoken agreement to perform without involving egos. In other words, each player shapes his part to best suit whatever is going on. The members of the rhythm section are always totally supportive of the soloist of the moment. The resultant collective creation then becomes far greater than the sum of its parts.... The performance you are about to see and hear is typical Astral Project fare, and I think each person is given a chance to shine. I would like to point out that the shifts in time and texture and dramatic use of dynamics that occur throughout our music are not worked out beforehand. They are the result of the interaction and empathy which we share, and have become a trademark of our performances. If one player musically suggests a direction while soloing, be it a change of tempo or harmonic density or whatever, the remaining players react instantly, aligning their parts with the new idea...."

Scott Aiges and the Spiritual Side of Astral Project
The first critic to explore the spiritual foundation of Astral Project was Scott Aiges in 1993, two years before he became the group's manager. It's worth quoting his article almost intact, for the insights and the quotations of the members, although I have added some commentary in brackets about the definitions of spirit and spirituality invoked.

Heaven Sent: Members of Astral Project Cultivate a Spiritual Union that Sends the Group's Music into the Stratosphere[8]

The Chinese call it "chi." [*Chi* is the life force of both the body and the universe; I take it to be different in essence from Spirit: rather, the manifestation of Spirit.] Mystical-minded Americans call it spirit, or soul. ["Soul" means something quite different to Christians: namely, that part of human beings which survives death.[9]] By whatever name, it is that vibrant life force that is sometimes imperceptible and sometimes impossible to miss. You can't see it, but you know when it's there.

   When the New Orleans jazz quintet Astral Project plays, you definitely can hear it. The band members hear it, too. So even though all of them are among the city's most talented and sought-after players for an impressive variety of jobs—everything from zydeco to bebop to funk-rock, from Latin jazz to big bands to Dixieland—they keep coming back to Astral Project.

   "If you study any kind of Eastern mystical writings," says band founder Tony Dagradi, who is no novice on the subject, "they talk about the different planes of existence. There's the physical plane, which we are on. And then the next, finer plane is the astral plane. And then there's the causal plane. And there's the super-causal plane. And supposedly as you get to each level, it's a finer and finer spiritual experience, higher and higher. So the astral plane is the next one. And supposedly everything on the astral plane makes a beautiful garden on Earth look like a toilet. So the music on the astral plane would be more uplifting than anything you heard on Earth." [Tony seems to be referring to music as capable of producing peak experiences.]

   That's why the New Jersey native collected the musicians he met long ago at the now-defunct club Lu & Charlie's into Astral Project....

   "It's more than a musical association. It's a spiritual association," pianist David Torkanowsky says. "It's a spiritual union. We're so intimate familiar with [one another's] musical tendencies and preference—I'm not saying there's no surprises anymore, but it's like ultimate comfort, ultimate trust in the music. Whenever you've been playing music with the same people that long, you achieve a certain understanding that goes beyond words." [Tork seems to be using the term "spiritual" to refer to strong rapport or collegiality.]

Anyone who has heard Astral Project must have asked, "So why isn't this band famous yet?" Mostly because the various members have been so busy with other projects that they haven't taken the time to find a manager who can boost the band's career in the commercial plane. The band hasn't even released an Astral Project album yet. [Such an album was released the next year; two earlier albums appeared under Tony's name.]

But while those are top priorities for the near future, they're not what really matter most.

"You have to make your priorities focus on a higher level, like a spiritual level," says guitarist Steve Masakowski during a break in a gig with saxophonist Alvin "Red" Tyler.... He says there's only one reason to keep going: "Just the enjoyment of playing. Because if you lose that, then you lose everything."... [Steve clarifies his ideas about music and spirituality below.]

Like the others, Dagradi uses Astral Project for a deeper level of communication than merely playing music.

"In the early history of [jazz], it was a very dance-oriented art form," Dagradi says.... "But there came a point in time where it splintered off. The dance forms became more pop-oriented. And the art forms became more intellectual, more spiritual, more involved in seeking an uplifting mode. [Tony seems to be using "intellectual" to mean "non-kinesthetic"; "uplifting" returns to the idea of peak experience.] And I really felt that very strongly listening to John Coltrane when I was in my teens and early twenties. That made just an incredible impact on me. He was immersed in different spiritual, mystical studies, and tried to apply that to his music. And his music to me is just the epitome of that."

Singleton, a multi-instrumentalist who seems to be fully immersed in every note he plays, likens the music to an immutable, if benevolent, force with a mind of its own.

"You have to stay out of the way of the music," he says. "And then the reward is you get something new that you didn't know before about yourself...."

"If I close my eyes, I can learn more, I can get more. You find it's a transcendent experience. It is a spiritual experience in a way. Because you find you become part of a larger thing. It reinforces your faith—in God and existence, human existence. It heals you." [James seems to be talking about both peak experiences and the sense of Oneness in existence; the original meaning of "healing" was "to make whole."]

The Group on Spirituality and Music

In Steve, James, and John, Tony Dagradi attracted a group of musicians who were not only supreme on their instruments but had strong resonance with his spiritual vision of jazz. James and John have meditated on and off for years. After the departure of Tork, who did not share the others' outlook on music, both the spiritual level and the unity of the group rose a great deal.

Steve's wife Ulrike, a Christian Scientist, has been his spiritual mentor. According to Steve, Christian Scientists "believe in a spiritual not a material existence." He classifies himself as "not a card-carrying member, but we talk about these things a lot and I believe in the philosophy they espouse." Not only does Steve understand that "There's a lot of commonality between a lot of different religions at the core"; he sees the commonality with quantum physics, as he has discovered from being "heavily into studying the writings of David Bohm and Niels Bohr and people like that—just seeing where the physicists, from the material side of exploring existence, are coming to the same conclusions as the mystics." Steve feels that "Tony has a heightened sense of spirituality, and I feel that I do, too. I don't talk about it much with the band members. But I feel we connect on a very high level, a very spiritual level."

In composing, Steve believes that

> "if you compose with a certain idea in mind, like a state of mind, a certain person, or a certain feeling or whatever, the music becomes almost incidental to the spiritual thought. I feel that that thought is somehow conveyed to the listener. It doesn't have so much to do with the music, although the music obviously was inspired by the thought. I always find it helpful to be inspired by a spiritual thought before I start composing something."

Ultimately, "I think music is always an expression of your life experience and your sense of spiritual existence. I know Tony and Joan have always been very devout practitioners of their spiritual path, always stayed very true to it, and I really respect them for that. I think that's reflected in Tony's music, in the way he plays. I like to think that it's the same with me, as well."

Steve went on to talk to me about releasing the ego while playing. The term is commonly used with several shades of meaning; here I take it to mean the conditioning and belief systems that prevent us from realizing we are unlimited beings.

> "I think that's a very important part. I think when we have a night when things happen on an extraordinarily high musical level, it's usually because everyone has released their ego to the music: just playing and not thinking consciously about the individual anymore but about the band, and the enjoyment of playing music together. You would think that that's always the situation, but sometimes it's not, depending on how people are feeling on any one particular day. With Astral Project I think we all realize that's what we strive for. But even so, it's still four individuals, and occasionally you can get sometimes get opposing views. Or maybe one or more of the people trying to control things a little more in a way that might not be devoid of ego. (laughs) That's just human nature. I think when we're playing our best it's when our egos are not involved with the music at all. I think that goes for anybody when they perform. As a group it's always helpful to keep your ego in check and just try to have the ultimate goal be to make great music together."

According to James, "We don't stroke each other's egos a lot. About once every five years, I'll hear Steve go, 'Yeah, James.' That means I did something serious, but it never happens otherwise."[10]

Steve and Tony's lives have been just about light; James and John have been through the dark side and back. James confirmed: "We really went way, way, way down; both of us almost died. Most of John's childhood friends went to jail or died." In spiritual practice we learn not to judge or to label existence, but to embrace its totality, its "good" and its "bad," its yin and its yang, its light and its dark.

"Saints" Anthony, James, John, and Stephen embracing the All, the "otherworldly" and the "this-worldly," performing miracles. Open your ears—and your hearts.

After the Award

Yet for Astral Project, winning awards did not mean an automatic increase in the number of performances over the next few years. In 1993, the group continued its monthly gig at Snug Harbor, interspersed with a few one-off concerts around town. Tony told a funny one-liner about the gig at Charlie B's, where the Cognac Hennessy Jazz Search had been held: "A couple of months later, Charlie called me up for a gig and asked, 'What did I pay you the last time?' And I said, 'The last time we worked there, we got $10,000!'" In late July and early August the group went on a short tour to Colorado. Of its performance at the Winter Park Jazz Fest, a local critic wrote that the group "used its exposure to turn serious listeners into believers. Astral Project is ... a band that successfully reaches into the creative skies without losing its footing on earth. The group (which played on several stages during the festival) may lack name recognition, but it sure doesn't lack anything else."[11]

In previewing Astral Project's performance at Snug Harbor on 4 February 1994, Scott Aiges wrote: "For such a high-powered band, it's amazing that they don't have any records out. But with three new projects about to be released, Dagradi and Co. will be coming soon to a record store near you."[12] That year, the group did issue its first recordings exclusively under its name. Recall that both *Lunar Eclipse* and *Dreams of Love*, although featuring the Astral Project lineup, had been released under Tony's name. (The third project mentioned by Aiges is presumably the CD by the Tony Dagradi Trio, *Live at The Columns*.)

Astral Project's *Acoustic Fusion*, the proceeds of which financed the group's first real recording, was a "play-along CD" that accompanied the June–July issue of *Jazz Player* magazine. The idea of "play-along," now a standard part of jazz education, is that in addition to hearing some well-known artists play and even solo on the tunes, budding musicians have a superior rhythm section to "accompany" them for several choruses, so they can practice soloing themselves. The magazine included the lead sheets of the compositions—all Tony's: "Astral Elevado," "The Call," "Child's Play," "Emperor of Love," "Miles," and "Morning Star." (For a discussion of this recording, see Lasocki, *A Higher Fusion*, chapter 6.)

The first Astral Project CD, *Astral Project, New Orleans LA*, which had a low-budget black-and-white cover of the group's logo, included a mixture of studio and live performances, some dating back to 1990. In addition to four of Tony's compositions—"Indian Folk Song," "Miles," "Oneness," and "Supersonic Hawk"—James and Steve contributed one distinctive, New Orleans-flavored composition apiece ("Bongo Joe" and "Sidewalk Strut," respectively). The CD also included two standards (Strayhorn's "A Flower is a Lovesome Thing" and Monk's "I Mean You"). It also included Carla Bley's "Útviklingssang"—Tony's feature from his days with her band, recorded with it in 1980—and an "instant composition" dedicated to Nat Adderley. The *Times–Picayune* claimed in August that year that Astral Project was "in orbit with the airplay [that] its new album ... is getting on National Public Radio's international network."[13] The CD won the Big Easy award for album of the year. (For a discussion of this recording, see Lasocki, *A Higher Fusion*, chapter 6.)

With the help of Steve's brother-in-law, Migo Sprenger, Astral Project made a highly successful and critically acclaimed tour of the Westphalia area of Germany as well as traveling further north to Bremen in late November and early December 1994.

The group went on a local music show, "LTV," on the Cox Cable network on 2 February 1995, to promote its new CD. John and Tork were interviewed in a relaxed mood by the show's presenter, Bernie Cyrus, director of the Louisiana Music Commission. Cyrus joked, "Well, I'm the star of this show, but these guys are the asteroids." When he put it to Tork that "Astral Project's kind of a fusion jazz thing: is it appropriate to say that?" the pianist responded: "'Fusion' is not really the word. We're just kind of an amalgam of different kinds of New Orleans music."

Notes

1. Fred Laredo closed Tyler's before selling it in January 1987. It took the new owner, Mike Kieffer, until July to get it reopened, and he sold it again in September 1988. See Jason Berry,

"Tyler's Fate not an Open and Shut Case," *Times–Picayune*, 22 January 1989, section JJ, J3.

2. See Fumar, "In Search of Modern Jazz."

3. See http://publications.neworleans.com/no_magazine/37.7.-JAZZALL.html; accessed 15 December 2004.

4. Charlie Kinzer, "The Astral Perspective: A Conversation with Tony Dagradi," *Jazz Society* (Baton Rouge, LA) 2, no. 6 (June 1990).

5. Wyckoff, "Astral Project Blasts off Jazz Month."

6. Kevin Patton, "Astral Project," *The New Orleans Art Review* 11, no. 2 (September–October 1992): 30–31. "Oneness" is also a reference to Tony Dagradi's composition of the same name.

7. Scott Aiges, "Astral Project Lands a Heavenly Award," *Times–Picayune*, 20 November 1992, section Lagniappe, L7.

8. Scott Aiges, "Heaven Sent: Members of Astral Project Cultivate a Spiritual Union that Sends the Group's Music into the Stratosphere," *Times–Picayune*, 2 May 1993, section Living, D1–D2, D6. For a discussion of such definitions, see Lasocki, *A Higher Fusion*, 261–63.

9. The *Oxford English Dictionary* does give an obsolete definition of "soul" as "The principle of life in man or animals; animate existence."

10. Quoted in Alex Rawls, "Let's Stay Together. How Does a Band Last 30 Years? Ask Astral Project," *OffBeat* 21, no. 5 (May 2008): 68.

11. Norman Provizer, "Mix of Sounds Works Well at Winter Park Jazz Fest," *Rocky Mountain News*, 4 August 1993, section Entertainment/Weekend Spotlight, 18C.

12. Scott Aiges, "Testing Boundaries with a Jazz Sax," *Times–Picayune*, 4 February 1994, section Lagniappe, L11.

13. Betty Guillaud, "Fire is a Word that Really Rings a Bell with Warren," *Times–Picayune*, 26 August 1994, section Living, E2.

10. QUARTETS, BIG BANDS, AND TRIOS

Quartets

The drummer Jeff Boudreaux, a former student of John Vidacovich's, started to play a regular gig at the Hyatt Regency Hotel's Mint Julep Lounge on 5 April 1988 with Tony, David Torkanowsky, and Bill Huntington. In an article about the gig in the *Times–Picayune*, Boudreaux praised Tony's attitude:

> "For a long time I went on jobs and didn't like the music, so I wouldn't have a good time and the job would last forever. But people like Dagradi and Vidacovich taught me that no matter what kind of music it is, you play your absolute best. I learned that gradually. Dagradi plays weddings, some of the corniest gigs imaginable. But man, I'm telling you, he burns them up."[1]

Boudreaux reminisced:

> "A couple of steady gigs I remember I did specifically with some of the Astral Project guys in the years after the World's Fair were at the Hyatt Regency Hotel, next to the Superdome. I knew someone working there and by chance got in with the food and beverage manager, who liked jazz. He put me in charge of the in-house music for a couple of years. It consisted of a jazz trio or quartet, Wednesday–Saturday, solo piano on the off nights, and a Sunday brunch. After I'd kept those gigs going for a while, James, Steve, and others began calling me 'Saul,' after the stereotypical hustling Jewish businessman who pulls deals out of a hat.
>
> "The Wednesday–Saturday gig, in the atrium, was usually a trio with Tony and Bill Huntington. Actually, it started as a quartet with Tork on piano, then was reduced to a trio most of the time unless the hotel had a high occupancy rate. It was a very pleasurable gig because we could basically play what we wanted to. It was special because we got the chance to work in that context with Bill, a true living legend and patriarch of jazz bass in New Orleans. Having Tony on the gig, whose time was as impeccable as Bill's, gave me a lot of freedom as a drummer, and the things I learned from Johnny about what the drums could do to outline harmony and form came to fruition in this context."

On 1 June 1989, the saxophonist Rick Margitza, who had temporarily moved back to New Orleans, had a gig at The Columns Hotel with Steve Masakowski, Huntington, and Boudreaux. Two weeks later, Margitza had been replaced by Tony, and the group was dubbed The Tony Dagradi Quartet. This quartet gig lasted almost exactly a year: every single Thursday through 21 June 1990, at which point Boudreaux, tired of scuffling for a living, left New Orleans to teach at the American Institute of Music in Vienna, Austria. In an interview, Tony praised the setting at The Columns: "They have been very rewarding gigs, mainly because of the artistic freedom. And the room tends not to have a club atmosphere—it's more like playing in somebody's living room."[2]

Boudreaux recalled:

> "The last main thing I was doing in town before I left for Europe was a weekly gig at The Columns Hotel with Tony, Steve, and Bill Huntington. I knew a girl who was waitressing there, and eventually crossed paths enough with the owner to get her interested in having

jazz. I'd always had the idea that acoustic jazz would be a perfect match for the atmosphere created by the hotel's Victorian architecture—very fine quality wood, with a warm, natural feeling—and the coziness of its bar and main meeting rooms. Before long we had a loyal following, doing mostly Steve's and Tony's original tunes in a more suitable setting than most Astral Project gigs. And maybe it also gave Tony a chance to get different things out of Bill and me for some of the same tunes he had been doing with Astral. Anyway, it was a very fertile Uptown setting.

"Lots of musicians used to come by, to listen and to sit in. Allen Toussaint used to come and listen nearly every week, pulling up in front with his old Rolls Royce, hanging out and always being courteous and appreciative, but also shy and mysterious. He had come often also to the Cafe St. Charles in 1984 to hear the James Drew Trio with James Singleton and myself. Most people didn't know he was such a big modern jazz fan.

"More importantly, a drummer named Brian Blade, who's now become world famous, used to show up religiously. He had just moved to New Orleans to study at Loyola, and had started with Johnny V. there. He was very young and lacking experience, but everyone could tell by the way he played and by his magnetic, almost angelic, personality, that he was a very special musician. He came nearly every week and would sit in the front for the whole gig; but he was so shy then that we had to practically drag him up to the drums to sit in on the last set each week. He always sounded great and he knew all of Steve's and Tony's tunes by heart. Because the gig ended after the street car went down to one an hour, I used to drive him home sometimes, hang out a little bit, maybe listen to a little music and talk about Johnny V.—what he'd been learning from him, and what I learned from him, etc."

(For more on Tony's involvement with The Columns, see under Trio below.)

A taste of wider fame arrived for Tony in April 1989, when a tape of drummer Chris Lacinak's quartet, of which he was a member, placed first in the Louisiana State Jazz Composers Series, then reached the semifinals of the Cognac Hennessy Jazz Search, at that time a national competition with more than 600 entries.[3] The other two members of the quartet were Brad Burris, bass, and Matt King, drums. Lacinak headed for New York a couple of years later. The Chris Lacinak Quartet gave an album release party on 27 June 1989 at Snug Harbor. He told me that the CD was called *New Arrival* and besides Tony it featured Steve Masakowski.

On the Slide

"You hate to be smug, but it's always gratifying to take out-of-towners over to hear the jazz at the Gino's Restaurant bar. It's especially nice when the visitors are from a major city, because they can't believe they're hearing musicians like this in Baton Rouge. If you're going to thank somebody, see Lawrence Sieberth, who's been playing there regularly for years. As a pianist, he's world class, and other musicians recognize that. They must look forward to playing with him since they certainly come back."[4]

By November 1988, Larry Sieberth was playing six nights a week, both solo and with other musicians, at Gino's in Baton Rouge, the state capital of Louisiana and the home of Louisiana State University. According to another article in the local newspaper, "With a reputation as a strong jazz player, Sieberth started getting some friends from New Orleans to join him on a casual basis. It resulted in some great musicians showing up for guest appearances, but their visits were often last-minute situations. 'I'd had Tony Dagradi and Red Tyler come up a few times,' he said. 'I just wanted to organize it better.'"⁵ So beginning on 1 December, Sieberth produced a series he laughingly called "Great Sax at Gino's," featuring, in successive weeks, Tony, Amadee Castenell (a regular performer with Allen Toussaint), Paul McGinley, Red Tyler, and A.N. Other. The bassist Bill Grimes of LSU and John Vidacovich had played with both Tony and Tyler.

Live at Gino's, recorded June–July 1990, presents a good sampling of work by Sieberth and a rotating series of guests, dubbed *I migliori*, Italian for "the best."⁶ Tony is featured on only one track, Duke Ellington's "Caravan," with Grimes and John, using an Ahmad Jamal "Poinciana" beat. Tony turns in a mature solo, well-developed and balanced, becoming temporarily more Coltrane-like when Sieberth drops out of the rhythm section. Tony ends, surprisingly, by growling the A sections of the out chorus (by flutter-tonguing?), with more solo on the bridge.

Big Bands

The *Times–Picayune* announced on 26 October 1990: "Tenor saxophonist Tony Dagradi brings his Astral Orchestra, an expanded version of his Astral Project, to the Sandbar at the University of New Orleans tonight for a modern jazz concert that will be broadcast live on WWNO–FM...."⁷ Tony remembers that this performance revived his *Portraits and Sketches* suite from 1982 with a ten-piece group. "I'm pretty sure David [Torkanowsky] and James [Singleton] were there at that gig. And for some reason I'm thinking Herlin Riley played drums on that." The performance was rebroadcast in October 1993 as part of WWNO's "Jazz over Big Easy" series.

On 23 November 1990, four works were performed at the sixth annual new-music festival at the Contemporary Arts Center to celebrate its recent renovation. According to the *Times–Picayune*'s classical-music critic, Frank Gagnard, Tony's work, written for the New Orleans Saxophone Ensemble, made the greatest impression:

> "Nothing on the program was richer and wittier than Tony Dagradi's 'Tango' for four saxophones, with such luxurious performances resources that Kidd Jordan chugged away at the rhythmic base on baritone sax. Dagradi rewardingly cast himself in the lead (on soprano sax) in another of his works, the lyrical 'Return.' Dagradi personified the festival's theme of the interaction between written and improvised traditions in New Orleans music. The compositions on Friday that departed from this theme and most strongly represented European classical traditions sounded, by comparison, bloodless and prissy.... Also written for the reopening of the CAC was jazz guitarist Steve Masakowski's episodic Piano Sonata No. 1, played by [his wife] Ulrike Masakowski."⁸

Tony is still "very pleased" with his arrangement of "Tango," and he included another one on his most recent CD, *Gemini Rising* (see pp. 161–64).

On 3–4 October 1990, Tony organized a significant big-band concert, which inaugurated the Freeport–McMoRan Theater at the Contemporary Arts Center, at the behest of its director, Jay Weigel. The band, which played both "familiar and unexpected" works by Duke Ellington, included such top New Orleans musicians as Clyde Kerr, Jr., trumpet; Victor Goines, Donald Harrison, Jr., Kidd Jordan, and Red Tyler, saxophones; John Mahoney, trombone; Ellis Marsalis, piano; Bill Huntington, bass; and John Vidacovich, drums. Tony played as well as conducted. He was reported as saying: "It was so successful that everyone looked at each other and said, 'Why don't we keep doing this?' Now ... the idea is to establish a repertoire big-band jazz orchestra."⁹ Accordingly, on 1–2 October 1991, in "a reprise of sorts of last year's Duke Ellington tribute concerts," Tony led a big band through "familiar and lesser-known [Count]

Basie compositions."

A year later, on 25 September 1992, Tony's big band performed Ellington's "New Orleans Suite," which was commissioned for the first Jazz and Heritage Festival in 1970 by one of its producers, the celebrated George Wein. According to Tony, the work had not been performed since, "because Ellington himself did not make it available. The score we are working from has been meticulously transcribed from the recordings."[10] Scott Aiges wrote in his review: "Everyone took a turn in the spotlight—but only one—and each musician nailed his solo with fiery elegance. Everyone played so well that it seems unfair to single out individuals. But I can't resist mentioning the moving duet of bandleader Tony Dagradi's soprano sax and James Singleton's bass on 'Johnny Come Lately,' David Sager's loving trombone solo on 'Blue Light,' Dagradi's heart-melting tenor sax on the suite's fourth movement, and Nicholas Payton's roaring Satchmo tribute."[11]

By 23 January the following year, the band had acquired a fitting if generic name: the New Orleans Repertory Big Band. At the Contemporary Arts Center once more they performed music written and arranged by Thad Jones who, according to Tony, "set the standard for what contemporary big bands should be." Tony waxed lyrical about Jones' arranging skills: his works are "very playable and draw upon the tradition of the big band, and yet they go beyond it—and I'm talking about rhythmically as well as harmonically. On a blues or '[I Got] Rhythm' changes ... he would create very interesting voicings ... much thicker, much more dissonant. Because the arrangements are so advanced harmonically and they demand that you use a lot of dynamic changes ... they create a lot of dramatic turns. So it's very enjoyable for musicians to play."[12] Tony was so enthusiastic about Jones' big-band saxophone writing, in fact, that he wrote a pair of articles on the subject.[13] Unfortunately, he was so sick in bed—a fever that wouldn't break—that he had to miss the performances. "We did the first rehearsal and I was OK, and then it was downhill from there."

What seems to have been the same band, now billed as The New Orleans C.A.C. Jazz Orchestra and conducted by David Torkanowsky, gave a series of concerts on 25–27 January 1996 with three singers, Johnny Adams, Germaine Bazzle, and George French, which were culled for a sprightly recording for Rounder.[14] On the successful recording, as well as playing clarinet and flute, Tony had tenor sax solos on two Bazzle numbers: laid back to the point of being covered up by the crazy ensemble on "I Love Paris" and rhythm-and-bluesy on "I'm Just a Lucky So and So."

On 28 November 1997, in what was labeled only a "Big Band Concert" at the CAC, Tony was advertised as leading "local young jazz musicians performing big band pieces from the Louis Armstrong Archives, Queens College."[15] A similar concert three years later, on 7 October 2000, gave more details:

> "The Contemporary Arts Center Big Band, under the direction of saxophonist Tony Dagradi, will stage a tribute to Louis Armstrong on Saturday as part of the Art for Art's Sake festivities, with trumpeters Kermit Ruffins, Charlie Miller, and [CAC composer-in-residence] Hannibal Lokumbe as the featured soloists [in the role of Armstrong]. The 15-piece CAC Big Band is staffed by first-tier players from the local modern jazz ranks, including pianist Peter Martin, bassist Roland Guerin, drummer Johnny Vidacovich, trombonists Rick Trolsen, Mark Mullins, and Craig Klein, saxophonists Clarence Johnson, John Ellis, and Brice Winston, and trumpeters Antonio Gambrell and Eric Lucero. The band is using the same arrangements that Armstrong performed with his big bands, as supplied by the Louis Armstrong Archives at Queens College in New York. They'll run through a program

of classic titles, including 'Basin Street Blues,' 'Rocking Chair,' and 'Up the Lazy River.' 'He did a lot of things with small groups,' Dagradi said. 'I think he felt playing with a big band was a special treat.' Dagradi and company are familiar with the Armstrong charts, as they used them for a previous Armstrong tribute. 'They're very simple,' he said. 'It was not meant to be difficult music to feature the band. It was meant to be a nice backdrop to feature Louis. He's the diamond in the setting, and we're the setting.'"[16]

Trio
The Tony Dagradi Trio, with James Singleton on bass and John Vidacovich on drums, which had already made a recording in 1986, continued a sporadic existence over the next several years. For example, they took part in a concert labeled "Free Jazz" with Kidd Jordan's Improvisational Arts Quartet at Tulane University on 11 December 1989, which Tony curated as part of his assistantship there, and had gigs at Snug Harbor on 31 August 1989 and 21 August 1991.

Tony Dagradi and James Singleton, probably early 1990s

On January 1st or 2nd, 1993, the expatriate drummer Jeff Boudreaux, visiting New Orleans from Europe for the winter holidays, revisited The Columns Hotel, with two of his colleagues from the Tony Dagradi Quartet who had performed there in 1989–90 (Tony and Steve Masakowski) plus James Singleton, replacing Bill Huntington.[17] Did this whet the hotel management's appetite for more of Tony? In any event, on 4 March, the Tony Dagradi Trio began working there regularly, as Jill Anding Webster reported in the *Times–Picayune*:

"The Columns Hotel, a Neo-classically styled mansion on St. Charles Avenue, has for some time been on the list of local historic places to visit. Now it's also showing up on the live-music lists, with its new weekly entertainment schedule which includes jazz musician Tony Dagradi and pianist Philip Melancon [Sunday brunch]. Music only adds to the charm of The Columns, which was built as a private home in 1883 and has enjoyed a new life since 1980 as a guest house, restaurant and bar. The Victorian Lounge, The Columns' lavishly furnished bar, has become a popular stop for tourists as well as a hangout for locals.

"'Its age and gentleness appeal to all people,' says owner Claire Creppel, adding that The Columns has attracted everyone 'from cabbages to kings.' Now, Creppel says, you'll also find a 'serious jazz crowd' gathering on Thursday evenings [8:00 to midnight] to listen to Tony Dagradi and his jazz group (three members of the five that make up Astral Project). Dagradi will appear in the room opposite the lounge each week during March and April, and then return in the fall after a European tour this summer to promote his new [sic] album, *Images from the Floating World*."[18]

Scott Aiges soon wrote in the *Times–Picayune*: "Look for a baroque ballroom, natural acoustics, preternaturally talented musicians, jazz standards and originals played with such soul that you'll have one epiphany after another."[19]

The trio in fact made one appearance before the fall, on 15 July. The ever-supportive Aiges advised:

"The Columns Hotel is a wonderful, stately setting for acoustic jazz — one made even better by the return of the Tony Dagradi Trio. As a tenor and soprano saxophonist, Dagradi plays with a searching soul that burns through on every tune. The piano-less trio format allows all the silences between the notes to take an even more important role. With Coltrane and a wandering spirit as his guide, Dagradi follows his muse to a very satisfying place."[20]

The Trio returned to the hotel for its weekly series on 28 October, spurring Aiges to keep on inventing superlatives in his weekly recommendations: "saxophone wizard," "three outrageously talented and free-spirited locals," "free-swinging jazz," "sleek trio," "transcendent jazz." The trio continued to perform at The Columns on Thursdays in February–May 1994, including a release party for their new CD (see chapter 11), "with a show in the Beaux Arts ballroom in which it was recorded."[21]

The Tony Dagradi Trio's spring 1994 season at The Columns had finished by 5 July, when the *Times–Picayune* announced: "Tim Laughlin, the red-headed clarinetist whose regular gig is at Kabby's Sunday brunch, will be performing Thursday evenings at The Columns with his regular sidekicks, the piano-playing John Royen and guitarist Hank Mackie. They're filling in for Tony Dagradi, who's off doing one of those European summer festivals that lure lots of local [i.e., New Orleans] talent to lure international tourists."[22] Tony recalls that he did a five-week tour with Steve Masakowski, James Singleton, and Jeff Boudreaux as the Tony Dagradi Quartet, based in Boudreaux's Vienna apartment, and performing in Austria, France, Germany, and Italy.

In September, the trio began its fall season at The Columns, beginning on Thursday 1st, then switching to Wednesdays for the rest of the year. On 3 October, it had a gig at the Maple Leaf Bar, presumably adjusting their repertoire to the more blues-oriented clientele. The Columns gig continued into spring 1995. On 20 or 27 April, the trio returned to Thursdays, and on 1 May also had a gig at the Pie in the Sky pizza restaurant. Aiges wrote on that occasion: "This Astral Project splinter group uses the trio of sax, bass, and drums to explore the shadows between the chords—and to give Dagradi, one of the most technically exacting and soulful sax players around, room to stretch."[23]

After a break for the summer, Aiges wrote on 1 September 1995, "Finally, school is back in session, which means it's time for the Tony Dagradi Trio ... to resume its weekly Thursday sets of sublimely spare modern jazz at The Columns Hotel."[24] On 11 November, the trio—another advertisement says quartet—took part in the annual Odyssey Ball at the New Orleans Museum of Modern Art; the theme was "Louis Armstrong: a Cultural Legacy," although the trio played its own repertoire.

Since then the trio has played only occasionally, including at Snug Harbor (12 April 1996, 29 October 2002, 23 July 2003), the Funky Butt (1 October 1997, 10 May, 17 May 1998, 22 February 1999), the Musical Bridges Sunday Evening Concert in the Southwest School of Art & Craft, San Antonio, TX (6 August 2000),[25] Le Salon, Windsor Court Hotel (April, June–July, November 2002), the Ogden Museum of Southern Art (4 June, 9 September 2004), and Snug Harbor (11 December 2005, after Hurricane Katrina). In December 2000, the same three musicians started playing occasionally as the Johnny Vidacovich Trio, but that's a story for John's book....

According to James, sometimes John had another gig, so Tony would find a sub for him in the trio. "I remember Steve [Masakowski] doing it at least one, because Steve and I had done duos together. Tony and I had done duos together, and I'm pretty sure Tony and Steve had done duos together. So it was a no-brainer. We all had the material together from Astral Project, so we could do that." At some point in fall 1993, one sub for John was his student Stanton Moore, nicknamed Stand-in because of the frequency with which he was playing in other people's groups.[26]

Tony and Steve were advertised as playing a duet live on radio station WWNO as part of the station's fund drive on 7 March 1994. The duet of Tony and James played three pieces—Tony's "Emperor of Love" and John Coltrane's "Equinox" and "Naima"—in a program that united jazz and classical music at the Contemporary Arts Center on 19 November 1995. The *Times–Picayune*'s classical critic, Theodore P. Mahne, wrote approvingly: "The common, sensual thread running through the three pieces gave them the feel of a single work. The performance by Dagradi and Singleton got things off to a hot start."[27]

A further sub, the jazz singer Phillip Manuel, turned out to be a special case. Tony and James Singleton had recorded with him in 1991–92 for his album *A Time for Love*.[28] Tony does his usual beautiful job of finding a "line" behind the singer on the heads and out choruses, not to mention the intros. His solos are conservative for him, sometimes even old-fashioned in the sense of Swing. He fits right into Manuel's gospel interpretation of "Fire and Rain," which the *Cadence* critic found "the most indelible track."[29] As Scott Aiges put it, "Does the world need another version of James Taylor's 'Fire and Rain'? Maybe not, but the New Age intro, soft gospel piano chords, and fluttering, blues-inflected vocals—all interspersed with Tony Dagradi's heart-tugging soprano sax— make for a strong rendition."[30] Tony himself told me that particular solo was his favorite moment on the album.

Manuel performed with Tony and James at Snug Harbor on 19 April 1994. But it was apparently not until January the following year that Aiges in the *Times–Picayune* could announce:

"Any time you get saxophonist Tony Dagradi and bassist James Singleton in a room, sparks of soul scatter over those lucky enough to listen. Usually, they play in a trio with the endlessly inventive drummer Johnny Vidacovich. But on Wednesday [18th], Dagradi and Singleton will instead be joined by singer Phillip Manuel at The Columns Hotel. Together, their three melodic instruments play a high-wire game of song with no safety net of chords or rhythm. And still the swing is sweet. Manuel has an exceptional range and a round, hollow tone that's a match for Dagradi's tenor sax. Adding original lyrics to Astral Project instrumentals and improvising with instrumental flair, Manuel sings in tandem with Dagradi's sax while Singleton digs hard into both rhythm and harmony. Manuel, one in a long line of New Orleans musicians, doesn't use all the schtick of Bobby McFerrin. But he's got the same warm and friendly presence and the chops to back it up. All three players are unfailingly soulful in the elegant setting of The Columns' baroque ballroom."[31]

In fact, that was already the first of two recording dates, two weeks apart, for the CD *Heart to Heart* (see chapter 11).

James told me: "We all went to Europe on that gig, because the artistic director of the Perugia festival, Carlo Pagnotta, was coming to town. He often comes to the Jazz Fest to snoop out what's available and what he wants to program on his festivals. We were told that he heard the trio record with Phillip on the radio on his way into town from the airport, and said, 'Who's that? I want that for my festival!' So we went to the winter version of the Orvieto festival: a great gig for six days."

The same trio, with Bill Huntington substituting for James, played at a party in Metairie for patrons of the Contemporary Arts Center in late January. With James back on the job, the Manuel trio performed again at Snug Harbor on 10 March and 25 May 1995, as well as at the Jeff Fest in Lafreniere Park in Metairie, LA (Jefferson Parish) on 14/15 October and "holiday jazz" at the Galerie Simonne Stern, at that time the oldest continuing contemporary art gallery in New Orleans, on 26 November.

A footnote: Tony has a few soulful bursts of solo on the track "You Showed Me What True Love Is" on Manuel's album *PM* (2007).[32]

Notes

1. Quoted in Vincent Fumar, "He'll be Drumming up his Own Jobs Now," *Times–Picayune*, 1 April 1988, section Lagniappe, 14.

2. Quoted in Fumar, "In Search of Modern Jazz."

3. Vincent Fumar, "Lacinak on a Winning Jazz Track," *Times–Picayune*, 21 April 1989, section Lagniappe, L6.

4. Calvin Gilbert, "Jazz at Gino's is Recorded for Takeout Orders," *The Advocate* (Baton Rouge, LA), 26 July 1991, section Fun, 8–Fun.

5. Calvin Gilbert, "Saxophone Series," *The Advocate* (Baton Rouge, LA), 25 November 1988, section Fun, 4–Fun.

6. I migliori, *Live at Gino's* ([New Orleans]: Chromatose Productions, [1990]).

7. Scott Aiges, "Hot Pix," *Times–Picayune*, 26 October 1990, section Lagniappe, L8.

8. Frank Gagnard, "Sound of New Music Draws a Crowd to CAC," *Times–Picayune*, 27 November 1990, section Living, D6.

9. Scott Aiges, "Jazz Month Gets into Swing with Tribute to Basie," *Times–Picayune*, 27 September 1991, section Lagniappe, L7.

10. Scott Aiges, "A Jazzy Salute," *Times–Picayune*, 25 September 1992, section Lagniappe, L8.

11. Scott Aiges, "Happy Times with David Byrne," *Times–Picayune*, 2 October 1992, section Lagniappe, L7.

12. Scott Aiges, "What a Big Band Should Be," *Times–Picayune*, 22 January 1993, section Lagniappe, L6.

13. Tony Dagradi, "Saxophone Solis by Thad Jones," Writing for Saxophone, *Saxophone Journal* 15, no. 2 (September–October 1990): 44–45, 58; "Saxophone Solis by Thad Jones: 'Cherry Juice,'" 15, no. 4 (January–February 1991): 52–54.

14. The New Orleans C.A.C. Jazz Orchestra, *Mood Indigo* (Cambridge, MA: Rounder CD 2145, 1997).

15. "November Cultural Calendar," *The Advocate* (Baton Rouge, LA), 26 October 1997, section MAG, 11–MAG.

16. Keith Spera, "All-Star Band Pays Tribute to Armstrong," *Times–Picayune*, 6 October 2000, section Lagniappe, 25.

17. Jeff Boudreaux told me that the event took place on New Year's Day, but it was advertised in the *Times-Picayune* for January 2nd.

18. Jill Anding Webster, "A New Beat at The Columns," *Times–Picayune*, 5 March 1993, section Lagniappe, L18.

19. Scott Aiges, "Just Call him Mister Medley," *Times–Picayune*, 2 April 1993, section Lagniappe, L9.

20. Scott Aiges, "Best Bets at the Clubs," *Times–Picayune*, 9 July 1993, section Lagniappe, L10.

21. [Scott Aiges], "In the Key of Jazz," *Times–Picayune*, 15 April 1994, section Lagniappe, L8.

22. Betty Guillaud, "Back Here Playing Jazz and Pulling 'Heartstrings' Here," *Times–Picayune*, 5 July 1994, section Living, D3.

23. [Scott Aiges], "Jazz," *Times–Picayune*, 28 April 1995, section Lagniappe, L12.

24. [Scott Aiges], "Let Jazz Add Some Pizzazz to Your Weekend," *Times–Picayune*, 1 September 1995, Lagniappe, L6.

25. "What's Up," *San Antonio Express–News*, 6 August 2000, section S.A. Life, 2H.

26. Scott Aiges, "Lifestyles of the Young and Funky Set to Music," *Times–Picayune*, 10 December 1993, section Lagniappe, L8.

27. Theodore P. Mahne, "New Concerto is Jazzy Smash," *Times–Picayune*, 21 November 1995, section Living, D14.

28. Phillip Manuel, *A Time for Love* ([New Orleans]: AFO Records 92–1128–20, cp1992).

29. David Dupont, review in *Cadence* 19, no. 8 (August 1993): 78.

30. Scott Aiges, review in *Times–Picayune*, 5 February 1993, section Lagniappe, L10.

31. Scott Aiges, "Three Pillars of Jazz," *Times–Picayune*, 13 January 1995, section Lagniappe, L9.

32. Phillip Manuel, *PM* (New Orleans: II Fire Records, 2007).

11. *LIVE AT THE COLUMNS* AND *HEART TO HEART*

Live at The Columns

Live at The Columns. Tony Dagradi Trio: TD, ts (1–4, 6–8), ss (5); James Singleton, b; John Vidacovich, perc; with Steve Masakowski, g (6, 8). Recorded at The Columns Hotel, New Orleans, Louisiana, April–November 1993. UPC 783287940925. Turnipseed Music TMCD.07, p1994.
1. Meditations (Antônio Carlos Jobim) (7:59)
2. Heart to Heart (TD) (7:05)
3. Limbo Jazz (Duke Ellington) (8:00)
4. Urban Disturbance (TD) (5:57)
5. New Day (JV) (11:05)
6. Body and Soul (lyrics, Edward Heyman, Robert Sauer, Frank Eyton; music, Johnny Green) (5:22)
7. Fall Out (TD) (8:40)
8. Blue Monk (Thelonious Monk) (7:50)

"Body and Soul" reissued on *What's in the Fridge? The Musical Spices of Louisiana* (Louisiana Film Commission, 1995).

The Tony Dagradi Trio (Tony, James Singleton, and John Vidacovich) recorded *Live at The Columns* during its regular weekly gig at The Columns Hotel in New Orleans in April and November 1993. Steve Masakowski made a guest appearance on one track. Although it's a fine example of the trio at work, James told me: "That band in that place: there were nights when it was just transcendent. The main session for the recording was the night when it didn't quite get that way. That was, I felt, a tip-of-the-iceberg CD. The music got so much more intense than that, but I do think it's pretty good."

The recording has grown on me. At first, I found Tony's solos too discursive—unlike his usual concentrated statements, where every note counts. But after repeated listenings, I've come to appreciate the "stretching out" for its own sake. The CD also provides the opportunity to hear Tony playing some well-known standards ("Blue Monk," "Body and Soul," "Meditations") and especially a lesser-known one (Duke Ellington's "Limbo Jazz") that catches the trio on a high musical and spiritual plane, giving us some idea of its "transcendent" moments.

The trio renders Antônio Carlos Jobim's "Meditations" in a style more calypso than Brazilian. Tony's extended linear solo—as with Coltrane or Rollins, you feel he could go on indefinitely—has a high spiritual level. During the solo, James plays stop–start motives, then switches to walking, adding to the excitement. John and James alternate solos: John melodic, James active. Tony re-enters and paraphrases the theme before bringing back the head.

The second recording of Tony's "Heart to Heart"—the first was on *Lunar Eclipse*, fifteen years earlier—finds Tony stating the head in Johnny Hodges fashion with little scoops and glissandi. In his solo, he moves far away from Hodges, spinning out motives, using the full range of the saxophone and a variety of tone colors, while James plays bursts of motives. The out chorus is abbreviated and reversed (BA).

"Limbo Jazz" is a rollicking calypso worthy of the Sonny Rollins Trio of the late 1950s. Tony catches Sonny's method of thematic development and even his vibrato, not to mention producing tones of golden honey, from low register to high, that should bring a smile to every jazz fan's lips. James takes an inspired solo, accompanied by John, beginning by developing motives himself, then moving to slapping the strings, guitar-like strumming, and back to slapping. John plays a solo based on the melody, then Tony returns with a paraphrase of the theme. The out chorus has a cute ending on a descending scale followed by three honks.

Tony's "Urban Disturbance," first recorded on his *Oasis* album (1980), finds our saxophone player at his most Coltrane-like in some obsessive working-out of a motive and quick squealing forays into the high register. John even plays some Elvin Jones-ish textures and accents behind him. After a tag, John takes an intense solo with real development, using the pitch of the bass drum effectively. Tony comes back for a linear solo before the head returns in varied form.

John's composition "New Day" had been around since Alvin "Red" Tyler's *Heritage* album of 1986. The trio version features Tony on soprano sax, a snaky bass-line from James, and lots of color from the composer. Tony takes his time with his solo, moving into squawks, then faster note-values, which the others pick up on and double the tempo. The solo becomes intense, featuring Coltrane-like shrieks and nice interplay with John on a repeated motive. An abrupt switch to the A section of the tune shows off Tony's shawm-like tone. On his solo, James also takes his time, developing that snaking line with flurries and droops, then, as John joins him, twanging the strings and ending with the head motive. John's own solo, using mallets on toms in a timpani-like manner, is clearly a set of variations on the theme. When the head returns, John employs more of a more parade style, doubling the rhythm on the first part of the A section.

On that old ballad "Body and Soul," made famous in jazz circles by one of Tony's heroes, Coleman Hawkins, Steve joins the trio, providing chordal support and helping out the lyrical atmosphere. Tony, using the full compass of the tenor sax, plays the head sweetly with some embellishment, but more like Hodges (or Getz) than Hawkins in conception. Steve's pretty solo sticks close to the tune, with arpeggios, flurries, then paraphrase. Tony ends with a solo that leads back into a restatement of the head, a brief unaccompanied cadenza, and one of his trademark resonant low notes.

As already mentioned, "Fall Out" was one of a group of three compositions that Tony wrote for the trio in 1982, "somewhat indicative of a tonal center, but 'out.'" He wrote the tunes "just from the saxophone, from an intervallic kind of thing, strictly as an exercise, and it was only later that we added the New Orleans groove. That definitely completed it." The piece is built on an Faug7 vamp and a simple two-measure bass ostinato consisting of the notes FBFDb. The form expands the common AABA song-type form into AABBCAA, where C is a free break over an F7 vamp. The melodies of both A and B are wild and angular, suggestive more of nuclear fallout than any other kind of falling out. Tony begins by playing the ostinato alone, then in parallel with James during the intro. Introducing the A section, John displays his incomparable rolling beat on the snare drums. Tony's solo, over a fast walking bass, uses a variety of motives, then a freer, more static passage, like a cadenza, while James strums a repeated note. John continues the press rolls into his solo, still hinting at the theme, developing rhythmic motives, and segue-ing into the rolling beat of the head. The complete intro and head return.

The final track, Thelonious Monk's "Blue Monk," is one of the few standards, and one of the few blues, also in the repertory of Astral Project. The trio takes the piece more slowly than Monk did, and Tony has a "lazy" way of stating the theme—perhaps a New Orleans approach?—holding back, then returning to the beat. His classic blues solo draws on the whole history of the blues in jazz. He begins slowly in the first chorus, then picks up speed in the second, with wails and staccato motives, moving on in the third, fourth, and fifth to bursts of variations on traditional motives, both fast and slow. James, for his solo accompanied by John, develops motives from the theme itself, then picks up speed in the second chorus, with descending glissandi, double stops, and slaps.

I asked Tony about the difference for him between playing in the trio and Astral Project:

Tony. The trio had a really different personality, because there wasn't any harmonic accompaniment, and I can play very differently with a trio.

DL. On *Live at The Columns*, I get the feeling of endless space. It seems that you could take your time; you could do anything you liked. It has almost a languorous feeling. With Astral Project, I don't get any sense of languor whatsoever. It's very tight.

Tony. The trio is just a looser mentality from the jump. We were dealing with more standards. More of a "Let's be a little looser, be more in the tradition." In Astral Project we have an agenda of repertoire that we want to get through, and there's very few if any standards. As I was going from the Trio to Astral Project, in the Trio I would feel very comfortable and, as you said, wide open. There were definitely nights when I would go to Astral Project and—this may have also been a time when the band wasn't performing a lot; we would show up at Snug Harbor or someplace—sometimes the guitar and the incessant piano would feel cluttered to me, and I would feel locked in, or locked out. Sometimes I'd say, "OK, it's great, but follow me a little bit more." David [Torkanowsky] has his own agenda as a player. He likes to hear things a certain way, and he's very groove-oriented and likes to have the piano be a very percussive thing. If you want to have some flexibility harmonically, I like the piano to be not so statically percussive—be reactive.

The critics generally responded positively to this album. The most succinct assessment came from Richard Cook and Brian Morton: "*Live at The Columns* finds the trio on home turf in New Orleans and enjoying themselves. Dagradi continues to retain an air of freedom while contenting himself with familiar structures, and his confidence in his own powers as an improviser radiates through an hour of music. Masakowski guests on a fine 'Body and Soul.'"[1]

Michael Ullman introduced the specter of originality: "The music is by and large energetic, intelligent, pleasing—something more than one has the right to hope to find at a late-night dinner club—but not startlingly original. Dagradi's solo on 'Meditations' finds him, to my ears, deciding too carefully what to do from chorus to chorus. The more raucous 'Limbo Jazz'—a rarely played Ellington tune—is better. Dagradi's 'Fall Out' becomes a feature for the magnificently recorded drums of John Vidacovich. The piano-less trio doesn't lead Dagradi to flights of harmonic fancy. He's a solid, grounded player, heard here on a good night in front of an appreciative audience."[2]

Jason Staczek was also preoccupied with questions of originality, but gave higher marks: "This is a wonderful record. A beautiful live recording of a sensitive ensemble breathing together with a decade's worth of shared musical past, with every subtlety of their performance documented in breathtaking relief.... The sound is very open, very airy. Dagradi is free to explore without the confines of a chordal instrument like piano or guitar.... On all the tunes, but particularly the Dagradi originals, you can feel the band pushing gently at the borders of elegant restraint, but held in check, perhaps, by their hotel surroundings.... To be honest, there is nothing groundbreaking or truly extraordinary about this record. Its beauty is in its honesty and simplicity, and its ability to transport you to another place and time...."[3]

The *Cadence* critic, David Kuner, put such questions of originality in their place in his final sentence: "The Tony Dagradi Trio is ... a regularly working unit whose compatibility goes a long way toward making [*Live at The Columns*] a success. Though the muscular sound of his tenor is leaner and less grainy, Dagradi was obviously strongly influenced by Sonny Rollins. Like Rollins he's a storyteller with a knack for creating melodies and building logical, tightly constructed solos. The absence of a chordal instrument (excepting guitarist Steve Masakowski's guest appearance on 'Body and Soul') lends a refreshing ambiguity to the harmonic patterns of the songs, and while the band seems interested in exploiting this freedom, they do so rather carefully and subtly. There's no truly 'free' playing here, but there's a good deal of freedom; and a strong sense of discovery pervades the whole affair, helped along by everyone's almost intuitive reactions to each other's moves. This is a strong effort that reaffirms the truism that jazz doesn't ... have to be boundary-shattering and innovative to be fresh and rewarding."[4]

A fellow saxophonist, Paul Evoskevich, well understood the challenges and rewards of playing in a trio, as well as Tony's mastery of his instruments: "The increased responsibilities for members of a pianoless/guitarless trio can be likened to a 4-cylinder automobile that's running on only 3 cylinders: everyone in the group has to work harder and assume much more responsibility. There is a trade-off for the increased freedom of not having to be at the mercy of the chords and voicings interjected by a piano or guitarist. Each member of the group has to be in complete control of their individual parts ... [and] to find ways to vary the textures of the music so it doesn't all sound the same.... Each tune is tightly arranged, which results in a cohesiveness that I don't expect to hear in groups like this.... For me, the sense of order established by the highly refined arrangements is a big plus for this band.... Bassist James Singleton and drummer John Vidacovich ... are very gifted musicians who are constantly poking and prodding Tony during his solos, while [creating] some excellent solos themselves.... the two of them create more excitement than I've heard come out of some 17-piece big bands! Tony Dagradi is not only a terrific jazz musician, he is also a marvelous saxophonist. He has technique and clarity that many classical saxophonists would envy. This recording showcases his tenor and soprano saxophone playing, both are which are quite extraordinary. At times I can hear bits of Coltrane in his playing, at other times his sound is reminiscent of Johnny Hodges. Most of the time his sound is his own, and a magnificent sound it is.... It takes extraordinary musicians to make music this exciting in a trio context...."[5]

Heart to Heart

Phillip Manuel, *Heart to Heart*. Manuel, v; TD, ts (1–6, 8–10), ss (7); James Singleton, b. Recorded live at The Columns Hotel, New Orleans, Louisiana, 4, 18 January 1995. UPC 783287951028. Turnipseed Music TMCD.10, p1995.
1. Love for Sale (lyrics, Brian Hooker; music, Rudolf Friml) (7:03)
2. Fragile (Sting) (5:42)
3. Heart to Heart (lyrics, Phillip Manuel; music, TD) (7:18)
4. It's Only a Paper Moon (lyrics, Billy Rose, E.Y. Harburg; music, Harold Arlen) (4:21)
5. Fever ("John Davenport" [Otis Blackwell], Eddie Cooley) (5:11)
6. Oneness (lyrics, Manuel; music, TD) (5:49)
7. Nature Boy (Eden Ahbez) (7:14)
8. Doctor Moon (lyrics, Manuel; music, James Singleton) (6:15)
9. Angel Eyes (lyrics, Earl Brent; music, Matt Dennis) (5:41)
10. Love is Here to Stay (lyrics, Ira Gershwin; music, George Gershwin) (6:21)

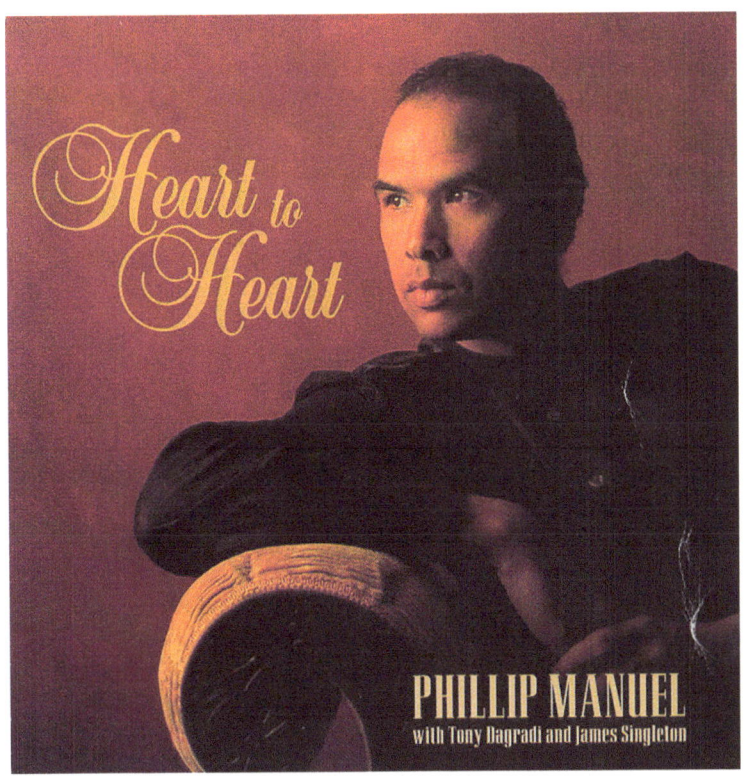

This fine CD by the singer Phillip Manuel, Tony, and James was recorded live at The Columns on 4 and 18 January 1995—a couple of days when everything fell into place. The arrangements, mostly the work of Tony and James, the fine intonation, the way Manuel and Tony coordinate so immaculately, the spirit of the recording: all are superb. James holds down the rhythm so well by himself that you don't feel the lack of a drummer, although Manuel's spontaneous finger snaps do come in handy from time to time. Tony's tone, rhythm, and versatility come out more strongly than ever against the simple accompaniment of bass (with the occasional finger snaps).

On the opening "Love for Sale," Manuel comes in like Bobby McFerrin to Tony's counterpoint, then Tony is off and running in his solo, happy as a sandboy. After Manuel's scat solo he renders the out chorus freely while Tony plays fragments of solo. Tony's fragile intro sets the scene for Sting's "Fragile." After the head, when he and Manuel generally render the same line in harmony, Tony finds his most luscious tone, at once sensuous and spiritual, leaving me speechless.

Tony's "Heart to Heart," first recorded on *Lunar Eclipse* in 1982 and also found on the then-recent *Live at The Columns* by the Tony Dagradi Trio, was named after Kirpal Singh's spiritual book *Heart-to-Heart Talks*.[6] But Manuel's lyrics treat it as a conventional love song: lovers needing to have a heart-to-heart talk:

Please come closer, dear [laughs from the audience]
I don't mean to bend your ear
But it's been so long since we talked
I think it's time we had a heart-to-heart

I thought I knew you well
No more secrets left to tell
Love left all alone falls apart
When all it needs is a heart-to-heart

Imagine what might happen if we dared to tell
Would love grow or whether closeness be too much
Will this honesty and trust be used against us, Could we
Walk away from this—I think not

Sometimes things get gray
And it's hard to find our way
Love isn't a cause you can charm
I think it's time we had a heart-to-heart

Tony immediately turns sentimentality to spirituality through his tone, his matchless phrasing, and his "presence."

Over a fast walking bass from James, Tony creates another appropriate "line" against Manuel's clear articulation of the cute old lyrics of "It's Only a Paper Moon." On his solo Tony develops a motive from the head, becomes bluesy, then returns beautifully to the motive. Manuel gets the audience to finger snap at the beginning of "Fever," forever associated with Peggy Lee. Glenn Brooks said of Manuel: "instead of Peggy Lee's classically aloof delivery (sounding like she's ready to get even with her lover, dammit), Manuel turns up the soul right from the beginning with some elegant cat howl scatting. Dagradi helps out by fluttering like a wounded bird in the background as Manuel pulls off 'Baby, you make me hard all day long.' Yow!"[7] Tony takes a solo of discovery, playing with the phrase lengths, and of course finding the blues.

On "Oneness," then recently issued also on *Astral Project, New Orleans LA*,[8] Manuel does understand the spiritual ramifications of the title.

Listen, here's a secret
That all those who are wise come to
It's simple, depending on your point of view
And how much you want the truth
That's the question and once you've heard my secret
The new life will reveal to you
No choice, only one thing to do

Love all, judge none, be last, first come
Take less, give some
Don't doubt, rare one

One whole, part of one dream
One love that could cure the world
And one day, in spite of everything you've planned
Only oneness will remain, this I tell you
The whole truth
Nothing but true
So help me, Heaven help us all
If we fail to heed the quiet call

To humbly look high
Pray long, draw nigh (?)
Take that, serve some
Don't doubt, rare one

Tony solo shows off his tone and sincerity against the simple accompaniment, to which Manuel now adds claps.

On "Nature Boy," an old Nat King Cole vehicle, Tony makes a magical entry on soprano sax, for the only time on the album, on the B section of head, before we hear the lesson the Nature Boy taught: "just to love and be loved in turn." Tony's solo, unusually, begins with the theme, then keeps up the sense of it more than usual. Next Manuel adds lyrics to "Dr. Moon," a rollicking piece by James, also recorded on John Vidacovich's *Mystery Street*, with Eric Traub rather than Tony.[9] The song begins free, then gets into a good groove. Tony is bluesy in his tenor solo, becoming freer in the coda.

On "Angel Eyes," Tony creates a line containing some imaginative curlicues on the head. His solo is plaintive and bluesy by turns. Finally on "Love is Here to Stay"—perhaps both love of God and love of humanity—Manuel plays with the tune, then adds some fun commentary afterwards. Tony's final solo, particularly strong rhythmically, leaves a heartwarming impression. Manuel aptly laughs and shouts "Yeah!" at the end.

The CD received five reviews, all positive. For Geraldine Wyckoff in *Jazz Times*, "Most interesting are the original tunes from Singleton and Dagradi, originally composed as instrumentals, to which Manuel has written lyrics."[10] In the *Times–Picayune*, Scott Aiges wrote: "Without the safety net of a rhythm or chordal instrument, they braid harmonies in ways that leave one breathless from the combinations of intellect and soul.... Manuel contributes thoughtful lyrics and delivers them with the necessary respect.... even when he tosses care to the wind, elegance rules."[11]

The other three reviewers, including Glenn Brooks, focused on Manuel. Jerome Wilson in *Cadence*, made a cute reference to "Phillip Manuel, a young singer from New Orleans who sounds like Al Jarreau with taste.... Manuel stretches his voice like silly putty, but always in the service of the grooves laid down by two major New Orleans players, Tony Dagradi and James Singleton. The absence of a drummer on this set was an accident, but that absence shows how good Manuel is at carrying and exploring a melody."[12] Howard Reich, soon to become an enthusiast for Astral Project, wrote simply in the *Chicago Tribune*: "Assisted only by the walking bass of James Singleton and the evocative saxophone playing of Tony Dagradi, Manuel creates new sounds in venerable standards and original compositions alike."[13]

Notes

1. Cook and Morton, *Penguin Guide to Jazz on Compact Disc*, 3rd ed., 313.

2. Michael Ullman, review in *Stereophile* 18, no. 4 (April 1995).

3. Jason Staczek on http://www.jellyroll.com/05/tonydagradi.html; accessed 5 December 2004.

4. David Kuner, review in *Cadence* 21, no. 10 (October 1995): 109–10.

5. Paul Evoskevich, review in *Saxophone Journal* 21, no. 1 (July-August 1996): 76–77.

6. Kirpal Singh, *Heart-to-Heart Talks*, 2 vols. ([Delhi]: Ruhani Satsang, 1975–76).

7. Glenn Brooks, review on http://www.jellyroll.com/06/philipmanuel.html; accessed 14 December 2004.

8. *Astral Project, New Orleans LA* ("Produced by the Astral Project," p1995, released spring 1994).

9. John Vidacovich, *Mystery Street* (Diamondhead, MI: Record Chebasco DIDX 029242, cp1995).

10. Geraldine Wyckoff, review in *Jazz Times* 25, no. 9 (September 1995): 109.

11. Scott Aiges, "Sass, Sophistication in the Blood Lines," *Times-Picayune*, 9 June 1995, section Lagniappe, L6.

12. Jerome Wilson, review in *Cadence* 22, no. 9 (September 1996): 97–98

13. Howard Reich, review in *Chicago Tribune*, 18 June 1995, section Arts, 21.

12. ASTRAL PROJECT, 1996–2000

In 2003, James told an interviewer about Astral Project, "I pushed the band to make its first CD. Once that was done, I sent them out. It wasn't a hard chore getting the band gigs after the CD went out. Everyone who heard it wanted to see us play live."[1] But evidence from the period suggests that finding gigs was still challenging. Lloyd Sachs reported in the *Chicago Sun-Times* in October 1996:

> "You would think that a band that embraces the funky majesty of Professor Longhair one minute and the regal glories of Duke Ellington the next faces a challenge in carving a coherent sound. But, Singleton said, the major challenge has been finding a way to market music that can't be easily categorized—and sell a band on the other side of up-and-coming status. At a time when many young genre-crossing bands are drawing attention from major labels, the fortysomethings in the Astral Project ... are drawing blanks....
>
> "'It doesn't help that we're all involved in so many projects of our own, we don't often present a unified front,' Dagradi said. 'In the end, though, records can't capture what we do when we play live. There's a lot of trust on the bandstand, the kind that tells you you can go anywhere. There's nothing to hold you back.'"[2]

Astral Project's fortunes had already begun to change that same year, when it finally hired a manager, Scott Aiges, a keen fan who had already written a number of highly favorable articles about the group's work. Four years earlier, he had put forward as the reason why Astral Project wasn't yet famous: "Mostly because the various members have been so busy with other projects that they haven't taken the time to find a manager who can boost the band's career in the commercial plane."[3] The idea of him becoming that person came up when he and Tony's wife Joan were both sitting vigil at the hospital bedside of Allison Miner, a strong proponent of New Orleans music, who died of myeloma on 23 December 1995.[4] Joan mentioned to Scott that Astral Project was now looking for a manager. He had recently resigned after six years at the *Times–Picayune*, in order to manage a rock band called the Continental Drifters. Now he readily agreed to take on Astral Project, too, and within a few years he was managing the group exclusively.

Under Scott's aegis, the group hired a booking agent and obtained a record deal—alas, both short-lived—and he set up some business practices that have stood it in good stead to the present day. Beyond that, as Tony told me: "because of his connections—he was a writer—his forte was really as a publicist. Wherever we went he was always sure to connect with the local writer and the local arts papers. And we always had a big spread announcing the gig, reviewing the gig. So he was always really on top of that."

As Scott set about managing Astral Project, the number of performances increased steadily. A European tour in June included Jazzclub Allmend in Oberengstringen, Switzerland, and a return to some of the towns in Germany the group had visited in 1994. The critics generally commented on the group's ability to switch groove and style.

Reviewing *Astral Project, New Orleans LA* in November 1994, Howard Reich, arts critic of the *Chicago Tribune*, had expressed the hope that "Perhaps a savvy Chicago impresario will be shrewd enough to bring them to town."[5] Exactly two years later, in early November 1996, the group did do a short tour of Chicago, playing among other places at the Green Mill jazz club on the north side—a regular gig once or twice a year that lasted through September 2009. The performance was extremely well received by the Chicago critics. Lloyd Sachs wrote beforehand in the *Chicago Sun–Times*:

> "Man for man, the Astral Project may be the strongest and broadest-based band to come out of the Crescent City since the Neville Brothers. Dagradi, a New Jersey native, accompanied leading funk and soul artists including Ike and Tina Turner before moving to New Orleans and forming the group in 1978; he roots his tenor and soprano playing in a Coltrane-inspired spirituality. Guitarist Steve Masakowski has impressed in both mainstream and fusion settings (not to mention a classical encounter with Luciano Pavarotti). And the nonpareil rhythm section of pianist David Torkanowsky, bassist James Singleton, and drummer John Vidacovich asserts a hand-in-glove mastery of groove-oriented jazz and roots styles."[6]

One reason for touring was the dearth of suitable performance venues in New Orleans, despite encouraging signs of change. Aiges' replacement as critic for the *Times–Picayune*, Keith Spera, noted in May 1996: "That a list of four clubs represents a dramatic upswing in the local modern jazz scene's fortunes speaks volumes about its shortcomings."[7] Tony told Howard Reich:

> "When I first got here, in the late 70s, it was the tail end of the good times—there were a lot of places to play. You could go any night of the week to hear straight-ahead jazz. It isn't like that now. There are a lot of great musicians here, but except for a few places, like Snug Harbor, it's hard to stay here and work consistently, which is why we've been touring so much lately."[8]

James produced and put up the money for Astral Project's second CD, *Elevado*, which was released around June 1997—curiously, a little late for Jazz Fest. This time the composing duties were divided more evenly: five tunes by Tony ("Astral Elevado," "Nose Dive," "N. O. Goodbyes," "O. F. O.," "Too Soon to Tell"), three by James ("Bulldog Run," "Gator Bait," "Lauren Z"), and three by Steve ("Burgundy," "Miller," "Paladia"), as well as Michael Pellera's "Carnival." Pellera even performed on one (other) track. James told me why: "In Europe, everywhere you go, people want a CD of what they just heard. I felt that, if Michael was going to be playing the gigs, I wanted to be able to say, 'Well, yeah, he's on "Lauren Z."'' Only one of Tony's compositions was new: the smooth ballad "Too Soon to Tell." The album won the award for best modern jazz album in the *OffBeat* Best of the Beat Readers Poll. (For a discussion of this recording, see Lasocki, *A Higher Fusion*, chapter 8.)

After playing a gig in Jackson, MS, the group was approached by a record company, Compass, based in Nashville, who licensed *Elevado* and signed a contract to make another CD. Tony noted: "The one thing that Compass did: they had a lot of advertisements, and they distributed the record. They got it reviewed, and they supported tours, so wherever we went they did publicity, and they made sure the records were in stores. That's what a distribution company does for you."

Elevado was generally well received by the critics. Moreover, the release of the album attracted a highly positive article in *Down Beat* by Howard Reich called "Sabotaging the Moment"—a reference to the group's ability to switch style and direction in an instant.[9] The critic called the group "one of the most distinctive and cohesive quintets in jazz of the 90s." He marveled that, "Revered by listeners in the Crescent City but almost unheard of everywhere else, Astral Project has managed to thrive (artistically, at least) as a working unit for nearly two decades—without a steady gig, record contract, or major management." He expressed his belief that it "stands at an artistic peak as it approaches its 20th birthday" and his hope that "With a Midwestern tour on the books for the fall and a European sojourn next spring, Astral Project's moment finally may be at hand." Finally, he quoted John as saying, "in a classic New Orleans lilt":

> "It's kind of amazing that we're still together, because it sure wasn't the money that kept us playing.... Maybe we stuck together because it always has been like going to play a ball game with the same guys for 20 years. We've been doing it so long now that we bend the rules like crazy. So when I play with the Project, I know I'm going to be set free.... I know I can go and bounce the ball all over the floor, wherever I want to go. The object isn't to win or lose but to keep the ball going in any bizarre way you want."

In 1998, as Geraldine Wyckoff wrote in a sympathetic article about the pros and cons of being on the road at their age, "Astral Project took to the highway, performing at prestigious clubs such as New York's Blue Note and Chicago's Green Mill, and traveling overseas to Denmark, Guatemala, and Brazil."[10] On 7 October, Astral Project gave a "concert by the sea" and clinic at the Rytmisk Musikkonservatorium (Rhythmic Music Conservatory) in a suburb of Copenhagen, Denmark. The idea of such clinics has been to perform for students as well as allow them to ask questions of the members of the group.

In mid-November, the group made a short tour to the Midwest, including a night in Bloomington, IN, at the Collins Living Learning Center, Indiana University. A Bloomington jazz fan remembers the gig as an attempt to cater to a younger audience.

> "The music was eclectic, a lot of it being in the jam band vein. It was quite a scene: people just packed into this tiny room, practically sitting on top of each other. I sat on the floor in the aisle. There was no room to move: definitely a fire-code violation. There was a lot of energy, and Tork was definitely playing to the room. His playing and behavior were more what you would expect in a blues band, not a jazz group. He stood at times while playing the piano, and I think he may have sung. He certainly spoke on the microphone. His general demeanor and appearance are much coarser than the other guys: that stood out at the Collins gig. I came away thinking that the group would do great in college-town bars."

The term "jamband" was coined by the critic Dean Budnick to describe "an eclectic mix of artists united in their devotion to unscripted, improvisational passages."[11] Scott Aiges told me that around this time he began to see the jamband crowd as Astral Project's true audience. For James, the reasons were both musical and spiritual:

> "When Tony started the band we were all in our 20s, so we were pretty crazy. We would do insane libations and run without sleep for days. Waking reality became dreamlike on numerous occasions. To me it's highly amusing that our current compositions capture that spirit more precisely than our earlier stuff. The people in those dives we used to play were ready, if not desperate, for some kind of transformative profound change. The freedom that we practiced was encouraged and rewarded. With today's jamband crowd I see an echo of that level of 'adult curiosity.' Of course, the jazz crowd has always been around, but it's really encouraging to see greater numbers of younger people hungry."

The group's stay in St. Paul on its Midwest tour proved significant because it encountered its old friend Bobby McFerrin, now a conductor of the Saint Paul Chamber Orchestra. James commented: "He sat in, and it felt as good as ever. We gave him our latest CD and he called us up a few days later and said, 'I've memorized your music. I'd like to perform with you again.'"

If 1998 was a good year for the group, 1999 turned out to be a bumper one. It released a new CD, *Voodoobop*, in time for Jazz Fest on 30 April, this time making the recording directly for Compass. The album was given a release party at Snug Harbor on 18 April 1999. The division of composition was broadened to include a new piece by John ("Deb's Garden"). There were also four pieces by Tony ("Fallout," "Protecting Circle," "Smoke and Mirrors," "The Whole Truth"), three by Steve ("Sombras en la noche," "Southern Blue," "Voodoobop"), and two by James ("Foxy Roxy," "The Queen is Slave to No Man"), as well as one standard ("Old Folks," on which John sings and Tony imitates Ben Webster). Once more, critical reception was highly favorable, and the album won the Big Easy award for album of the year. According to a report, it "gained airplay on more than 150 jazz stations across the country."[12] (For a discussion of this recording, see Lasocki, *A Higher Fusion*, chapter 10.)

Bobby McFerrin/Astral Project Midwest tour, June 1999; from left to right, James Singleton, David Torkanowsky, Tony Dagradi, Bobby McFerrin, John Vidacovich, Steve Masakowski

After a quick trip to the Green Mill, Chicago, in late May, the group undertook a three-week tour of the Midwest, including seven festival gigs with Bobby McFerrin, who kept the promise he had made the previous November. Tork was unavailable for some of the gigs and was replaced by Howard Levy from Chicago on piano and harmonica. The editor of *Down Beat*, Ed Enright, wrote a feature article in the form of a travelogue about the Ann Arbor-to-Cleveland segment. Besides ribbing the members of the group for their propensity to get lost on the way to gigs, and to have near-accidents on the road, Enright makes some telling musical observations and extracted some good quotations.

"The group agreed that the highpoints of the gigs had been when McFerrin interacted one-on-one with individual band members. 'One night we were in Indianapolis playing "Moondance," and Bobby signaled that everyone lay out except him and Steve,' Singleton recalls. 'They got into this beautiful spontaneous composition. And Bobby's sound people instruct the lighting crew that when Bobby goes up to one of us and appears to be interacting with us individually, to cut all the lights and focus on those two.' McFerrin agreed: 'One thing I like is when Tony and I are playing, and I'm standing right next to him. I actually like being that close and look[ing] at his face and the way he breathes. And when we trade things together, that to me is very cool. The highs for me at just standing by each member of the band, playing off of that energy: standing behind Johnny when he plays, watching Steve's fingers on the guitar board. To me, those are the moments: inviting that energy and that person to feed off of it and play with it.'"[13]

In August, Astral Project took third place in the *Down Beat* Annual International Critics Poll, a survey of 104 of the world's top jazz writers, in the category "acoustic jazz groups deserving of wider recognition." That same month, the group left New Orleans again, this time for Europe. James recalls that "Tork bailed out at the last minute," and Larry Sieberth substituted on keyboards. The tour began with two performances at the Oslo Jazz Festival on the 11th and 12th. According to James: "The Oslo gigs were a little rough. Traditional festival, sparse crowds. Larry hadn't settled in yet and still rocked the house. Then at the Copenhagen Jazzhaus, it really blossomed with Larry. The crowd were screaming." At the Brecon Festival in Wales, the group's performance drew a positive response from Alyn Shipton, the critic of *The Times* (London), who has since become well known for his book *A New History of Jazz*:

"There are always two festivals at Brecon—the outdoor stroller programme on several open-air stages, and the more formal indoor concerts. Outdoors, from time to time, the elements took a hand this year, a rain squall scattering the crowd during a sublime set from the New Orleans funk band Astral Project. The group played on undeterred, and introduced British audiences to a sound that's a local legend in Louisiana, built around the powerful saxophone of Tony Dagradi and guitarist Steve Masakowski. While it was good to have a band of such quality playing on the stroller programme, which seldom has many headline acts, they would have benefitted from a more sympathetic indoors setting, where the weather and variable sound quality would have been less likely to disrupt them."[14]

The group in fact seems to have played a further set indoors, as the critic Peter Bacon later wrote that he treasured the memory of "Astral Project storming through a wondrous set in a standing-room-only Castle Hotel lounge."[15] James recalls that Astral Project actually played three gigs at Breckon: "the first was the weakest, but filmed by the BBC. We sold out all the

CDs: 200+! Many queries of 'Is Larry on the CD?'"

Shipton cites Astral Project in *A New History of Jazz* as an example of "a discernible contemporary tradition" in New Orleans "fighting to be heard above the endless repetitions of 'The Saints'": "At a venue such as the Snug Harbor ... are bands such as Astral Project, taking a new spin on post-bop jazz with the funky New Orleans street beat of drummer Johnny Vidacovich combined with the hard-edged saxophone of Tony Dagradi and the guitar of Steve Masakowski."[16]

If world fame did not immediately ensue for Astral Project from its renewed association with Bobby McFerrin, its date book became fuller in 2000 than ever before. James told a reporter: "Now we are building up gradual momentum, with the catalyst being the addition of a manager and a booking agent, both of which have freed us up to focus on being creative."[17] On 14 January, the group played a gig at the Funky Butt, about which Philip Booth wrote: "Vidacovich's drums, and the playing of his bandmates, are a great place to hear the cumulative sound of jazz's past, and a viable model for the music's future track."[18] In a further review, Booth noted, perceptively:

"Jazz as we know it, the modern mainstream sound inspired by the bebop revolutionaries, has largely been developed by players who built their music around bands, as opposed to the stars-and-sidemen model so prevalent these days. Think of John Coltrane's classic quartet, Miles Davis's quintets, or Bill Evans's trios. Shared experience on the bandstand, for Astral Project, has similarly translated into the band members' intuitive understanding of one another's playing, as well as a remarkable ease in making the kinds of connections and transitions that other outfits couldn't achieve, even with constant practice."[19]

On 7 May, Astral Project gave its annual performance at Jazz Fest, inspiring a short, favorable report by Keith Spera:

"Astral Project drummer Johnny Vidacovich was in a particularly chatty mood at the Jazz Tent. He delivered a lengthy soliloquy on the fact that he and his bandmates are locals and did not need to ride eight hours in a van to make their Jazz Fest appearance. 'I live just over on Bienville Street: it took me about five minutes to get here,' he said.

"Their local pedigree established, Vidacovich and company got down to the business of making top-flight modern jazz. The latter part of their set favored new compositions. On 'Big Shot,' pianist David Torkanowsky two-fisted the keys, working them furiously. The ballad 'South by Southwest' featured an especially pleasing melody, one guided by Tony Dagradi's lush saxophone and guitarist Steve Masakowski's supple lines. The finale, 'Burgundy,' suddenly veered into Professor Longhair's seasonal anthem 'Go to the Mardi Gras,' with Torkanowsky popping up and down on his piano bench and the audience on its feet, clapping in time. Even without Vidacovich's speech, that moment made clear that this particular modern jazz band could hail from nowhere but New Orleans."[20]

Another witness, Brian L. Knight, wrote: "The jazz tent brought out national figures like Sam Rivers, Diane Krall, McCoy Tyner, and Joe Sample; but the tent's energy belonged to New Orleans' own Astral Project, who may just be one of the finest-sounding jazz bands around.... Astral Project has been together as a group since 1978, and after listening to their latest album, *Voodoobop*, you will discover that they show no signs of letting up."[21]

A short European tour followed for Astral Project in mid-July, with gigs at the Midtfyns Rock

Festival in Ringe, Denmark, and Europe's largest jazz event, the North Sea Jazz Festival in The Hague, Netherlands, whose director hired the group after hearing it at Jazz Fest in New Orleans. During a tour of the East Coast in August, James told an interviewer, "Our CDs are very eclectic, so it's hard for people to pigeonhole us. That's a great victory. We do still go and play the jazz clubs like the Blue Note in New York, but we've been playing these jazz festivals that have exposed us to these younger fans who like the jamming."[22]

Notes

1. Quoted in Scott Iwaski, "Astral Project Bringing Eclectic Sound to S.L.," *Deseret News*, 28 July 2000, W03.

2. Lloyd Sachs, "Arkestra Plays on as Founder Sun Ra Would Have Wanted; Astral Peaks," *Chicago Sun–Times*, 29 October 1996, section Features, Jazz, etc., 32.

3. Aiges, "Heaven Sent."

4. John Pope, "Music Manager, JazzFest Pioneer Allison Miner Dies," *Times–Picayune*, 24 December 1995, section Metro, B5.

5. Howard Reich in *Chicago Tribune*, 13 November 1994, section Arts, 33.

6. Sachs, "Arkestra."

7. Keith Spera, "Jazzed Up: Modern Jazz Musicians Finding More Clubs to Call Home," *Times–Picayune*, 31 May 1996, section Lagniappe, L18. The four clubs in question were Dona's Bar & Grill, the Funky Butt, the New Showcase Lounge, and Snug Harbor.

8. Howard Reich, "Shining Time: Astral Project just may Be New Orleans' Best," *Chicago Tribune*, 20 October 1996, section Arts & Entertainment, 9.

9. Howard Reich, "Sabotaging the Moment," *Down Beat* 64, no. 10 (1 October 1997): 40.

10. Geraldine Wyckoff, "The Project Comes Together," *Gambit Weekly*, probably January 1999.

11. See the review of Dean Budnick, *Jambands: The Complete Guide to the Players, Music & Scene* (San Francisco: Backbeat, 2003), by Philip Booth, in *Journal of Popular Culture* 38, no. 3 (2005): 574. Booth complained that although Budnick's book made room for "jazz-rooted ensembles, including Medeski Martin and Wood, Charlie Hunter, and Soullive ... overlooked are The Bad Plus and Astral Project."

12. Philip Booth, "Fresh Gumbo," *Jazziz* 17, no. 5 (May 2002): 39.

13. Ed Enright, "On the Road with Bobby McFerrin & Astral Project," *Down Beat* 66, no. 11 (November 1999): 32–34, 36–37.

14. Alyn Shipton, "Brecon '99, Powys," *The Times* (London), 17 August 1999, Features, 37.

15. Peter Bacon, "A Beacon of Great Jazz," Peter Bacon's Jazz Diary, *Birmingham Post* (England), 11 August 2004.

16. Alyn Shipton, *A New History of Jazz* (London & New York: Continuum, 2001), 876.

17. Quoted in Kristin Ciccone, "Astral Project Celestially Showers the States with Stellar Grooves"; available from http://www.jambase.com/headsup.asp?storyID=656; accessed 2 January 2005.

18. Philip Booth, "Future Jazz: A Report from the IAJE in New Orleans"; http://citypaper.net/articles/020300/mus.jazz.shtml; accessed 27 September 2006.

19. Booth, "Fresh Gumbo."

20. Keith Spera, "Spera's Spins," *Times–Picayune*, 8 May 2000, section National, A07.

21. Brian L. Knight, "New Orleans 2000—A Hazy Recap," *The Vermont Review* (2000); available from http://vermontreview.tripod.com/Concert%20reviews/nawlins00.htm; accessed 11 December 2006.

22. Quoted in Iwaski, "Astral Project Bringing Eclectic Sound to S.L."

13. NEW GROUPS AND INSTRUMENTS

By 7 November 1997, Tony was announced as having started a "new band," the horns from which were said to be augmenting the rock-fusion groups Twangorama and Woodenhead for a performance at the Howlin' Wolf.[1] According to Tony, it was just him, the trumpeter Erik Jekabson, and the trombonist Mark Mullins playing with the two rock groups that day.

In March 1998, however, Tony did actually begin a new group, as the *Times–Picayune* reported:

"With Astral Project, saxophonist Tony Dagradi is one fifth of the city's foremost acoustic modern jazz ensemble. But his new electric quintet will fly on a slightly different plane. Featuring keyboardist Larry Sieberth, guitarist Scott Goudeau, bassist Mark Brooks, and drummer Julian Garcia, the group takes its cues from Chick Corea's electric band and latter-day Miles Davis. And, promises Dagradi, it will be funky. 'This is an exciting departure for me,' he says. 'Playing in an electric setting requires a different perspective than a straight acoustic format. It's an exhilarating experience, and it gives me the opportunity to investigate other modes of expression.' The Tony Dagradi Quintet makes its debut Sunday [15th] at Snug Harbor."[2]

By their next advertised performance on 7 February 1999 at Snug Harbor, the group had acquired a name, X-Ray Vision, and Garcia had been replaced by Ricky Sebastian. An ad for the group's performance at Snug on 14 July notes that in this quintet Tony "stretches out on smooth jazz and contemporary R&B."[3] Chris Severin sometimes substituted on bass, and Darrell Lavigne on keyboard. In 2005, Tony described the group as "fun," but noted: "I haven't worked with them in a long time."

The New Orleans Saxophone Ensemble (aka Quartet) continued to play occasionally through the 1990s, including an appearance at Jazz Fest in 1995. By 30 September 2000, when the group played a double bill with the violinist Leroy Jenkins at the Contemporary Arts Center, NOSE had come to consist of Tony and three younger saxophonists: Aaron Fletcher, alto sax (a finalist in the Thelonious Monk International Saxophone Competition in 2001), Brice Winston, tenor sax (of Los Hombres Calientes, later featured with Terence Blanchard), and the baritone player Alonzo Bowens. The group was advertised at the Zeitgeist Multi-Disciplinary Arts Center on 12 April 2001. At Jazz Fest two weeks later, "The New Orleans Saxophone Quartet, a group with just three gigs under its belt," played a battle of the bands with Winds of Change. A further gig ensued at Snug Harbor in September. The same four players were named for a performance at the Solarium Concert Series, Bultman Solarium, on 19 January 2003, in "original compositions and arrangements of jazz classics by Thelonious Monk, Duke Ellington and John Coltrane."

In 2000, while on sabbatical, Tony started another new group, this time a larger one called Inside Out. It made its debut at the Funky Butt on 25 January, then had a regular gigs there weekly on Tuesdays through 27 June, as well as a debut at Snug Harbor on 17 June. After that it was heard from no more. An advertisement for their performance at the Funky Butt on 1 May mentioned: "Inside Out's eight players, including five horns, do original music and fresh arrangements of Mingus, Ellington, Wayne Shorter, and Miles Davis material."[4] The (first) debut featured Jamil Sharif and Eric Lucero, trumpet; Jeff Albert, trombone; Scott Bourgeois, alto saxophone; Jonathan Lefcoski, piano; Mark Anderson, bass; and Mark DiFlorio, drums. Tony told Keith Spera that he had been dreaming of writing for multiple horns for a long time:

"I was always crazy about the Gil Evans Band's gig at the Village Vanguard on Monday nights. Writing for multiple horns has always been intriguing to me, but something that I didn't get to that often.... It gives you much more to work with."[5] According to Tony, the "revolving cast of characters" in Inside Out also included Chuck Arnold and Mark Braud on trumpet, Derek Dougay on alto sax, Kelvin Harrison (Donald's cousin) on alto sax, and James Singleton on bass (for one gig). Tony commented: "It really only existed during my sabbatical. That was the only time I had to call seven people and call the club owner. I was trying to do something different. But I came to the conclusion that it requires so much time, and it's my time. I need more time, so I'm back to thinking small is much better."

In December 2000, Tony founded a series of concerts entitled Jazz Underground, held in the "smoke-free, all-ages" Underground Café of the Danna Center at Loyola University. At first performing himself with various local and guest musicians, he framed these concerts as tributes to famous jazz artists, using punning titles to attract a young audience. In December 2002, the Loyola newspaper reported:

"As the semester draws to a close, The Jazz Underground Series is preparing for its spring lineup and is looking for a sponsor for the series. Now in its third year, it has grown from four shows a year to six. The series' creator, Tony Dagradi, an associate professor of music and a tenor saxophone player for the band Astral Project, coordinates the series. He said he based the series on something similar that he had done as a graduate student at Tulane. The idea behind Jazz Underground is to give people an intimate jazz club setting. But attendees exchange the smell of a smoke-filled room for the food, coffee and beer that the Underground provides. Local professionals are matched up to the tribute artist they are most likely to emulate and play that artist's music. The lights are dimmed, and sofas are moved to create a semicircle around the musicians, making a cozy atmosphere in which to chill out. 'To be able to create a jazz club atmosphere, we wanted to find a really cool place on campus,' said Reid Wick, publicity coordinator for the College of Music.... Attendance has been good with about 100 people per show, but sometimes it's standing room only, organizers said. For the tribute to John Coltrane an estimated 300 or more showed up, Wick said. 'It was so full, we couldn't put another person in there.'... Wick said that the program's goal is three-fold: it gives another cultural enrichment opportunity, develops an audience for jazz, and pays tribute to musicians who deserve it."[6]

And Tod Smith noted on allaboutjazz.com, "Adding to these events is WWOZ jazz radio personality and historian Michael Gourrier. Contributing insight into the lives of the performers and introducing the artists, Gourrier's presence makes the Underground a total New Orleans modern jazz experience."[7] Altogether, Tony took part in the following shows:

Horace Silver (Silver Serenade), 5 October 2000; with Rick Trolsen, trombone; Peter Martin, piano; Chris Severin, bass; John Vidacovich, drums.

Thelonious Monk (Monk's Dream), 2 November 2000; with Michael Pellera, piano; Chris Severin, bass; Adonis Rose, drums.

Art Blakey (Art Blakey's Message), 1 February 2001; personnel not advertised.

John Coltrane (Trane Tracks), 8 March 2001; with Clarence Johnson III, tenor sax; Jon Cowherd, piano; Roland Guerin, bass; Brian Blade, drums.

Dizzy Gillespie and Charlie Parker (To Be or Not to Bop), 27 September 2001; with Rex Richardson, trumpet; Aaron Fletcher, alto sax; Victor Atkins, piano; Chris Severin, bass; Adonis Rose, drums.

Wayne Shorter (Shorter Moments), 18 October 2001; Irvin Mayfield, trumpet; Peter Martin, piano; Chris Severin, bass; John Vidacovich, drums.

Alvin "Red" Tyler (Graciously), 7 November 2002; Astral Project.

Sonny Rollins (Sunny Side Up), 13 March 2003; with Roland Guerin, bass; Ocie Davis, drums

Tadd Dameron, 25 September 2003; with Jamelle Williams, trumpet; Larry Sieberth, piano; Roland Guerin, bass; Adonis Rose, drums.

Joe Henderson (Mo' Joe), 11 March 2004; personnel not advertised.

John Coltrane (Chasin' the Trane), 23 September 2004; with Tim Price, saxophone; Victor Atkins, piano; Chris Severin, bass; Stanton Moore, drums.

Tim Price wrote about the second Coltrane tribute: "Tony Dagradi ... should be way better known. He sounds beautiful, and his command of the language of the tenor comes right from the heart.... We played some unique Trane tunes like 'India,' which I voiced for [electronically enhanced] bassoon and Dagradi's soprano, and we did 'Naima' like a bright bossa with an open feel. Tony played 'Soul Eyes' as his ballad. It was very, very inspirational for me to do this...."[8]

For the rest of the year, Tony left the performing to others (Wes Anderson, Alvin Batiste, Henry Butler, Evan Christopher and Tom McDermott, Joe Krown, Jason Marsalis, Larry Sieberth, Rick Trolsen, John Vidacovich), although he still coordinated the series.

After five years of concentrating on Astral Project, on 22 March 2005, Tony started yet another new group, this time indeed a small one: an organ trio featuring Brian Coogan on organ, and Jason Marsalis or Simon Lott on drums. It performed at d.b.a. on 22 March and 17 May, and Snug Harbor on 26 June. (After Hurricane Katrina, in November 2005, Coogan and Lott performed with Steve and Tony as Astral Project.) Of the Snug Harbor performance, with Coogan and Lott, Nerissa Cohen wrote:

"[Dagradi] proceeded to use the waning moments to remind us why he has held his spot at the top of N.O.'s music scene for so long. He's a great sax player. His tone is unique and beautiful. His technique is as spellbinding as his imagination. I've heard him play no less than fifteen times this past year, and every single solo has left me on the edge of my seat. Channeling the spirits of Coltrane et al. in one riff, and rivaling any of the [Dave] Koz's and [David] Sanborns in the next, he's always setting the groove, stretching the limits, and making full use of the talented players behind him."[9]

In the summer of 2004, Tony told me that he was learning to play the bagpipes. I suggested that he write a piece called "A Drone for Joan's Tone."[10] He countered with "The Let's Get Reel." Both bagpipes and puns soon petered out.

Tony "performed on tenor and soprano in an evening that Pandit Ajoy Chakrabarty," an Indian vocalist, "organized to bring Indian classical music and jazz together" in 2004. In March 2005 he was excited about playing the bamboo flute from India called the *bansuri*,[11] and learning to perform Hindustani (north Indian) classical music by working with Andrew McLean. McLean, a local *tabla* player and singer, studied under Ustad Ali Akbar Khan and Pandit Swapan Chaudhuri.[12] Tony finds the formal aspects of Indian music appealing, particularly the mixture of improvisation and written sections, often repeated. He is also impressed that Indian musicians practice on scales in a similar manner to jazz musicians. "It's exactly the same things that are in my book *Essential Scale Studies*, which is just a series of sequential exercises on scales. In India they have something called *paltas*: basically a shape that you play sequentially through whatever raga scale you're in." *Paltas* (literally, turn) is in fact a general term for exercises, especially specific types of ornaments comprised of permutations of notes.[13] Tony also appreciated that "in India the classical musicians are the improvisers. And they are considered to be spiritually advanced because they can do that. Not necessarily that they are—I understand that—but they are considered to be, and truly, the great players really are." On 8 April he played a "World-Spirit Music Concert" at Wild Lotus Yoga, using both *bansuri* and saxophone, with Andrew McLean and Friends (Benny Dominic, guitar; Dan Carroll, percussion; Seán Johnson, vocals). In November 2006, Tony could still tell a reporter that his iPod had "a whole lot of Indian classical music" on it.[14]

Notes

1. "Local Rock," *Times–Picayune*, 7 November 1997, section Lagniappe, L8.

2. "Dagradi Gets Plugged in," *Times–Picayune*, 13 March 1998, section Lagniappe, L9.

3. "Nontraditional Path to Trad Jazz," *Times–Picayune*, 9 July 1999, section Lagniappe, L9.

4. "Jazz," *Times–Picayune*, 28 April 2000, section Lagniappe, L22.

5. Keith Spera, "Horns Aplenty in Inside Out," *Times–Picayune*, 21 January 2000, section Lagniappe, L9.

6. Bill Brown, "Jazz Goes Underground: Music Series Takes over Danna Center Basement," *The Maroon* (Loyola University, New Orleans), 6 December 2002; available from http://maroon.loyno.edu/media/paper542/news/2002/12/06/News/Jazz-Goes.Underground-338020.shtml; accessed 29 June 2005.

7. Tod Smith, "Jazz Underground"; available from http://www.allaboutjazz.com/articles/newo0202.htm; accessed 29 June 2005.

8. Message written 3 October 2004; see http://forum.saxontheweb.net/archive/index.php/t-15717.html; accessed 15 November 2006.

9. http://www.liveneworleans.com/detail.php?id=741.

10. A pun on Chick Corea's *Tones for Joan's Bones*. Joan does call Tony "Tone."

11. The *bansuri* is a flute made of a single length of bamboo with (traditionally) six fingerholes. After at least two millennia of associations with shepherds and folk musicians, it was introduced into Hindustani classical music in the twentieth century by Pandit Pannalal Ghosh, who developed the now customary alto size, added a seventh fingerhole, and adapted the classical vocal style to the instrument. See http://www.musicalnirvana.com/instruments/bansuri.html; accessed 15 December 2005.

12. See Arvindkumar Parikh, "N.O. Man Fuses Jazz with Music of India," *Times–Picayune*, 28 May 1998, section Picayune, 3A1. As the title of this article suggests, McLean has also fostered a fusion of Indian classical music and jazz, working with such jazz saxophonists as

Tim Green of 3NOW4 and Tony's former student Clarence Johnson III. See also, for example, "Indian Music," *Times–Picayune*, 17 October 2003, section Lagniappe, 30; "Concerts," *Times–Picayune*, 17 September 2004, section Lagniappe, 31.

13. See "Brief Glossary": http://www.aacm.org/aacm/discography/glossary.html; accessed 15 December 2005.

14. See http://www.clevescene.com/search/rss.php?eventSearch=1&date=2006-11-09&section=events; accessed 15 November 2006.

14. SIDEMAN, 1992–2005

Between 1992 and 2005, Tony increased the frequency of his performances as a sideman on recordings for other New Orleans musicians—of course, jazz but also soul, blues, and even rock.

In November 1992, John Vidacovich took part in a video series on New Orleans drumming, *Street Beats: Modern Applications*, produced by Dan Thress, and also featuring Herman Ernest, Earl Palmer, and Herlin Riley.[1] During his interview with Thress, John is joined by three of his Astral Project colleagues, Tony, Tork, and James, for six exemplary performances: "Carnival," by Michael Pellera; "Her Mind is Gone" and "Big Chief," the first written by Professor Longhair and the second associated with him; "Cake Walk," by Alvin "Red" Tyler; John's own "New Day"; and James's "Bongo Joe." John's comments on his playing in these performances show how much he had thought about what types of groove to play on each tune, and how he can switch on a dime from one groove to another.

The *Cadence* critic Dale Smoak claimed that John's *Banks Street* (1996)[2] "straddles the fence between modern jazz and party music."[3] Even the *Times–Picayune* contrasted John's jazz experience with his knowledge of other New Orleans genres: "Mr. Adams isn't the only Johnny to serve two masters. Johnny Vidacovich is best known these days as the drummer in high-flying modern jazz ensemble Astral Project, and as one half of the vaunted Vidacovich/James Singleton rhythm section. But he was also Professor Longhair's longtime [sic] timekeeper, and is well-versed in the ways of the New Orleans second-line street beat. *Banks Street* ... continues to work both sides of the street."[4] John, an inimitable fuser of styles, saw the album as simply the music of his home town, as John Wirt reported: "While many label Vidacovich's *Banks Street* a jazz record, the drummer prefers to call it ethnic music. 'If you listen to it, you hear familiar street beat sounds and claves and stylistic colors that are characteristic of a bunch of music from around here from way back,' he explained."[5]

The tenor saxophonist Eric Traub appears on the first five tracks, Tony on six altogether, one overlapping with Traub, although Tony doesn't solo on James Singleton's loping "Bulldog Run," soon to be a hit on Astral Project's *Elevado* (1997). The overlap comes as a tenor chase on the title track, and Tony switches to soprano for a further, Coltrane-like solo just before the out chorus. Tony plays tenor plaintively in unison with the right hand of the composer on Michael Pellera's plaintive "The Cry." When it segues to the jaunty "Gothic," Tony finds the plaintive edge of jauntiness on the head, and he turns in his best solo, with beautiful phrasing and some unusual phrases, sometimes going a bit "out," and ending delicately. On the curious "Blue Monday," also by Pellera, John's parade rhythm persists throughout, Tony double-tracks soprano and tenor on the head against the composer's insistent comping, and then Tony takes a curiously meandering soprano solo. Too blue?

"Gator Bait," another wonderful New Orleans-flavored theme by James soon to be on *Elevado*, is played in unison by tenor and piano right hand again. Tony has a solo in the out chorus, Coltrane-ish plus wails. The tune of "Don Juan, the Indian" (by John himself) features a smearing, double-stopped bass line from James Singleton and a sonorous tenor line by Tony over a basic cymbal beat supplemented by basic bongos. In his ensuing solo Tony is at his most Coltrane-like in the intensity and the altissimo-register sonority, although the blues—and New Orleans—are never far away. As John reaches his poem to recite, he switches to toms, while Bill Huntington's guitar adds the briefest splashes of *Bitches Brew* color and the bongo background intensifies. The track simply fades out.

John's eponymous album *Vidacovich* (2002), his third as a leader, is one of my favorites from New Orleans.⁶ It shows off the leader to joyous effect in small-group settings with some excellent local musicians as well as his old friend Jeffrey Meyer, the percussionist, who acted as co-producer. Tony has a blast on seven of the ten tracks.

Two of the pieces are "settings" of John's poems. "Jack Shee" (music by Meyer) starts with Michael Pellera's insinuating solo Hammond-organ line and a cymbal wash, over which Tony eventually enters with short, haunting bass-clarinet phrases as John adds drum rolls and accents. A similar organ-and-drum texture accompanies the poem, after which Tony returns to haunt again. "Message from General Child," to music by Pellera, opens with a vamp, then a couple of choruses of his bluesy Rhodes piano against nicely varied drums and bass (Matt Perrine). John declaims the whole poem against the earlier vamp. Michael then switches to Hammond organ as Tony enters in his best R&B groove—jabbing, growling, rolling, wailing—before ending with the vamp followed by some churchy chords on the organ.

On the opening track, Michael Pellera's "The Zone," a great NOLA piece, we are immediately introduced to John's press rolls, the rocking guitar of Shane Theriot, and Matt Perrine's sousaphone, which adds a festival spirit to the bass line. Tony laps up this kind of accompaniment and fashions a blissful solo. John's "Deb's Garden" is named for his wife, and she does have a garden—according to John, now a more beautiful than ever. It's performed by tenor, sousaphone, and drums alone. Tony was familiar with this piece, because it was included on Astral Project's *Voodoobop* (1999). He contributes a lyrical, rhythmically varied solo, with a nice climax. Then he switches to a riff-based contrapuntal line behind Perrine's solo.

"Second Opinion," composed by Pellera and Meyer, is a joyful parade piece with a whooping sousaphone line from Perrine. Tony double-tracks soprano and tenor saxes on the head and out chorus. He begins his solo with only drums, strongly rhythmic, including some repeated-note figures, and he sticks to this approach when Perrine enters on the second chorus. "Snowalkin'" by John and Pellera is a nice angular piece, on which Tony again double-tracks soprano and tenor on the head, although he doesn't take a solo.

Meyer's "Coffee" is heard in two versions. First, at a slow tempo, John sings about the virtues of the beverage and the considerable quantity he consumes, accompanied by his drums and Perrine. Then the tempo doubles, and Tony comes in on tenor to play the same piece with only drums, taking off, as Geraldine Wyckoff put it, "with apparent caffeine-injected velocity."⁷ He delivers a boppish solo, with nice switches of rhythm and of course a few wails. After a drum solo in John's inimitable style, based on the melody, Tony returns for the fast out chorus and an abrupt stop. Imaginative!

Solomon Burke (1940–2010), "The King of Soul and Rock 'n' Roll" as well as 375 lbs and proud of it, made a live recording with a big band at The House of Blues in New Orleans on 1 May 1994.⁸ Tony came in to fatten up the sound of the horn section in the studio.

The New Orleans blues and gospel singer Johnny Adams (1932–1998), known as "The Tan Canary" (although he made an album called *A Tan Nightingale*), branched out into jazz and just plain crooning on his later albums. On *The Verdict* (1995), made with well-known jazz musicians, mostly from New Orleans, Houston Person plays a sultry tenor sax.⁹ Tony comes on board with his soprano sax on "Down That Lonely Lonely Road," wailing appropriately. Geraldine Wyckoff observed: "Adams doesn't completely abandon his R&B roots, and we're glad when we hear that rhythmic sense on James Black's 'Down That Lonely Lonely Road,' enhanced by saxophonist Tony Dagradi...."¹⁰ Tony comes back on the intro and heads of "Come Home to Love," helping to set the bittersweet feeling of the track, mournful in mood but upbeat in message.

It's a shame that Tony got to record with Tommy Ridgley (1925–1999) only when the veteran

New Orleans blues singer was 70 years old, by which time his voice sounded worn out and he had a shaky sense of pitch. The three different crack bands on *Since the Blues Began*, which included the guitarist Snooks Eaglin and George Porter Jr. on the bass, certainly give Ridgley a good run for his money.[11] Tony plays a lyrical solo on "Running After You," which also contains a scintillating short solo from Eaglin. On "The World is our Stage," Ridgley croons like Johnny Adams, and almost makes it. Tony's all-too-short solo sounds funky and lyrical at the same time. On "You Mean Everything to Me," Tony takes a sultry blues solo, then joins in on the out chorus.

The New Orleans clarinettist Tim Laughlin plays in a traditional idiom. *Blue Orleans* (1996) features him with a variety of Crescent City musicians in a mixture of standards and originals.[12] On the title track, an updated traditional piece, Tony takes a solo in a 1930s style and Tork contributes a bubbly Hammond organ. Lawrence Gibbs commented: "Laughlin uses famed New Orleans musician Tony Dagradi and members of his Astral Project to help add the 'contemporary' touch to this music.... The title track is a laid-back blues with a little something extra.... Dixieland meets Rhythm and Blues as Tony Dagradi's soulful tenor saxophone completes the picture."[13]

After working in New York and Melbourne, Australia, the singer and composer Denise Mangiardi spent about five years in the 1990s in New Orleans, where she befriended the Astral Project circle and made three CDs with them.[14] She has a unique style of singing and composing, part jazz, part folk. *A River of My Own* (1998) contains eleven poetic original compositions, an old Billie Holiday vehicle, plus a setting of a poem by John Vidacovich, mostly in her own arrangements.[15] The songs and her voice have a delicate, almost "smooth" vibe to them. In supporting the singer and adding his solos, Tony picks up on exactly that vibe, playing delicately, veering towards but never quite reaching smooth: soprano sax on "River of My Own," "Precious Stones," "Rainbow Chasers," and "Transformation"; tenor sax on "The Keeper." Playing tenor on "Rocks and Streams," which has a more hard-booting arrangement, he's more hard-booting.

On at least eleven occasions between May 1997 and September 2000, Tony went on tour with Clarence "Gatemouth" Brown and Gate's Big Band, including such important venues as the Montreux Jazz Festival, the North Sea Jazz Festival, and the Lionel Hampton Jazz Club in Paris. Some of the fruits of their work are found on the CDs *Gate Swings* (1997) and *American Music Texas Style* (1999).[16]

On *Gate Swings*, Brown's tribute to the Swing bands of the 30s and 40s, Tony takes tenor sax solos on "Flying Home," "Gate's Blues Waltz," "One O'Clock Jump," "Take Me Back Baby," and "Too Late Baby." He plays in R&B style, mild for him, on "Gate's Blues Waltz" (one measly chorus) and "Too Late Baby," and a Swing style reminiscent of Johnny Hodges on "Take Me Back Baby." Much more engaging are the exchanges with another New Orleans tenor sax player, Eric Traub, on "Flying Home" and "One O'Clock Jump." I wish the exchanges had been longer, but of course Brown was the star.

Nevertheless, the critics spoke highly of the Swinging saxes. The *Down Beat* critic Frank-John Hadley commented of the album: "One big plus is the featured playing of Tony Dagradi: what jumps out of the bell of his tenor on five numbers is both exciting and unpredictable."[17] The blues critic Art Tipaldi: "If this is K.C., there must be a nod to Count Basie, whose flyin' 'One O'Clock Jump' centers Brown's guitar as lead instrument—until New Orleans' Tony Dagradi and Eric Traub do a tenor battle reminiscent of the early duels of Ben Webster and Lester Young in some after-hours jam.... Lionel Hampton's 'Flying Home' double-times the tempo and doubles the tenors as Traub and Dagradi again put sax valves [i.e., keys] through a screamin' workout."[18] And another blues critic: "The material might seem a tad clichéd, but in these hands there's no room for moldy-figgery: everything here sounds as urgent as tomorrow's headlines. The sax soloists—Eric Demmer, Eric Traub, and Tony Dagradi—blow as if they were trying to rip the roof off every Dew Drop Inn between Houston and the state line.... personal favorites include ... the final workout on Lionel Hampton's immortal flag waver ['Flying Home"], complete with lusty sax breaks by Traub and Dagradi (both of whom are smart enough to avoid attempting any recreations of Illinois Jacquet's legendary 1943 solo)."[19]

On *American Music Texas Style*, Tony was allotted tenor solos on only two tracks: "Front Burner" and "Without Me Baby." The first matches him with Traub again, to good wailing effect. The second is a pleasant outing, but he doesn't work up any head of steam.

Towards the end of his life, the former Count Basie Orchestra trombonist Al Grey (1925–2000) made a recording in the Big Easy called *Echoes of New Orleans* (1998).[20] James Singleton tells a story about this session:

> "The owner of Snug Harbor, Jason Patterson, asked me if I could play for a gig with Al Grey. I told him I could make the gig, but not the rehearsal, so could he find someone else? He couldn't and got back to me. I repeated that I couldn't make the rehearsal and he said that was OK. When I got to the gig, Grey was snippy and announced to the audience, 'Here's the bass player who didn't make the rehearsal.' But he actually liked my playing and announced, 'The bass player who didn't make the rehearsal plays good.' Then he offered me a solo. I was feeling irritated by this time, so I said, 'I'm going to play a solo by myself.' 'Oh,' announces Grey, 'the bass player who didn't make the rehearsal wants to play a solo,' but he let me. So I played 'Willow Weep for me' with all my usual slapping and loops. The audience went wild. Grey was impressed.
>
> "After the gig, he asked me if I could find a sax player and another trombonist for the record session he was doing: didn't pay much, but it was a gig. I said, 'Sure,' and I brought Tony and Rick Trolsen along. During the session, he offered to let me do a solo on one number, but he insisted on me being accompanied by piano and drums. Naturally, I was much more restricted in what I could do. Afterwards, Grey says, 'Here was your big chance for fame, and you blew it!'
>
> "Then someone proposed sending out for beers. Grey insisted: 'Red wine.' But he was a diabetic and should never have been drinking alcohol."

Tony adds: "The reason Grey needed the extra horns for that session is that he could never have made it through to the end by himself without the added support. And after the red wine, the session went down real fast...." He also recalls that Grey had recorded all the tunes on a little hand-held tape recorder to remind himself what to play, then sang the parts for the session musicians to pick up.

The pieces Grey chose were a mixture of old Traditional and Swing numbers ("Basin Street Blues," "Caravan," "Cottontail," "I Got it Bad and That Ain't Good," "St. James Infirmary," "St. Louis Blues," and "Struttin' with Some Barbecue"), presumably in tribute to New Orleans, one standard ballad ("Nancy"), and three of his own compositions ("Diz Related," "Echoes of New Orleans," and "Over and Under"). Tony, with his intimate knowledge of jazz saxophone history, was the perfect choice for such an album. Chameleon-like, he modifies his style on every number. In the older ones, he throws off echoes of Johnny Hodges ("St. James Infirmary" and the two blues), Coleman Hawkins ("Struttin' with Some Barbecue"), and Lester Young and his imitators ("Cottontail," including some repeated notes with different tones). On Grey's pieces, Tony reflects the hard-booting Jazz at the Philharmonic tenors on "Diz Related," and throws in some R&B influence on "Echoes of New Orleans" and "Over and Under," especially in the latter over the bouncy piano accompaniment of Victor "Red" Allen. My favorite solo is on "Caravan," where Tony relaxes into his normal style, using a harder tone, constructing phrases of pleasingly different lengths, and allowing the Coltrane influence to come forth, all against effective comping from Allen.

Not understanding the angle of the album, the British critic Christopher Hillman showed his snobbery and even brought out that British dirty word "provincial": "... it has to be said that [Grey's] approach, and that of his backing group, is less successful on the good old Dixieland numbers than on those of more sophisticated origin (among those, three of his own compositions) with, naturally, a climactic tour-de-force on 'Caravan.' Throughout, he dominates the music, and although the other musicians are of adequate standard for a provincial supporting group on a live occasion [sic], they take up too much space in relation to the quality of their contributions. My overall feeling is that Al Grey with just a rhythm section would have made for a better recording session."[21] Take that, New Orleans!

On his debut CD, *Cloud 9* (1997), the pianist Michael Pellera began his tradition of playing short solo pieces between the ensemble numbers, on some of which Tony solos.[22] The title track is a fairly modern piece built on a bass ostinato; Tony's soprano goes to town tunefully. Thelonious Monk's "Green Chimneys" is given the parade-rhythm treatment, somewhat hampered by Bill Huntington's static bass. Tony's funky tenor carries on regardless, gradually increasing in energy. After the gospel piano intro on "Sister," Tony's delicate tenor becomes funkier and more intense, with the singer Phillip Manuel intoning and wailing behind and Steve Masakowski's guitar adding fuel to the fire.

The *Cadence* critic David Lewis complained: "Dagradi fabricates passion during his double-tempo soprano lines in 'Cloud 9' and his tenor solo in 'Sister,' but this CD sounds bloodless until Monk's 'Green Chimneys' kicks into life.... Unless you are a Dagradi or Monk-covers completist or deeply into New Age jazz, you can pass on this."[23]

Pellera's *Son of Sky* (2001), which followed the same pattern,[24] received a laudatory notice from Jonathan Tabak in the *Times-Picayune*: "Michael Pellera didn't set out to make a typical jazz recording. 'Sometimes I get discouraged with a public that only wants to hear standards played with a swing feel,' the 45-year-old pianist said recently. 'But I have to make a statement that is uniquely mine and try to create some kind of hybrid that hopefully can find an audience that wants to stretch a little.' That statement is *Son of Sky*, a remarkable new CD that strips away tired formulas to reveal an absorbing, refined modern jazz expression that could only come from the Crescent City. The songs are all original, rarely following the standard melody–solos–melody structure, and they all possess a rhythmic nuance and lyricism that reflects New Orleans style (as opposed to mimicking 'New York jazz'). Of course, it helps to have Johnny Vidacovich on drums and Tony Dagradi on sax, players who have helped define the modern New Orleans sound as members of Astral Project (with which Pellera has enjoyed a long association), as well as the versatile young bassist Mark Anderson."[25]

Several tracks were "improvised at the recording sessions with minimal discussion as to the direction of each piece." "Ciao bella" is based on John's poem "Watch the Mountains Grow." The track begins with John saying "Ciao bella" (Hi, beautiful), a phrase that young men in Italy hurl at passing women. Its relationship to the egoless mountain-watching of the poem seems obscure. To a funk beat, Tony on tenor sax then plays fragments reminiscent of 1960s Wayne Shorter as well as growls, all nicely paced, against splashy chords in the piano, an active, contrapuntal bassline, and irregular rim shots from John. Next, Pellera takes a short dissonant solo. While the music continues in the earlier vein, John recites the poem quickly in a sing-song manner. The track ends with a second spoken "Ciao bella" and a brief drum figure.

"2 People," short at under two minutes, is also improvised by the four musicians. Without a poem to hang its hat on, the tonal-ish line by Tony, backed by occasionally "out" chords from Pellera, is merely pleasant. On Pellera's "Titan," by far the longest track on the album at seven minutes, Tony does well in navigating the ambiguity of the slow march rhythm in the drums, Pellera's heavy rhythmic comping, and the faster pulse in the bass. The title track is a rather static piece set to a parade rhythm, on which Tony takes a short free-ish solo.

The post-grunge alternative pop-rock band Better than Ezra used Tony as well as other prominent New Orleans musicians such as Mark Mullins (trombone) and Larry Sieberth (keyboards) as session men on the sessions for three albums: *Deluxe* (1995), *Friction, Baby* (1996), and what allmusic.com claims to be their best, *How Does Your Garden Grow?* (1998), which was made in their own recording studio in the Crescent City.[26] Tony looms large toward the end of the first track on *Garden*, as David Gerard described: "The opening number, 'Je ne m'en souviens pas,' is worth the price of this disc alone. A trippy bit of spoken word against a breezy jazz-funk backdrop (featuring jazz vibraphonist Karl Berger, and the animated flute of Tony Dagradi), [it] easily rivals the sonic alchemy of the Beasties and Beck."[27]

¡Cubanismo!'s album *¡Cubanismo! in New Orleans: Mardi Gras Mambo* (2000), celebrating the mixing of Cuban and Big Easy cultures, provided a rare opportunity to hear Tony play the baritone sax on the opening "Marie Laveaux."[28] Alas, he wasn't given a solo.

Although the electric bassist and keyboardist Al Arthur hired some prominent New Orleans musicians for his album *Mantis* (2000), including Tony, Cranston Clements (guitar), Brian O'Neil (trombone), and his regular drummer Freddie Staehle, the vapid songs and static accompaniment produce a smooth funk (oxymoron?) that rapidly palls.[29] Tony clearly found it hard to rise above the prevailing atmosphere, especially on tenor, where his style sounds like that of the Carla Bley days, particularly on "Crying Again." His solos on soprano on "Cool Breeze" and "Night Flight" are more lively and inventive.

On *The Way it Is* (2002) by the blind blues singer and guitarist Snooks Eaglin (1936–2009), Tony is billed on the opening "Can You Hear Me?" but in truth I cannot hear him in the performance.[30] In any case, the track sets a funky standard for the CD, and at the end Eaglin rightly says to his colleagues, Jon Cleary and the Absolute Monster Gentlemen, "That's a good groove there, boys."

On the following "Boogie Rambler," which appropriately begins with Eaglin's swinging boogie line, Tony punctuates the vocal line, then trades solos with the guitarist, essaying a mixture of R&B and Charlie Parker bebop, with fast runs and quintuplet figures. One reviewer wrote: "Eaglin's unique guitar technique—that combination of percussive finger-strumming, rhythmic leads and spidery solo flights—really shines on a driving version of Charles Brown's 'Boogie Rambler,' where Tony Dagradi's swinging sax lines are a perfect foil for Eaglin's elastic string bends."[31] On "Lock Doctor," a medium-paced blues, Tony plays more in R&B style, including nice pitch bends, but is allotted only one chorus to the guitarist's two, and ends before he sounds warmed up.

"Ghost of a Chance," the strangest of tracks, might more aptly have been titled "I Can't Get Started." Tony sets out the theme in a lugubrious style, before handing over to Eaglin; he returns to make it almost a duet, but in a halting fashion, where it's not clear who's trying to state the theme and who's playing a solo. When it's clear that the solos proper have begun, the musicians play closer to jazz than to R&B, but every time Tony gets in a few licks in his warm ballad style and seems set fair to take off, he gets cut short and Eaglin takes over, unconvincingly. The track ends abruptly, with only a little cadenza from Tony to redeem it.

All in all on this CD, at three tracks out of eleven and noticeably less solo space than the leader, Tony was given a ghost of a chance to show his paces.

The New Orleans drummer Wayne Maureau hired some fine musicians for his *Sidewalk Safari* (2001), notably Tony and Larry Sieberth (keyboards), and wrote five pieces for the occasion, but Tommy Sciple's over-recorded electric bass weighs down the proceedings.[32] Nevertheless, Sieberth has never played better on recordings, and, buoyed by the quality of the piano or keyboard, drums, and percussion (Michael Skinkus), Tony contributes some exciting solos on "Children of the Night" and "Guess What" (tenor) and "The Passage" (soprano). Evidently not as in practice as in the 1980s, he plays saxophonist's flute on the smooth jazz "The Real Guitarist" and "Scattered Showers."

The "horn" (in this case trumpet plus saxophone) arrangement on "Good Life," the first track on Kim Prevost's *Talk to me* (2002), was made by Tony and the pianist Darrell Lavigne.[33] It has a good-time feel that matches Prevost's happy voice, and Tony has a rollicking tenor solo. The arrangements on "Eleanor Rigby," "Give Me Your Love," and "I'll Be Lovin' You Right" are attributed to Tony and Prevost's husband, the guitarist Bill Solley. "Eleanor Rigby" is given a boogaloo feel, a little out of keeping with the celebrated "lonely" people depicted in the Beatles' song. "I'll Be Lovin' You Right" comes right out of Motown. "Give Me Your Love" sounds like a disco piece from the 70s, and I was waiting for Prevost and Solley to dance the hustle; but perhaps we have to wait for the video? Alas, Tony doesn't receive any further solos.

Jim McNeil is a Mississippi folk singer–songwriter who sings of love and loss. For his *Give me my Wings* (2005) he hired some of New Orleans' best jazz musicians,[34] and the *OffBeat* critic saw a "disparity between the sadness of the emotional lyrics and the liveliness of the music, performed by McNeil, Larry Sieberth, Victor Atkins, Tony Dagradi, and Johnny Vidacovich."[35] I wouldn't say "liveliness": rather, there's a relentless quality that drives home the sad point until it's almost unbearable. Tony is supportive to the singer as always, throwing in hints of R&B on tenor; wailing and crying on soprano.

Notes

1. *Street Beats: Modern Applications, New Orleans Drumming*; videotape; interviewer: Dan Thress; includes six short performances by members of Astral Project ([Miami?]: DCI Music Video, 1993); reissued as part of the DVD *New Orleans Drumming* (Miami: Warner Brothers 905772, 2004).

2. John Vidacovich, *Banks Street* (Diamondhead, MS: Record Chebasco RC1496, cp1996).

3. Dale Smoak, review in *Cadence* 22, no. 12 (December 1996): 95.

4. [Keith Spera], review in *Times-Picayune*, 8 November 1996, L21.

5. John Wirt, "Vidacovich Adds Life to his Sound with Hereditary New Orleans Beat," *The Advocate* (Baton Rouge, LA), 28 June 1996, section Fun, 17–Fun.

6. John Vidacovich, *Vidacovich* (New York: PawMaw Music 02, cp2002).

7. Geraldine Wyckoff, review in *OffBeat* 15, no. 5 (May 2002): 88.

8. Solomon Burke, *Live at The House of Blues* (New Orleans: Black Top CDBT–1108, 1994).

9. Johnny Adams, *The Verdict* (Cambridge, MA: Rounder CD 2135, 1995).

10. Geraldine Wyckoff, review in *Jazz Times* 25, no. 4 (April 1995): 80.

11. Tommy Ridgley, *Since the Blues Began* (New Orleans: Black Top BT–1115, 1995).

12. Tim Laughlin, *Blue Orleans* (Berkeley, CA: Good Time Jazz GTJCD–15004–2, 1996).

13. Lawrence Gibbs, review in *The Clarinet* 27, no. 1 (December 1999): 24–25.

14. For more on Denise Mangiardi, see her website http://www.denisesongs.com/about/; accessed 6 October 2013.

15. Denise Mangiardi, *A River of My Own* (Bailey, CO: Crow Hill Publishing CHP–011298, 1998).

16. Clarence Gatemouth Brown, *Gate Swings* (Verve/Polygram 314 537 617–2, 1997); *American Music, Texas Style* (Verve/Blue Thumb 314 547 536–2, 1999).

17. Frank-John Hadley, review in *Down Beat* 64, no. 9 (September 1997): 43.

18. Art Tipaldi, review in *Blues Revue*, no. 35 (March 1998): 37–38.

19. David Whiteis, review in *Living Blues*, no. 135 (September–October 1997): 58.

20. Al Grey, *Echoes of New Orleans* (New Orleans: Progressive PCD–7108, cp1998).

21. Christopher Hillman, review in *Jazz Journal International* 52, no. 4 (April 1999): 31.

22. Michael Pellera, *Cloud 9* (New Orleans: Pajacis Music PAJ–001, cp1997).

23. David Lewis, review in *Cadence* 24, no. 5 (May 1998): 126.

24. Michael Pellera, *Son of Sky* (New Orleans: Pajacis paj–002, c2001).

25. Jonathan Tabak, review in *Times-Picayune*, 26 October 2001, section Lagniappe, 24.

26. Better than Ezra, *Deluxe* (New York: Elektra 61784–2, 1995); *Friction, Baby* (New York: Elektra 61944–2, 1996); *How Does Your Garden Grow?* (New York: Elektra 62247–2, 1998).

27. David Gerard, review in *The Boston Globe*, 1 October 1998, section Calendar, 8.

28. ¡Cubanismo!, *¡Cubanismo! in New Orleans: Mardi Gras Mambo* (New York: Hannibal HNCD 1441, 2000).

29. Al Arthur, *Mantis* (New Orleans: privately published DM102000, 2000).

30. Snooks Eaglin, *The Way it Is* (New Orleans: Money Pit Records 1111, 2002).

31. Scott Jordan, review in *Gambit Weekly* 23 no. 23 (4 June 2002): 29.

32. Wayne Maureau, *Sidewalk Safari* (New Orleans: privately produced, 2001).

33. Kim Prevost, *Talk to me* (New Orleans: STR Digital Records, cp2002).

34. Jim McNeil, *Give me my Wings* (New Orleans: privately produced AL–20051, cp2005).

35. Burke Ingraffia, review in *OffBeat*, September 2006.

15. ASTRAL PROJECT, 2001–05

In 1991, Tork had been quoted as saying of the other members of Astral Project: "I hope they all outlive me, so I can play with them the rest of my life."[1] In May 2001, after a good decade of arranging—or not arranging—substitutes for himself, the over-committed keyboardist removed himself from Astral Project permanently. Following a "high" gig at Jazz Fest on the 5th and a "magical" one at Snug Harbor the next day, he decided "maybe now's the time to jet." The Times-Picayune announced on the 25th:

> "Keyboardist David Torkanowsky has left Astral Project, the modern jazz ensemble he co-founded 23 years ago. According to saxophonist Tony Dagradi, Torkanowsky's involvement with solo projects and as a sideman for the likes of smooth jazz saxophonist Boney James could not be reconciled with the band's increasingly busy touring schedule. 'It became a conflict to try to schedule around that,' Dagradi said. Torkanowsky could not be reached for comment.
>
> "Michael Pellera will fill in on piano through July 9—he'll be with the group Saturday at Snug Harbor—after which Astral Project will continue indefinitely as a four-piece. The band was a quartet early in its history [1986–87], after the departure of original percussionist Mark Sanders and before the addition of guitarist Steve Masakowski. They became a de facto quartet once again as Torkanowsky missed more and more gigs. Now the band plans to start writing for four people instead of five. 'It opens things up to different orchestration,' Dagradi said. 'It's a change, but we're looking forward to it.'"[2]

The remaining four members of Astral Project did toy with the idea of permanently hiring another pianist, such as Pellera or Larry Sieberth, both of whom had substituted with the group on many occasions.[3] But Pellera was tied up with his longstanding regular gig at the Windsor Court Hotel[4] as well as teaching at NOCCA, and Sieberth had a restaurant gig at Mr. B's and other commitments. So Astral Project decided to continue as a quartet. Steve comments: "It put more of a burden on me than on anybody else in the band, because I basically had to cover the piano's function and relearn how to approach the music. But I felt very comfortable doing that because I've always done a lot of gigs without piano players and also a lot of guitar trio stuff. So I was used supplying my own accompaniment when I solo. It's definitely a more open texture without the piano." John had favored the idea, as Geraldine Wyckoff reported: "'I was really looking forward to the vacant lots of opportunity,' quips Vidacovich, who [has] used the chance to look at new ways to integrate his drums into the music. 'A piano is like another drum to me. It's like a big drum and it's powerful, and David is a rhythmic person. So now I have even more options.'"[5]

Without Tork or another pianist, Astral Project did begin to appreciate John's "vacant lots of opportunity." Wyckoff again: "'There's more space in the band; there's more space on stage,' says Dagradi, while the other members jump in with, 'There's more space sonically, in the van, in the elevator, at the dinner table!'"[6]

Pellera did note one drawback to Tork's departure: it affords fewer opportunities for saxophone and guitar to play the melody line of the tunes in unison. "Once you get a trumpet and a sax, it starts to sound like Horace Silver records, or Art Blakey, or Miles; it almost makes the music automatically dated. It's really hard to make it sound new. But when you put a guitar with a saxophone, you have the strength of the two players and a kind of hybrid sound.... 'Sombras en la noche': that's a perfect example. The piano's playing, then they come in together—

it's great. Now they can't do it as much, because Steve has to hold down the fort with the harmony." Still, some tunes do still feature sax and guitar together. The saxophonist Kevin McNerney, commenting on an Astral Project performance at the University of North Texas on 5 October 2005, noted: "[Dagradi's] guitar-and-tenor unisons with Masakowski were dazzling ... they pulled it off with jaw-dropping speed and accuracy."[7]

The end of 2001 brought two separate trips to Europe. In October, the group had no fewer than ten dates in the area of Nancy, France, organized by the longstanding festival Nancy Jazz Pulsations. That had one big practical advantage: the group could stay at the same hotel each night. Scott Aiges went along as translator. James stayed on in Europe for a tour of Austria, Germany, and Romania with the Romanian saxophonist Nicolas Simion. On 10 November, his colleagues returned to join him for a one-off performance at the Jazz Tage [Jazz Days] festival in Ingolstadt, Germany.

In February 2002, Astral Project became the house band for the variety show *Crescent City* on the public-radio station WWNO. Steve wrote the theme song "Crescent City Strut" for the show (and the group used it at once for the closing number on its next CD). The producers planned a couple more shows that year and hoped to move to weekly broadcasts and syndication. The show was still going in 2005, with ten broadcasts a year (five in the spring and five in the fall) from Le Chat Noir cabaret theater and piano bar, and even survived Hurricane Katrina, but ran out of funding and closed on 9 May 2006. Steve was the music director. Astral Project, dubbed "the world's greatest house band," was given regular slots on the show, by itself and with a variety of local guests, both singers and instrumentalists, including Theresa Andersson, Troy Andrews, Germaine Bazzle, Troi Bechet, Topsy Chapman, Jeremy Davenport, Donald Harrison, Leroy Jones, Tim Laughlin, Ingrid Lucia, Phillip Manuel, Ellis and Jason Marsalis, Mark Mullins, Fredy Omar, The Pfister Sisters, Wanda Rouzan, Kermit Ruffins, and Jamil Sharif.

Astral Project publicity shot, *ca.* 2002; from left to right, John Vidacovich, Tony Dagradi, Steve Masakowski, James Singleton

The viability and creativity of the quartet formation were demonstrated by the group's self-produced CD *Big Shot*, released in time for Jazz Fest in April. The album contains eleven newly recorded originals: five by Tony ("Heart of the Matter," "Hymn," "Retro-Active," "Spherical," "X-Ray Vision"), four by Steve ("Big Shot," "Crescent City Strut," "Vengeance," "Vigil"), and two by James ("Magic Lantern," "Pandemonium"). Steve commented: "I think one of the things we've consciously decided to do ... is to start playing the new compositions before we go into the studios, as opposed to learning the new tunes for a record date and letting the tunes evolve."[8] Tony agreed: "we had a chance to let the material gel on the bandstand before going into the studio."[9] Steve also noted: "Astral Project has always been considered a New Orleans band. This is our first record that takes advantage of the New Orleans sound, of that music that's around us in the city. It's really a New Orleans album. That's what we've always been about. And this album really demonstrates that."[10] It won the award for best contemporary jazz album by a Louisiana artist in the *OffBeat* Critics' Choice poll. The big hits have been its two opening pieces, "Big Shot" and "Spherical," both New Orleans flavored. (For a discussion of this recording, see Lasocki, *A Higher Fusion*, chapter 12.)

The main reason for Astral Project to produce the album itself was financial. Because most of the sales had been made off the bandstand, or through stores in New Orleans such as the Louisiana Music Factory, Tower Records, and the Virgin Megastore, the group simply made far more money being independent. Tony noted: "Our profit margin is way greater, exponentially greater, than if we had dealt with a record company." Of course, the backside is reduced distribution, and to some extent publicity, nationwide. The balance of national to local publicity is illustrated clearly by the number of reviews: *Elevado* received nine outside New Orleans, *Voodoobop* six outside and one local, *Big Shot* five outside and four local.

On hearing *Big Shot*, at least one critic felt that Astral Project was playing far better now as a quartet:

"Puzzingly, [the quintet] together just sounded like an amazingly overqualified bar band, switching styles with the proficiency of shoplifters without assimilating them into an original sound. Last year's self-produced bonanza, *Big Shot*, changed all that. Astral Project seems to have blossomed following the departure of pianist David Torkanowsky; perhaps when he left the band in 2001 this simply reduced the number of forceful personalities pulling at the band's center. Whatever the reason, *Big Shot* has a startling clarity with clean lines and bright texturing; there's a distinctive group aesthetic here, which brings all the material under one tent, from post-funk rooted in second-line rhythms ('X-Ray Vision,' 'Big Shot') to a latter-day lament that references the N'Awlins funerals of old. Masakowski's solos swivel and soar, and Dagradi counters with earthy yet visionary statements; and as you might expect after all these years, bassist James Singleton and drummer John Vidacovich lock so easily into their rhythms it's as if they're taking each other's pulse."[11]

The group even found itself the subject of a short favorable article/interview in *Down Beat* by the magazine's editor, Jason Koransky:

"One could excuse the members of Astral Project if they get a little weepy and sentimental at their annual New Orleans Jazz & Heritage Festival gig. After all, this was where they debuted as a band in 1978, and every year since, without fail, they have improvised before increasingly larger and more receptive crowds at their hometown's musical blowout.

"But they don't get sentimental. They just play. And at their 2002 JazzFest show in

April, saxophonist Tony Dagradi, guitarist Steve Masakowski, bassist James Singleton, and drummer Johnny Vidacovich played with jubilant intensity. This proved to be a significant show. It was their first appearance at the fest as a quartet. Gone was pianist David Torkanowsky, whose relationship with the band came to an end last May. Since Torkanowsky's departure, the band has recorded a new album, *Big Shot* ... which layers sometimes infectious, sometimes gorgeous melodies above vicious, New Orleans-rooted beats. Without piano in the mix, the groove flows deep on *Big Shot*, and this runs over in the group's live show."[12]

In August 2002, Scott Aiges took a job with the city of New Orleans and began easing out of his position as Astral Project's manager. Yet even before then, the number of gigs had clearly begun to decline. For example, the group did not undertake a Midwest tour in the spring, or any kind of tour in the summer. Astral Project's reduced schedule continued in 2003, although the radio show *Crescent City* had picked up to a performance almost every month. A second Midwest tour in early October incorporated no fewer than three clinics or master classes: at Edgewood College in Madison, WI (3 October), Indiana University (8 October), and The University of Chicago (11 October), in each case during the day, followed by a gig in the evening. The clinic at IU, which I attended, took the shape of performance–questions–performance. The audience, mostly jazz majors, were understandably concerned about how to launch their careers, on which subject the members of Astral Project had copious practical advice.

A similar pattern of performances ensued in 2004. Two recordings by Astral Project came out that year: its second self-produced CD as a quartet, *The Legend of Cowboy Bill*, and a commercially issued CD of its stunning performance at Jazz Fest on 24 April. *Cowboy Bill* contains nine new original compositions: five by Tony ("Delicately," "Down Time," "Nowhere to Hide," "Second Thoughts," "Too Close for Comfort"), two by Steve ("Dark Sage," "Open Space"), one by James ("Cowboy Bill"), and one by John ("Saint Paul"). The Jazz Fest show—in effect a CD release party—featured seven compositions taken from the *Cowboy Bill* repertoire.

On 12 March 2005, Astral Project made its first complete videorecording, *Astral Project Live in New Orleans*: in fact live at Snug Harbor, which had been its home from home since 1980. The result, culled from the best of two sets, featured seven previously recorded pieces from the current repertoire ("Cowboy Bill," "Dark Sage," "Delicately," "Saint Paul," "Sidewalk Strut," "Spherical," "Too Close for Comfort," "The Whole Truth") plus a new ballad feature for Tony, Billy Strayhorn's "Blood Count." (For a discussion of these two recordings, see Lasocki, *A Higher Fusion*, chapter 14.)

Since Scott Aiges resigned as manager in 2002, Tony, a full-time professor, has been booking the group again—a time-consuming task.

"My time is limited. I make all the calls: book the gigs; call the promoters. I don't think I have time to be a publicist, too. I can do a little. But I'm doing it all right now. Everybody wants to have their own room. Booking the hotels, and getting maps: that's easy—nothing to that. That's busywork. The hard part is making the connection, getting somebody to answer the phone, getting somebody to call you back, waiting for the callback, getting everything to look good on paper, then calling them back one more time to make sure: 'We are doing this, right?'

"I can do clubs, quickie tours. If we have an anchor gig at a festival that drops in our lap, that's easy to book around. We basically need a booking agent. That will be my vision of the future. If I have somebody that's feeding me the gigs, I can book other gigs around them."

Astral Project has not undertaken tours of Europe after 2001, only tours of the Midwest in the spring and fall, or only the fall, plus a regular slot once a month at Snug Harbor. And yet, Tony notes with surprise, "We probably made as much money as we've ever made, or more. I'm not sure how that happened." Doubtless it helped not having to split the proceeds with a pianist and a manager.

Notes

1. Anthony Clark, "Jazzcats," *OffBeat* 4, no. 5 (May 1991): 33.

2. Keith Spera, "Five nor [recte Now] Four," *Times–Picayune*, 25 May 2001, section Lagniappe, 25.

3. Sieberth had substituted as early as 29 November 1991 (Contemporary Arts Center). Pellera worked on the European tour that year.

4. First advertised on 24 May 1991 (at that time, five days a week).

5. Geraldine Wyckoff, review of *Big Shot* in *OffBeat* 15, no. 5 (May 2002): 81.

6. Wyckoff, review of *Big Shot*.

7. Kevin McNerney, "The Little Easy," http://themusingsofkev.blogspot.com/2005/10/little-easy.html; posted 6 October 2005; accessed 10 December 2006.

8. Clinic, 8 October 2003.

9. Clinic, 8 October 2003.

10. Quoted in Jason Koransky, "Backstage with ... Astral Project," *Down Beat* 69, no. 7 (July 2002): 12.

11. Neil Tesser, "Audio Review," *Chicago Reader* 32, no. 26 (28 March 2003), S3, 36.

12. Koransky, "Backstage with ... Astral Project."

16. AFTER HURRICANE KATRINA

The Hurricane

On 29 August 2005, a hurricane named Katrina—level 5, the highest level on the scale, and 200 miles wide—headed straight for New Orleans, prompting mayor Ray Nagin to call for the evacuation of the city. When the hurricane abruptly turned to the east and dropped a level in force just before it hit the Gulf coast, it seemed that New Orleans might be spared. But a storm surge topped the Industrial Canal on the east side of the city, flooding part of its Ninth Ward as well as two neighboring parishes. The levees on two drainage canals at 17th Street and London Avenue, coming into the Crescent City from the lagoon called Lake Pontchartrain, developed breaches three or four hundred feet long, causing Gulf water to flood about 80 percent of the city. This was no "act of God": "a design or construction flaw caused them to collapse in the face of a force they were designed to hold."[1] Areas on higher ground, such as the historic French Quarter, escaped with little damage, but many neighborhoods were soon sitting in water up to 20 feet deep. Nagin exhorted everyone to leave, but some had no means of transportation or were stuck in their attics or on their roofs. The Superdome filled up with 10,000 people. Federal aid was slow in coming. Criminals began looting and killing, forcing the police and National Guard to attend to them rather than continue rescue efforts. By 1 September, the mouth of the 17th Street Canal had been sealed with sheet metal, preventing lake water from reaching the breach in the levee; within four days, that breach had been closed with over 200 enormous sandbags and lumps of concrete, dropped from army helicopters. It took until 4 September to transport the thousands in the Superdome to the Houston Astrodome. The flood waters around the city became contaminated by gasoline, other toxic chemicals, and dead bodies. On 6 September, Nagin ordered the forced evacuation of everyone not involved in official disaster work. Aid poured in from concerned citizens around the country. Then began the long, slow clean-up—the Big Difficult.

Tony wrote to me about his experience:

"When Katrina hit, Joan was on her way back from the northeast after having dropped our son Dominic off at Carnegie Mellon. I had driven up with them both but had to leave early for an Astral Project gig in Fayetteville, AR. I was not paying attention to the weather; the last news cast that I saw said Katrina was moving east. On her way back, Joan called me and made me pack up a few things and take our two cats along. We met up in Jackson, MS, where we stayed for a night or two before traveling to Shreveport. When it became obvious that we couldn't return to New Orleans for an indefinite period of time, we drove east, making stops at my brother's home in Arlington, VA, Joan's father's house in Baltimore, and my mom's summer house in Shipbottom, NJ, before ending up in New Haven for the remainder of our 'vacation.' It was several weeks before I found out that Loyola would continue to pay salaries. Because Joan made me leave quite early, I can say that I did not see one drop of rain from Katrina."

On the way to Shreveport, he joked with an interviewer: "My wife and I were told we should evacuate to Houston, but who wants to go to Houston?"[2]

And what was the future of jazz in New Orleans—indeed, of the city itself? On 12 September, the publisher of *OffBeat*, Jan Ramsey, resuscitated the magazine's weekly e-mail newsletter and penned the following pertinent editorial:

"What Will Happen To New Orleans Music?

"As I write this, I am wondering if Katrina will create a permanent diaspora of New Orleans musicians. Or will they return to the city that gave them inspiration? Already I've heard from so many people who are in Lafayette, various places in Tennessee (especially Nashville), Baton Rouge, and Austin.

"I hate to say this, but unless we are committed to getting our city back—and that means everyone in the music community—there will be no more music in New Orleans. Austin seems to be licking its chops at the prospect of sucking up so much musical talent and so many music businesses. Basin Street Records has already landed there....

"For all those people who love New Orleans and her music, come back to the city as soon as you can, please! There have been numerous (too many to count) benefits to help New Orleans residents. Some have been earmarked for the city's musicians. But no one has come forward to administer these funds for local musicians.

"And what about all the music businesses that have been displaced because of Katrina? There are no FEMA funds to help these people."[3]

Philip Booth, declaring "Music, Tragically, is Missing," wrote of the city: "Everyone has scattered—they didn't have a choice. Many of these folks likely will settle into new residences, new jobs and new lives elsewhere. Could you blame them if they decide not to return and rebuild? So I wonder, and I agonize, and I think back on so many unforgettable musical experiences: digging the intense playing of Astral Project...."[4]

Midwest Tour, September 2005

Astral Project already had a Midwest tour booked for the end of September, less than a month after Katrina, and the show went on. James drove his van all the way from Los Angeles to Chicago and met up with his colleagues there for the first gig on the 23rd. Howard Reich eagerly awaited the visit: "The band's shows at the Green Mill, its local venue of choice, tend to be exuberant affairs that convey New Orleans' party ambience, though driven by first-rate jazz improvisation. There's no telling if that mood will prevail this time around, but considering the caliber of its personnel, Astral Project likely will put on a hard-hitting show regardless of its emotional tone."[5] In his review, he wrote of the "emotional weight" of the occasion:

"For the first time since they and their families had been scattered across the country, the musicians of Astral Project came together again, to make music for an audience eager to hear them.

"Not surprisingly, their first set Friday night sounded more like a catharsis than a concert, the band playing harder, faster, and with more ferocity than ever. Exulting in the muscularity of its work, attacking beats and offbeats with extraordinary force and precision, Astral Project seemed to be raising its fist against the vicissitudes of Katrina.

"'This is the best thing that's happened to me in about three weeks,' the band's volatile drummer, Johnny Vidacovich, told the crowd, which roared its approval.

"'We're kind of water-logged right now,' he added, though whenever the band played, it sounded as crisp and tautly drawn as the skins on Vidacovich's drums.

"Never an ensemble to understate its message, Astral Project on this occasion played on a particularly grand scale, yet without bombast. There's so much musical content in its repertoire and expressive control in its technique, in other words, that even its large-scale statements sounded well calibrated for the room and the mood.

"From the opening number, 'Big Shot,' Astral Project unleashed its signature sound, a lean, tough, rhythmically unyielding approach to jazz improvisation. In many instances, saxophonist Tony Dagradi and guitarist Steve Masakowski lit up explosive unison lines, while bassist James Singleton and drummer Vidacovich aggressively pressed rhythms and tempos forward.

"Judging by the huge tone and soaring lines that Dagradi produced in 'Delicately,' the band might want to consider changing the name of the tune to 'Explosively.' For here again, Astral Project recast its standard repertoire to fit the tenor of its post-Katrina identity.

"Perhaps no moment more eloquently addressed what these musicians must be feeling than Dagradi's searing solo on Billy Strayhorn's ballad 'Blood Count.' Gently caressing its sinuous phrases at one moment, blowing full throttle the next, Dagradi poured as much heart and pain into this tune as it possibly could hold. His throaty low notes and wide-open vibrato and otherwise nostalgic view of this music said a great deal about what has been lost in the great city of New Orleans.

"Then again, the inarguable fact that Astral Project still swings—though its personnel may never again call Louisiana home—suggests that musical New Orleans endures, at least in fleeting performances such as this."[6]

At a clinic at Indiana University four days later, Steve confirmed that the occasion had been intense for the group, too:

"There's a lot of frustration; a lot of conflicting moods. It was very special the first gig of the tour we played in Chicago. Many people from New Orleans came to the gig, and there was a real emotional kind of vibe there. It was a very special moment, I think, for all of us. We hadn't played in a long time. We were displaced, and everybody evacuating to different parts. These tunes became a vehicle for that emotional expression. Survival at this point (laughs). We're really a gypsy band right now (laughs loudly). No place to go, so we're working."[7]

A journalist reporting on the group's gig the next night at the Iron Post in Urbana, IL noted that the members "are taking everything in stride, even though their lives are in total upheaval. The quartet delivered an exceptionally lively, lost-in-the-music-and-moment performance at the Post.... Vidacovich joked that people should buy the band's CDs, even though they had been inundated with flood waters. The manufacturer, he said, assured them that all people have to do is wipe them off. He said he and the other band members were glad to be in Urbana; that the Post audience always makes them sound better."[8]

Kevin Lynch, previewing Astral Project's performance the day afterwards in Madison for a hurricane relief benefit, had interviewed Tony by phone about the future of New Orleans.

"'The poor economic section will be the last to come back, and that might be a negative effect if they don't find their way back,' Dagradi says. 'Not having those really beautiful funky people there. That's where the loss of culture is gonna happen. The people really are a city's culture.'

"'We're all kind of shell-shocked,' Dagradi says. 'The mayor had invited everybody to come back to New Orleans, and now we have to get out again. It's been really frustrating, and I personally think it'll take longer than anybody thinks to get back in and make it feel like a city again.

"'We'll do the best we can to persevere and find work and survive. Musicians will be in the same position as anybody else. They'll live somewhere else until they get situated. Then it'll be hard to come back.'"[9]

An announcement of Astral Project's performance in Louisville as the main act for the Highlands–Douglass Big Rock Jazz Fest on 2 October quoted Tony as saying that touring was "a haven of normalcy."[10] By that time all the members of the group "have determined that their homes are still standing and are 'relatively water-free.' But 'there are a lot of question marks.... The hardest thing has been not knowing.'" On the way back to New Orleans, the group called in at Denton, TX on 5 October, with what the publicity called "an impromptu stint" at the University of North Texas.[11]

Back in NOLA

Tony and Joan Dagradi returned to New Orleans to live on 22 November 2005. Their house had virtually no damage. But he spent a couple of weeks clearing away tree limbs from the yard and putting a new floor in the garage which, being next to the sidewalk, did get flooded.

Tony returned to his teaching job in the spring semester. He told me on 1 March 2006: "It's been incredibly busy for me with no real let-up in sight. All of the faculty at Loyola are teaching overloads and we are going to be adding an additional 'Spring II' semester that will go to the end of July." The coordinator of jazz studies, John Mahoney, reported that the university "had a slightly smaller freshman class in jazz studies (and other music majors) but not as small as we had feared."[12]

Fortunately, part of Tony's busy-ness was returning to his old haunt The Columns Hotel on 18 January for a regular weekly gig, which lasted through 25 July 2007, mostly billed as "Tony Dagradi & All That Jazz." In late March 2006, he wrote to me, "So far it's been a revolving cast of characters; mostly young, usually good. Johnny V started the gig but is now doing a steady Wednesday night at Snug. Some of the other players include Simon Lott, Dylan Hicks, and David Mahoney on drums and Peter Harris and Greg Smith on bass."

Overlapping with The Columns, starting on 13 April 2007, Tony began another gig, at least once a week, at a relatively new venue called Club 300 Jazz Bistro, primarily in a quintet with the club's co-owner, the jazz singer Mary Jane Ewing. Guests in the quintet included the Chicago trumpeter Brad Goode, Fred Sanders, piano, and Tony's guitarist colleague in Astral Project, Steve Masakowski, Alas, the club closed at short notice after its lease ran out in late July 2008 (Tony's last gig there was on the 26th).[13]

Fortunately, there are some recordings to give us a taste of Tony performing at Club 300. Ewing released a CD entitled *I Love Bein' Here with You* in two different versions: the first privately in May 2007,[14] and the second commercially the following year.[15] The first version includes nine short tracks by Ewing with Tony on tenor sax; Chuck Chaplin, piano and Fender Rhodes; Peter Harris, bass; and Doug Belote, drums; four tracks from "Mary's U.S. Rock Ensemble"; and two tracks in a folk-influenced popular style. On the jazz tracks, Ewing displays a full, straight-ahead voice, with good diction even at fast tempos, although she is not really a "jazz singer" in the sense of melodic nuance, playing with the rhythm, or improvising. She sticks closely to the melody and does not seem particularly interested in the popular lyrics. The exception is the longest track, "Spring Can Really Hang You up the Most," where, although she doesn't quite have the low notes demanded by the song in a couple of spots, she persuades you that spring may really have hung her up a few times, and Tony creates a touching interlude in his best ballad style. On the other jazz tracks, Tony contributes some brief but effective intros, solos, interludes, and postludes, at all tempos, as well as accompanying on the head and out chorus, although I have the feeling that he would have preferred not to have Chaplin's busy comping.

The only tracks that survived onto the second version of the CD were "Cheek to Cheek"; "I Love Bein' Here with You," which includes a wonderful short, bluesy solo; and "The Song Is You," where his fast, effortless solo continues behind the out chorus. Steve Masakowski on guitar is added on several tracks, and has most of the fills on "So Nice to Come Home to," the solo on "Spring Can Really Hang You up the Most," and the longer solo on "What a Little Moonlight Can Do." Tony is shown to best effect on "One Note Samba," where he takes a funky then wailing samba solo.

A stunning video example of a medium-tempo ballad solo, "Invitation," was recorded at Club 300 during a Ewing Quintet date on 20 June 2008, with piano, bass, and drums.[16] Over the four minutes of this solo, Tony never once lets up the intensity, switching constantly and abruptly from variations on fast Coltraneish runs to slower, anguished forays into the high register, reaching a climax about three-quarters of the way through with a series of heart-rending "screams."

In 2007, Tony finally relegated his 1958 Mark IV tenor saxophone (see p. 47 above) to back-up and had his 1937 Selmer Balanced Action instrument fixed up.

Jim Germann (Hollis and Germann Music) in Pittsburgh did a fantastic restoration job and overhaul, working with me to modify and update some of the keywork. Afterwards, artisan Sherry Huntley re-cut the original engraving design. The horn was then silver-plated by Anderson Plating in Elkhart, Indiana before ultimately being assembled and perfected by Jim. The process took a number of months, but the result is a sonically amazing and visually distinctive instrument.[17]

Tony has taken part in three post-Katrina revivals of groups. First, his beloved trio format, starting with Club 300 on 24 May 2008, when John Vidacovich was "on the drums and on the cymbals." Then he had a few trio gigs at Snug Harbor (7 July 2009 with Roland Guerin, bass, and Troy Davis, drums; 28 July and 6 September 2009, and 26 August 2010).

Tony revived the New Orleans Saxophone Ensemble/Quartet under the updated name Sax Traxx for a performance at Snug Harbor on 1 February 2007. He described this latest line-up, featuring Alonzo Bowens, Khari Allen Lee, and Jason Mingledorff, as "arguably the best incarnation." As the Tony Dagradi Sax Quartet, it performed in the Ogden Museum of Southern Art's "After Hours" series on 5 April, along with an interview conducted by Alex Rawls, then of OffBeat, and at Snug Harbor on 16 August. Under the original name, it appeared in the New Orleans Jazz Historical Park Concerts on 17 March, gave workshops at Tipitina's on 15 and 22 April, and performed at Snug Harbor on 16 August. Under a name spliced, perhaps inadvertently with another famous group, the New Orleans World Saxophone Quartet, it performed at Club 300 on 30 June. A sax version of The Name Game?

Tony also revived the Jazz Underground series at Loyola University on 21 September 2006, and began it by participating himself in The Second Annual Coltrane Festival, along with his former student Clarence Johnson III and a rhythm section of Michael Pellera, Chris Severin, and John Vidacovich.[18] Further Coltrane Festivals followed in 2007, with Vidacovich, Victor Atkins, and Khari Allen Lee, and in 2008 and 2012 with unnamed colleagues. Tony was advertised in the Jazz Underground series, also called Montage, once or twice a year after that: "On 52nd

Street" (6 March 2008); "Fleur Debris" (a flowery but fragmented performance?) with the funky rhythm section of David Torkanowsky, George Porter Jr., and Simon Lott (4 February 2010); jam sessions (30 September 2010 and 17 March 2011); "Celebrating Cannonball and Coltrane" with Khari Allen Lee (29 September 2011); and an "All-Star Jam" with Steve Masakowski, Vidacovich, Roland Guerin, and pianist Mike Essenault (28 February 2013).

The calibre of these Underground concerts is demonstrated by the youtube video of the complete performance of the concert on 5 March 2009, in which Tony, Jamelle Williams, trumpet; Rex Gregory, alto; Michael Pellera, piano; Roland Guerin, bass; and Troy Davis, drums play all the pieces from Miles Davis' classic CD *Kind of Blue*, which had just celebrated its 50th anniversary.[19] The drummer Kevin O'Day wrote: "Dagradi was on fire, playing John Coltrane's parts with precision, and soloing with high energy and even a good sense of humor, interacting with the rhythm section in a way that had the whole band tuned in to his ideas, ready to respond."[20]

Tony began to give performances once or twice a year at churches in New Orleans. At Holy Name of Jesus Church on 27 February 2008, he led a performance of Coltrane's spiritual suite *A Love Supreme*, with Fred Sanders, Roland Guerin, and Troy Davis. (At Loyola's Lenten "Sacred Words and Music" celebration on 18 March 2009, he performed all the music from his CD *Sweet Remembrance*, 1987.) In March 2008 and 2010, Tony took part in the annual "Bach Around the Clock," a 28-hour tribute to Johann Sebastian, at Trinity Episcopal Church, on the second occasion playing Bach's Cello Suite No. 3, reading directly from the cello music. On 17 April 2011, he was one of the "spotlighted" performers in a new Jazz Vespers service at that church. On 6 April 2013, he was advertised as going back to "Bach Around The Clock" with the Ignatius Saxophone Quartet (something to do with Loyola, do you think?), comprising Tony, John Reeks on alto, Ray Moore on soprano, and Ward Smith on baritone.

On 4 March 2010, Tony dusted off his baritone sax, lubricated it well, then launched into Baritone Madness, at the Jazz Underground, with Roger Lewis, the bari player from the Dirty Dozen Brass Band. Just over a year later, on 20 March 2011 at Snug Harbor, this bari-foray spawned a new ensemble, Baritone Bliss—no craziness here, only ecstasy—with no fewer than five bari players, Tony, Roger, Tim Green, Calvin Johnson, and Dan Oestreicher, plus Roger's wife Marie Watanabe on piano and the celebrated Herlin Riley on drums. The group played at JazzFest on 4 May; there's a short raucous clip of part of one number on youtube, with Oestreicher playing a bass line on bass sax.[21] Baritone Bliss also played at JazzFest in 2012 (4 May).

Tony has been playing at least once a year with the Loyola University jazz faculty, two of whose complete performances are on youtube. The faculty septet from 6 March 2009 includes John Mahoney, trombone; Nick Volz, flugelhorn; Larry Sieberth, piano; Brian Prunka, guitar; Jesse Boyd, bass; and Wayne Maureau, drums.[22] The quintet from 18 March 2011 consists of the same musicians minus Volz and Prunka.[23]

On *Jazzin' up Christmas*, a CD by the John Mahoney Big Band released in 2009, Tony "illuminates a 13-minute 'O Come, O Come Emmanuel' with an epic tenor solo.... The melody of 'O Come, O Come Emmanuel' dates to the Renaissance, but Dagradi found it fertile ground for soloing. 'We just let him play,' Mahoney said."[24]

In recent years, Tony has also had gigs at Chickie Wah Wah, the Contemporary Arts Center, Harrah's Casino, the Maple Leaf, and Snug Harbor with such New Orleans musicians as Shane Theriot, guitar; the pianists Jeff Gardner and Larry Sieberth; Rick Trolsen, trombone; the singers Leah Chase and Stephanie Jordan; Bill Summers, percussion; Stanton Moore, drums; and the New Orleans Jazz Orchestra. He told me in December 2005, "Over the years I've played with

The Temptations numerous times at various venues around New Orleans: Rosy's Jazz Club, the Orpheum Theater, the Audubon Zoo, etc." He has kept up his association with the former Motown vocal group in recent years, performing with it at the Gretna Festival in Gretna, LA on 2 October 2010 and 6 October 2012. On 3 November 2011, as we can see on youtube, he played as a guest artist with the Louisiana State University Jazz Ensemble in Baton Rouge, including a joyous performance of his "Second Thoughts" and Sammy Nestico's "Ya Gotta Try" as a "tenor battle" between the two tenor sax players in the ensemble and Tony following.

Astral Project, 2005–14
Steve Masakowski summed up the group in 2005:

> "I think one of the most important things about Astral Project is the longevity and sticking to an idea through that whole period. We've weathered all these different changes in the music environment: In the 1970s, it was a very experimental time. People were into fusion; people were starting to get into electronics. And then the jazz world went through a neo-classic period. We've seen these trends happening within this 27-year period. But we've all stayed focused on what we do: expressed ourselves through the music, not necessarily being influenced by political or market forces. The idea of Astral Project to me is contemporary New Orleans music—we're all from New Orleans; we're all influenced by New Orleans music; but we also listen to lots of different types of music from around the world. That's the thing that I really like in this band: we're really open to a lot of different types of music, but based in this New Orleans sound and consistently staying on that track throughout our history. And I think that has a lot to do with our evolution and longevity and survival."

Of course, since its inception the "idea" of Astral Project has also been a spiritual one: to give its listeners a taste of the astral plane. Jazz as entertainment, to be sure, in the New Orleans tradition; but also, jazz as spiritual sustenance.

When I asked Tony about his plans for the group in 2006, he mentioned that, after making two albums with the quartet, he would like to record with extra musicians to create more variety of texture. "We've avoided that in the past, primarily because to my mind, when people are added to Astral Project, we play to them; they don't really play to us. "

> "I'd like to do a quintet or a sextet version of something ... tenor, trumpet, guitar, maybe piano, and rhythm section. I'd like to do a couple of things where we have numerous horns, and there could be overdubs—soprano/tenor, bass clarinet— that I would all play, plus trombone, trumpet, so maybe five or six horns in different types of groupings. That's all in the back of my mind: nothing's formulated."

He cited as models for such a venture Wayne Shorter's *High Life* (1995), which employed orchestral winds and strings as well as synthesizer, and Michael Brecker's *Wide Angles* (2003), which featured the saxophonist against the backdrop of his "Quindectet," a fifteen-piece band.

In practice, Astral Project made another CD with only the quartet of Tony, Steve, James, and John: *Blue Streak*, recorded in June 2007 and released in time for Jazz Fest 2008. It features a suite of compositions by Tony entitled "Cobalt Dreams": "Angel Song," "Blue Streak," "Cannonball," "Cobalt Dreams," "Double Helix," "Fallen," and "Lavender Sleep." According to the liner note, "the artistic premise for this multi-movement work was an examination of the blues as form and concept.... traditional blues language and mannerisms are merged with contemporary sensibilities and rhythmic influences of New Orleans." The suite is not presented as such on the CD, but rather mixed with compositions by Steve ("Entropy," "North Wind," "Once Was") and James ("Dike Finger"). Steve explicitly linked his pieces to "the circumstances we found ourselves in and the uncertainty of what was to come" after Katrina. (For a discussion of this recording, see Lasocki, *A Higher Fusion*, chapter 16.)

John told a journalist in 2008 that Astral Project "has as much a future as it does a past. There's 30 years that led us up to now: that's a pretty good foundation."[25] The group's performances at Jazz Fest have continued to be recorded by MunckMix through the time of writing (2014). Since March 2012, however, the group has been winding down: brief tours close to home and a gig only every few months in New Orleans....

Notes

1. John M. Barry, "After the Deluge, Some Questions," *New York Times*, 13 October 2005, Late Edition—Final, Section A, 27. A report commissioned by the Louisiana Department of Transportation and Development, and issued by a group of engineers and storm researchers called Team Louisiana in March 2007, argues that the U.S. Army Corps of Engineers used obsolete measurements. When the flood-control system of levees and floodwalls was designed in 1965, it relied on land-height measurements from 1929, but the city had sunk 1–2 feet in the meantime, and by 2005 the levees were as much as 5 feet too low. Moreover, the Corps never used a storm-surge model released in 1979 by the National Hurricane Center. In addition, the Corps ignored its own models that suggest the Mississippi River Gulf Outlet, a navigation channel completed in the early 1960s, would funnel storm surge into St. Bernard Parish and New Orleans. See http://www.cnn.com/2007/US/03/22/new.orleans.levees.ap/index.html; accessed 23 March 2007.

2. Kevin Lynch, "Sending out Big Easy Spirit: Astral Project Finds Solace in New Orleans Jazz," *Wisconsin State Journal*, 29 September 2005; available from http://www.madison.com/archives/read.php?ref=/wsj/2005/09/29/0509280421.php; accessed 15 November 2006.

3. Jan Ramsey, "What Will Happen to New Orleans Music?" *OffBeat Weekly Beat Newsletter*, mislabeled 3, no. 33 (25 August 2005); in fact issued on 12 September 2005.

4. Philip Booth, "Music, Tragically, is Missing," *Sarasota Herald-Tribune* (Florida), 8 September 2005, section Florida West, E1.

5. Howard Reich, "Astral Takes Distinctive, Jazzy Sound on the Road," *Chicago Tribune*, 23 September 2005, edition Chicago Final, section On The Town, 11.

6. Howard Reich, "Astral Project Blows its Blues away," *Chicago Tribune*, 26 September 2005, section Tempo, 1.

7. Steve Masakowski, Astral Project clinic, Indiana University, 27 September 2005.

8. Melissa Merli, "Next Wall to Wall Already in Works," *The News–Gazette* (Champaign, IL), 2 October 2005, F.

9. Lynch, "Sending out Big Easy Spirit."

10. Martha Elson, "Touring Jazz Group Really on the Road," *The Courier–Journal* (Louisville, KY), 30 September 2005, edition Metro, section News, 03B.

11. Lucinda Breeding, "Help for Back Home," *Denton Record–Chronicle* (Texas), 29 September 2005, section Denton Time, 6.

12. Quoted in Antonio J. Garcia, "Jazz Education in New Orleans, Post-Katrina," *Jazz Education Journal* 39, no. 3 ([December 2006]): 51.

13. See http://maryjaneewing.com/bio.html; accessed 17 March 2013.

14. See http://blog.nola.com/entertainment/2007/05/latest_cd_releases_as_of_tuesd.html; accessed 18 March 2013.

15. Mary Jane Ewing, *I Love Being Here with You* ([New Orleans]; Mid-Atlantic Records, [2008]).

16. http://www.youtube.com/watch?v=N_PF-kl6R0Y; accessed 18 March 2013; a transcription of the solo can be downloaded from his website, http://www.tonydagradi.com/home.cfm.

17. Tony Dagradi, "Equipment Notes," in *Sax Solos over Jazz Standards* (New Albany, IN: Jamey Aebersold Jazz, 2011), iii.

18. http://www.loyno.edu/newsandcalendars/release.php?id=1091; accessed 27 September 2006.

19. https://www.youtube.com/watch?v=AuFYSelYOGY; accessed 18 March 2013.

20. Quoted on http://www.tonydagradi.com/brianbtonyd.cfm; accessed 18 March 2013.

21. Released 15 May 2007: see http://www.youtube.com/watch?v=_1PJBd7ycW4; accessed 17 March 2013.

22. https://www.youtube.com/watch?v=wEGgMUQqgDw; accessed 18 March 2013.

23. https://www.youtube.com/watch?v=y3SS-3jY3EU; accessed 18 March 2013.

24. Keith Spera, "Jazzin' up Christmas—Loyola University Professor John Mahoney Unleashes his Big-Band Sound on the Music of the Season," *Times-Picayune*, 1 December 2009, section Living, C 01.

25. Quoted in Rawls, "Let's Stay Together," 68.

17. TEACHING

As we saw in chapter 7, Tony was hired in 1990 as the saxophone teacher at Loyola University. In 2006 he became a tenured full professor. He told me about his experience at Loyola: "It's been very good for me. I've learned a lot about teaching. I've learned to be a better teacher." I wondered how he coped with having to teach classical music:

"Very few of my students want to do only classical: one in a hundred might just be a classical saxophonist. Most of my students are interested in jazz and contemporary saxophone things, almost as a survival thing, because that's what there is to do for a living. Classical: you have to really be dedicated to that. I don't consider myself a great classical saxophone player. I know the repertoire; I can direct people; but it's not of interest to me to perform classical recitals."

He felt that playing classical music on the saxophone is "really a different animal."

"You have to approach the saxophone differently in many ways: sonically, technique. I try to get even my jazz students to play classical literature just for the discipline of it, just to be able to control their tone and their technique. But there's a real difference in the mentality. And that's true about the difference between jazz and classical, anyway. The jazz performer is the composer of the piece, whereas the classical artist is really the interpreter of the music."

Tony usually has about a dozen students, "give or take one or two," which is considered a full load for instructors who are also doing other kinds of teaching, a regular full load being eighteen students. And what do those students do after graduation?

"A lot of the students go on to be music directors, band directors. So they have a degree in maybe education rather than performance. And if they do get a degree in performance, it doesn't necessarily mean they're going to go right into it."

They're not trying to be jazz saxophone players? "Well, they're all working on it. But some of them aren't as motivated, inspired, to do that."

Asked by an interviewer in 2009, "When you meet with students for the first time, what's the first thing you tell them about what they need to do to be successful, or to do what they want with their music?" Tony replied:

"The first thing is to learn how to make a beautiful sound. (Laughs.) I'm not talking about a lot of notes—just taking one note and making it sound beautiful. That would be the first thing.... That opens a can of worms. After you're an accomplished musician, after you can technically play the instrument, then you have to decide what you want to play. What kind of music makes you feel good? I tell my students, if somebody called you for a festival or recording session, what ten tunes would represent you as an artist? That's a big question. And if you're a composer, that's great. You really should be a composer, because that's how you can make some money. If you're a jazz artist, you are a composer by very nature."[1]

What students need to do beyond the degree to have a career is an important theme, which Tony addressed at a clinic:

"What you do to fulfill your degree requirement as a jazz major is so minimal compared with what you need to know as a musician and the experience you need to gain. That piece of paper—I shouldn't say it too loudly—is worthless. All I want to say is: You have to do so much work on your own: you need to be listening, transcribing, trying to generate gigs and find situations where you can gain real experience playing. You need to get on gigs and gain that experience as a sideman or as a leader, supplementing that degree. The jazz degree is pointing you in certain directions. But don't think of that as the be-all and end-all, and that once you have that jazz degree you are a jazz player."[2]

At Loyola, Tony directs the top jazz combo (of at least five combos) and teaches an improvisation course, both twice a week. In addition:

"When I started, I was called upon to do a woodwind methods class: that's teaching woodwinds to people who don't play woodwinds, who are going to teach other people who don't play woodwinds. That I had to do my first couple of semesters there. I also taught a jazz history class to non-music majors, a common-curriculum jazz history. And both of those courses are still going, but other people teach them now. But I never wanted to be a lecture professor. I did that because I could, and they asked me to, but really my other duties started to fill up. Also, when I started, I was pretty much doing everything I'm doing now *and* doing that other stuff. Nobody was paying attention to my hourly load early on. I was getting blown out. Not that they were trying to do that to me: nobody was paying attention, and I didn't understand how they were counting up the hours. Now I do. I'm not doing as much and I'm doing it better."

Tony helps John Mahoney to direct the two Loyola Jazz Bands, which have generally given two joint concerts a year, in April and November. He has also been playing in the Loyola Faculty Jazz Septet in February or March each year.

Tony has also been expected to serve on university committees, such as the common-curriculum committee, which makes recommendations on the courses that form Loyola's core undergraduate curriculum. In 2004 he mentioned: "I'm on the grants and leaves committee: that's kind of a fun one. I don't mind that one. It seems like at least we're getting something done in a fairly methodical way."

Tony has been able to take two sabbatical leaves himself. In the academic year 1999–2000, he was replaced by John Ellis, a New York-based saxophonist who studied at The University of New Orleans. Tony worked largely on finishing his workbook *Essential Scale Studies for Improvisation* and seeing it through the press.[3] "That's the big evidence of that sabbatical. The university liked that. And then the other facets of my proposal for the sabbatical were just composition, and that's harder to document, but I could certainly show them some music that I wrote." Was it helpful to have such a long time off? "Absolutely. I never waste time. I'm very motivated to produce stuff. So if I wasn't teaching I'd be doing a lot of other stuff: compositions." Normally, teaching takes almost too much time away from composing and practicing:

"School definitely takes a lot of time. That's the big negative of school for me: how much time it takes away from just being creative. I have to practice in between students a little bit, to keep that up. It's very hard to get a groove writing during the school year."

Tony designed *Essential Scale Studies* to fit the full range of the saxophone, but with suitable modification in range the studies can be used for any instrument. He told me about this workbook:

"I showed it to various members of the faculty at Loyola. The flute teacher, Patti Adams, looked at it and she said, 'Oh, yeah, it's all the same stuff I teach.' Even the vocal faculty: Phil Frohnmayer looked at it and he goes, 'Yeah, this will be good for my vocal students.'"

The book is based on the premise that "at the core of any outstanding player's technique is a firm grasp of the intervallic relationships that make up the language of jazz" (Introduction). I find this a remarkable insight: a scale is seen not as an ordered series of pitches with fixed intervallic relationships, as one might define it, but a source of relationships among intervals. Tony continues: "On the bandstand, intervals and short melodic phrases must be strung together in a cohesive manner to create a complete musical thought in the form of an improvised solo." Here he rightly emphasizes that the intervallic relationships students will learn through the exercises are raw material that must be put together, like words in sentences, to "tell a story."

The exercises are described as "diatonic," which Tony defines as "the notes contained within the scale." This is essentially true, except that he does throw in some chromatic "approach notes" (the lower chromatic neighbor) at the end of a couple of sections. The exercises are set out methodically: patterns based on major scales, patterns based on pentatonic scales, seventh-chords, patterns based on diminished scales, and finally patterns based on whole-tone scales. It's amazing how much variety can be produced from diatonic material using the extra scales. The exercises are notated only in C, students being encouraged to transpose them not by writing them out, but mentally while working on their instruments—a necessary skill for the improviser in practical situations. Some sample rhythmic variants are given, and the student is encouraged to develop more. All in all, an extremely useful resource, and much more fun than the usual type of "etude book."

Tony had actually taught scale studies for improvisation before, on a 42-minute CD published by *Saxophone Journal* in 1994, with accompanying musical examples printed in an issue of the magazine.[4] It's rewarding to hear him reading what would otherwise have been the text of an article, in his by then combination New Jersey/New Orleans accent, as well as playing the scale studies and a couple of short jazz solos with James Singleton on the bass. (In addition, the CD includes four short excerpts from *Dreams of Love*, the recording by Tony and Astral Project—to what purpose, is not made clear.) The bulk of the CD takes the student through the various scales and associated chordal patterns: major scales, diatonic sevenths and their inversions, pentatonic scales, fourths, circle of fifths, i/V/I patterns, diminished scale, whole-tone-scale, and altered dominant scales. Among the sound general advice, Tony emphasizes developing a fine, personal tone on the instrument, learning as much as possible about the history of jazz and saxophone, and once more transposing all the exercises from C major by ear rather than writing them out—a form of ear training.

In the late 1980s, Tony recalls, he had been making some transcriptions of solos by other saxophone players, primarily John Coltrane. At Tulane, for the equivalent of a master's thesis he had to write two papers, so he made transcriptions and analyses of solos by Coleman Hawkins and Lester Young, also taking the time to learn how to produce their sounds. He found it a good experience to have to write about music. He sent the papers to *Saxophone Journal*, which was interested in publishing them, but eventually had to reject them because of difficulties with the copyrights of the transcribed tunes. The papers were never in fact published, but the magazine invited him to do a regular column entitled "Writing for Saxophones." Between 1990 and 1995, he went on to publish no fewer than eighteen articles, many of them analyses of solos, even including one of his own. He remarked: "I can be very analytical. When I'm playing, I'm not thinking like that at all. I'm not concerned with any of that, other than I know the mechanics of it. But for the purposes of the article, that's how you need to convey what's going on." Besides his own solo, the eight he analyzed were performed on *Jazz Player*'s "play-along" CDs by rank-and-file jazz soloists: Greg Abate, Gary Campbell, David Demsey, Jeff Holmes, Mel Martin, Jon Metzger, Miles Osland, and Greg Yasinitsky.

The series "Writing for Saxophones" begins with two articles analyzing the voicing techniques and harmonic devices in some saxophone "solis"—sections of big-band writing for the saxophone section—written by Thad Jones for the Thad Jones–Mel Lewis Jazz Orchestra.[5] Tony had heard this band at the Village Vanguard as a teenager traveling into New York from his home in New Jersey (see p. 6). He then devotes two articles to what he calls the "linear compositional styles" of Charlie Parker,[6] justifying taking a look at Parker's style of improvising rather than his composing by noting: "To be a great soloist in the jazz idiom an artist must above all else be an accomplished composer."[7] He goes on to illustrate Parker's "penchant for chromaticism," use of the upper extensions of chords, alteration of chords and even scales, and employment of a group of licks or formulas in different harmonic and rhythmic contexts. Tony does end by relating the improvisation to composition in his remark that each of Parker's compositions "represents the crystallization of his ideas, rhythmically, harmonically and melodically, and can be thought of as a perfectly fashioned improvised chorus."[8] After Parker, Tony goes back to Duke Ellington, discussing how he voiced the saxophone section. Tony points out that "some of the harmonic elements which he pioneered include 'blue note' voicings, dissonance through the use of altered intervals, pedal points, clusters, and the use of instruments in extreme (uncharacteristic) registers." Tony then presents his own Ellington-style saxophone soli, incorporating those features.

Tony then devotes an article to two types of harmonization in his own arrangement of "Amazing Grace" for the New Orleans Saxophone Ensemble (recorded on the group's half record; see p. 33).[9] First, a traditional approach using triads and seventh chords, as in a gospel choir, to create a "full, funky and soulful" effect. Second, reharmonizing "by placing triads in the upper three voices in opposition to a dissonant and tonally unrelated bass part"—a technique that Tony says he learned from Herb Pomeroy at Berklee.

Responding to reader requests, Tony then turns to two- and three-part writing, addressing the fundamental question "How do you create the illusion of interesting chords with only two or three available pitches?"[10] His answer: voicing, which creates a variety of colors even with the simplest of intervals; passing dissonance; interesting inner parts that move with the lead line; employing upper extensions of chords even at the expense of basic chord tones, which tend to be supplied by the rhythm section; and taking advantage of the "nebulous" quality of voicings build on fourths.

Introducing his next two articles, Tony comments that his previous ones "presupposed a certain amount of knowledge and experience on the part of readers and were perhaps, to some, difficult to follow."[11] More reader feedback? In any case, he now goes "back to basics" for "beginning writers and arrangers," and his basic advice is eminently practical. In the first article, he recommends listening to all kinds of music, including from other cultures; studying music theory; reading about orchestration in classical music; reading about jazz composing and arranging; learning to play the piano; scrutinizing scores; making reductions of scores; transcribing what interests you ("improvised solos, saxophone solis, piano accompaniments, or entire orchestrations"); and learning the characteristics of all instruments. The second article discusses how to handle levels of dissonance. Finally, "Reharmonization Techniques" focuses on reharmonizing passages to include passing chords on every note of the melody.[12] A promised next installment apparently never appeared.

I wondered whether publishing such articles was expected of Tony at Loyola.

"I don't know that it was expected. I mean, that really was going on as I was beginning Loyola, and maybe I thought it was expected, and it just seemed to happen right at that same time. I figured it would be a good thing to keep doing for a minute. But then after a bit, it started to take a little bit too much time, and I would really be wanting to sit down and practice and write music, and I would have this article due. I'm pretty fast doing the transcriptions. I'm slow writing."

Eventually, Tony felt that he could not write articles at the same time as pursuing his other musical interests:

"I would really be wanting to sit down and practice and write music, and I would have this article due. The editors of the magazine always liked what I did, you know, and when I said 'I don't think I can do it anymore,' they said, 'Man, all your stuff was great: any time you want to do it again, just let us know.' Haven't called them yet. I have other things that I do better than that. That's just really a decision. Things that mean more to me—composing and playing—are really what I do, and that's where I want to devote whatever time that I have."

Tony's most significant contribution to publications in jazz pedagogy is his most recent, written during his second sabbatical from Loyola in 2009–10, and published in 2011. It's a volume in the Jamey Aebersold Jazz series, in the "play-along" format made famous by Aerbersold, called *Sax Solos over Jazz Standards: 12 Modern Etudes in Solo Form Based on Standard Changes which Explore Motivic Development, Chromaticism & Modal Techniques*.[13] Besides the written "etudes" by Tony, there is a CD which alternates tracks: first Tony performing an etude with a rhythm section, then the rhythm section playing the same chord changes (taken from a "standard" tune) for the reader to improvise on. He expounded at length on the purpose of this volume in an article in the "Master Class" column in *Down Beat*.[14] In the volume he presents "sophisticated and balanced melodic statements based on standard changes that can serve as models for practice and study. While these solos are carefully 'composed,' each is designed to evoke the spirit of an improvised performance." Students of jazz need "solid technical skills ... a firm grasp of the intervallic relationships that make up the vocabulary and language of jazz combined with a thorough understanding of harmony and form." Students also need to develop skill in "the length and arrangement of individual phrases within a composition as well as the overall form." Ultimately, "technical, theory, language skills, and experience must all come together ... to create a cohesive melodic statement." In Tony's etudes, "all of these elements come into play." Moreover, the etudes cover "many facets of post-bop and contemporary playing styles ... including ... pentatonic scales, various types of chromaticism, the development of melodic ideas, and even 'outside' [the harmonies] sensibilities."

One of the impressive features of the CD is that Tony created the rhythm section himself. He remarks that he produced the CD

> "by recording my tenor over a 'virtual' sequenced rhythm section. I developed the sequenced tracks in Digital Performer, using sampled sounds from Native Instruments' Kontact and Kore libraries for the drums, bass, keyboards, and percussion parts..... Creating rhythm parts that felt organic and interactive was a real challenge. Fortunately, in a sequenced environment there are many ways to tweak individual parts and entire passages until they 'feel' right. In the process, I learned a lot about my own concepts of rhythm section interplay and formulated some interesting strategies to simulate what happens so effortlessly on the bandstand."[15]

Sax Solos over Jazz Standards is already in the "best seller" category on Jamey Aebersold's website and has received enthusiastic reviews. David Demsey in *Saxophone Journal* commented: "What separates Dagradi's book from the pack is—Dagradi himself. He has a gift for creating a balance between the spontaneous movement of improvisation and the 'textbook' outlining of patterns.... There is a harmonic and melodic clarity in his playing that clearly outlines the harmony, without being pedantic or patterned."[16] One of the all five-star reviews on the Aebersold website goes so far as to say that "This is the best Aebersold volume to date. Why? Because it goes way beyond the 'play these scales over these chords' approach. It contains real and very masterful solos over great standard changes. [The etudes] contain musical grammar I would never think of myself. Tony is a killer player, and this volume puts you right inside his head and heart.... the solo over 'In Your Own Sweet Way' ['Silver Lining'] is very moving—does soloing ever get any better than that? These solos are great to memorize, and play on piano, too."

Tony on Soloing

Tony. Jazz is about composition. Jazz is composition. You're composing spontaneously. Classical music is improvisation that's been gone over and pruned and polished, and you get all the imperfections out. But it's the same thing: composition. Only in jazz you're doing it spontaneously, and you're applying the same kinds of organizing factors.

DL. But one of the differences between good jazz and bad jazz is that the players who are not so good don't have a highly developed compositional sense. They just throw a bunch of licks at you. It's chaos.

Tony. Yeah, there's definitely different levels. Some people learn to improvise where they're just regurgitating things that they know. You might have a certain bags of licks that you know, and can put them together in different orders. And that's one sort of a step.

DL. That can work if you put them together skillfully.

Tony. Right. That's definitely a step along the way. In fact, one of my saxophone teachers —Andy McGhee at Berklee around 1971: that's how he described it to me. And he was a very good player, sort of a bebopper. He described that process and said, "You're just putting together things; put together what you know in different ways." And that's a step: one way of doing it, and we all do that to an extent.

DL. One thing I like about your solos, especially, is that I do get a sense that the stream really develops from beginning to end.

Tony. I'm trying.

DL. You're not throwing in your clichés, either. It really seems that you are trying to compose something that hangs together. When it's finished I get the satisfying sense that it's really a unit that was conceived spontaneously, and you weren't just taking lick A and lick B and lick C and stringing them together.

Tony. I think that's something I've always done unconsciously. I was never attracted to practicing a lick and just plugging it in. It never appealed to me as a way to do it. For me, and it's very hard to get students to do this—very hard to teach jazz, really—the object of practicing certain licks is first of all to get the technique under your fingers, and second and most important, to look at a solo from a compositional perspective and understand that it works because certain things are happening in the melodic line. You get from point A and point B, and it sounds right because certain things have happened. You have to find a way to explain that to yourself. There may be certain resolution tendencies, and this is resolving this way, and this is resolving that way. When you're improvising in a real-life situation on the bandstand, that's when you have to apply those concepts, and set yourself little puzzles to solve. That's the way I think of it. You're getting from point A to point B. Sometimes you look ahead, and sometimes not. The best playing I do, I feel I'm being very melodic and that really at my very best is when I'm just a spectator. I go, "Wow, this is great: everything is working perfectly."

DL. The solo plays itself.

Tony. Yeah. That's what everybody looks for. And I think everybody feels that at whatever level they're at. You could be just a beginner, and the reason that it's so exhilarating is that you get lifted above where you usually are in the process. Because you have the input from other people, and all of a sudden you play a note and you find something that happens and it's exhilarating and you say, "That's it, yeah." It might sound terrible, but it might be a little above where you usually are, and people get a sense of that. Then you're constantly looking for that next plateau of achievement, of artistry. That's what I look for. And I think: Astral Project, we're all in that same bag. We're looking for that place where it feels good, where the music is playing itself.

Tony on Touring and Soloing

Tony. You might do a whole tour where you play the same solo. I know I do it. If you go on tour what's interesting is that whether you play a couple of nights in a row or play fourteen nights in a row, you're working on the same solo, you play the same things, and the drummer knows to react at the same time to something you're doing. The hard part comes when you start to be conscious of it. You go, "Oh, I'm playing the same thing. I gotta do something different." You might start to realize you're doing a similar thing and you might yourself be bored with it. And that's the point where you start to question your stuff. There might be a couple of nights of not feeling very good. So the struggle is to break away from that. You might have played really well, and then you have three or four nights where you're struggling to break away from the things that you would normally do. After struggling for a couple of nights, you get to that thing where you go, "Oh, wow, here it is: here's some new stuff." And what you have to do when you're struggling, I think, is to be open to some other things: purposely and consciously force yourself to try something that you haven't done before. And that necessarily leads you to places you've never been before. It might take you a little while to evolve a new bit of vocabulary, a new bit of pacing, or something. That's the process. We all do that.

DL. Would that be the main reason for having a bad night?

Tony. Yes, very much so. Could be not so much anything that happened during the day, not so much anything you're doing badly: it's definitely a mental thing. It's like you're not satisfied; it's like you're consciously breaking habits. It's just part of the process. If you're going to continue to play good music, you're going to have some bad nights. There's no way around it. You're going to have nights where you'll be at a consistent level, sonically, rhythmically; you'll be able to pull it off and sound like you played a solo; but you might come away thinking, "Oh, that was just the worst shit I've ever played." People might have enjoyed it, and they might have clapped, and you might have had the same stage mannerisms, and so forth—look like you played a good solo. But inside you go, "Man, I hope I get past this thing soon."

DL. Wouldn't that vary from tune to tune?

Tony. It does. I know I have nights where I've really struggled and been dissatisfied, and then I'll get to a tune and I'll momentarily forget the struggles and go, "Oh, yeah, finally I played something good tonight." I'll have nights like that. And then I'll have nights where, from beginning to end, everything just seems like, "Yeah, I'm glad I came tonight." Hopefully you want to have a happy medium. You don't want to be at the extreme other end. You do want to get that extreme high. Keep the downward undulations shallow.

Studying with Tony

Patrice Fisher on Learning from Tony (from a phone interview in February 2005)
In the late 1970s, the harpist Patrice Fisher founded a group called Jasmine.

Patrice. Tony played with Jasmine sometimes, from 1984 to 1988.

DL. And he played flute with you as well as sax?

Patrice. Yes, he played flute with us, because I would rather have a flute player than a sax player. Tony could play flute as well as sax. But after I heard him play sax, of course, I wanted him to play sax. And he was one of my flute teachers.

DL. Really?

Patrice. I studied classical music, both harp and flute, up till my last year of university, then I got sidetracked by the jazz people. But there wasn't any way to learn jazz on the harp, so I learned jazz flute and tried to transfer it.

Tony gave me some interesting flute lessons. He would tell me to imagine that I was in a tunnel, and the tunnel was changing colors when the harmony of the tune changed. That's how I learned to improvise! No classical teacher would ever tell you something like that.

DL. Well, I've heard of classical teachers on other instruments teaching like that—"Imagine this movement is a cloud sailing in the sky"—much to the scorn of their students....

Patrice. Tony was very helpful, teaching me the flute. I actually wrote a piece called "Tai Chi Cycling" because of him. It was one of my assignments from Tony's flute lessons.

DL. I know the piece from your album *Foreign Affairs*. Did you ever do Tai Chi?

Patrice. There's a story that goes with the piece. I used to take my bike to the French Quarter on the weekends and ride around. The route I took back to my house was on Esplanade Avenue. Now it's nicely restored, but at that time it was falling down. Someone started chasing me, trying to mug me. I started pedaling faster and faster to get away from him. But the faster I pedaled, it seemed like I was going in slow motion, stuck in time, as if I was doing Tai Chi. Then I turned around and the stranger was gone.

DL. Did all that go into the composition?

Patrice. I wrote it right after I got home. But it was an assignment from Tony to work on a blues progression and try to find a little phrase that you could repeat throughout the progression. I didn't exactly use the standard blues progression, but I did have a little phrase that I repeated all the way through the song. Tony liked it, so every time he plays with us and I ask him what song he wants to play, he always picks "Tai Chi Cycling."

DL. So you were taking composition lessons with him as well?

Patrice. No, I was taking jazz flute lessons, so I could learn to improvise. And in order to learn to improvise, he had to teach me a lot about theory. So this lesson, which led to the composition of "Tai Chi Cycling," was about how to improvise on the blues changes.

DL. Sounds enterprising.

Patrice. And Tony would also have me transcribe other musicians' solos and try to figure out what they did. So there was a lot of theory involved.

When I asked Tony (in 2004) to name some of his more famous former students, he cited Rebecca Barry, Scott Bourgeois, and Clarence Johnson III.

> "Clarence is a real strong player. He has phenomenal ears and perfect pitch. He can hear if a note is a few cents sharp or flat, and he can learn a tune in its entirety just by hearing it a few times. Rebecca is really motivated; she's got a good business head on her shoulders. I'll bet she'll be the most successful professionally at performing. Scott's also teaching a little bit a Loyola. I don't know if he's doing the improv things. He definitely does some of the combos; he does the workshop band."

In 2005, even before Hurricane Katrina, Bourgeois moved on to New York. He had also been playing with 3NOW4, co-led by Astral Project's bassist James Singleton and the pedal steel guitar player Dave Easley. Otherwise, "There's lots of people that have graduated that are fine players; they just have to find their way professionally. It'll take a while."

Rebecca Barry (from a phone interview in April 2005)

DL. What is your musical background? Did you play as a child?

Rebecca. Yeah, I played sax. I started in like sixth grade, and continued on through high school. I studied classical when I was in Alabama—Fairhope. And I went to Interlochen, you know: spent a summer there. So when I got to Loyola, I really didn't know much about jazz. Tony was how I got into it, man. He pretty much introduced me to every player that I started liking—until later when I got into some newer guys. But I remember him hipping me to Coleman Hawkins, Lester Young, Jan Garbarek, Michael Brecker. I had never heard Michael Brecker until Tony played him for me. So that was a big influence on me.

DL. Those people were big influences on him, too.

Rebecca. Oh, absolutely, man. But the thing about Tony, though, is—I've gotta say this—I always know if it's Tony playing. A lot of people aren't like that today, you know? He's got his own style, and that's kind of a rarity to me in some ways. A lot of people are copying Trane and Wayne, and he has his own style.

DL. My three-year-old can recognize him after about four notes.

Rebecca. You can't say that of a lot of people, you know.

DL. He has a very beautiful sound, all his own. On soprano as well.

Rebecca. That's a hard instrument to get a good sound out of.

DL. Sax players have told me that the soprano is a bear to master. Tony makes it sound easy.

Rebecca. Yes! He was probably my biggest influence on sax. I used to go every week and listen to him at The Columns Hotel, man, with Singleton and Vidacovich. Wednesday or Thursday nights, every week I used to go down there.

DL. When you were taking lessons with Tony, did he do some classical music with you as well?

Rebecca. We went over classical. Like, I won the concerto competition there. But that wasn't so much his bag. We went over it, but I studied with John Sampen at summer camp. Tony, he hipped me to some more modal, "out" sounding classical. I had been more into the regular concertos like the Paul Creston.

DL. And the French school? All those French concours pieces as well?

Rebecca. I played Pierre Max Dubois. You know, I haven't played classical music in such a long time.

DL. Hard to remember now?

Rebecca. Because there's no call for it.

DL. So what was a lesson like with Tony? Did he play as well as hear you play; play CDs?

Rebecca. We would listen to music and he would show me patterns. He covered basics. We did everything from technique to working on your ear. I think there's one thing that Tony does that a lot of teachers don't do—he doesn't influence how his students sound. The kids that come out of Loyola have an individual sound. As a teacher, he gave me great ideas to build from, but ultimately I developed my own sound. That can be a rarity. If you go to certain schools, you can hear the players all sound the same.

DL. I'm sure he wouldn't force you to play like him. That would be out of character.

Rebecca. Or play like anybody, you know what I'm saying? It wasn't a necessity to play like John Coltrane. He did focus on developing your saxophone skills, you know? Technique. Which is important: something you have to stress as a teacher. I think it's also important to make sure that the kids develop their own sound.

DL. Did he comment on your sound as you were developing it?

Rebecca. He recommended mouthpieces. It took me a while to get a jazz sound. I wish I could remember how exactly, but it really happened more from transcribing. He encouraged me to transcribe more. Different mouthpieces work for different people. And he influenced that.

DL. So when you say "transcribe," you would take solos down from recordings?

Rebecca. I would figure out what they played on a recording.

DL. And a wide variety of sax players?

Rebecca. I transcribed him. I've got a couple of the Astral Project records I did. The first one had "Bongo Joe" and all that. While I was at Loyola I transcribed Coleman Hawkins, Lester Young, Joe Henderson, John Coltrane, Junior Cook, Sonny Rollins: I did a ton, man. I didn't really concentrate on one person.

DL. That was good training. You must have played in some kind of combo at Loyola. Was he the director of your combo?

Rebecca. No, he wasn't ever the director of my combo. I will say this, though: I remember doing a sax quartet with him that was a lot of fun. He used to write charts for it.

DL. The New Orleans Saxophone Quartet?

Rebecca. Yeah. He did it with the Loyola kids: we would play his charts. Some classical stuff. He played with us. And it was a lot of fun, man.

DL. Did he encourage you to go out and get gigs as a sax player?

Rebecca. I know that he would always get me into his gigs, because it's expensive when you're in college and on a budget. He would put me on the list at the door of the club. I don't know so much that he encouraged me to get gigs, but he encouraged me to sit in, which helped me to get gigs.

DL. Who did you sit in with?

Rebecca. Well, I used to sit in with him, like at The Columns. I actually went to The University of New Orleans and had Steve Masakowski for improv. I used to sit in with Steve all the time. Michael Pellera was a big influence on me. I'd go down to the Windsor Court and Johnny

Vidacovich would be playing with him and Bill Huntington. I was probably an annoying pest, man. I wanted to play with the best players, and that was the way I could get to play with them.

DL. So you sat in with Tony's trio at The Columns?

Rebecca. Yeah. Also Steve had a trio on Tuesday nights at Snug. I used to go sit in there all the time. I'd sit in with whoever. James Singleton.

Clarence Johnson III (from an interview in March 2005)
Johnson, a native of New Orleans, first met Tony at the Loyola Jazz Camp:

Clarence. I remember Tony coming in late, because he had another gig or something, and he came in for the last couple of days of class and conducted the master class. And of course we were all blown away. It wasn't until later that I got to hook up with Tony for lessons and a more personal capacity. As a matter of fact, I was still in high school, and I was doing some type of school report that had to do with music business that Tony helped me and a couple of buddies out on. That was even before I got out of high school.

DL. You went to interview him?

Clarence. We went to his house and we interviewed him. He gave us a great interview: a lot of great information. So, as I said, the foundation was being laid long before I got to Loyola. And we got an A on the report, too, so it was cool!

DL. When you were "blown away" by Tony at the camp, was it his teaching? They always play concerts as well.

Clarence. Well, it was a group of friends that I use to hang with, and we'd all heard of him and heard him play. We'd never met him personally. When he did the master class, that was the first chance we had to hear him up close and in person. And he was doing a lot of the things common to the saxophone, such as the overtone series, displaying different multiphonic techniques.

DL. So he was playing and demonstrating?

Clarence. Oh, yes. That's exactly what the master class was. We'd sit around with our instruments, and he'd pretty much for the duration of the entire day give us a group lesson, if you will. Show us different things. It was great, man.

DL. He's good at multiphonics, is he?

Clarence. Oh, yeah.

DL. He doesn't use them a lot in his solos.

Clarence. He may not use them as much as he used to. But he was one person that I actually learned using that from. Not only that but he turned me on to some other great jazz masters who used them as well: John Coltrane, Joe Henderson....

DL. Did you study classical sax as well as jazz at Loyola?

Clarence. Yeah, Tony, actually, had a lot of classical literature. And when I got to UNO, for a couple of semesters I actually studied with a classical saxophonist, Kelvin Harrison.

DL. Gave a recital?

Clarence. Gave a classical recital. So I've done it all, man. There was a hard piece. And the teacher I had before Tony, Victor Goines, he plays with the Lincoln Center Orchestra, he was one of my first, and he was the one who instilled discipline in me through reading classical literature. So I've got some background in that, as well.

DL. What was on that recital? Do you remember?

Clarence. It was a piece by Marcel Mule, the great classical saxophonist. We did the Caprice. I forget the entire name [probably Mule's edition of Eugène Bozza's *Improvisation et caprice pour saxophone solo*].[17]

DL. It was tough, huh?

Clarence. Very tough. In fact, Tony was the first guy to introduce me to Marcel Mule. He had all kinds of different recordings and material from him. So there's another example of him helping me out.

DL. One thing I've noticed about Tony's playing is that he uses staccato a lot more than other saxophone players.

Clarence. Right.

DL. And you use it even more: it seems to be a big part of your style—staccato bursts.

Clarence. Well, you know, I think that has to do a whole lot with New Orleans being such a rhythm town; such a town for drummers. The rhythm thing. Especially with him working with Fess, he's got that whole New Orleans rhythm thing happening, and it's all the Second Line down here. You're always thinking rhythm, even though you're playing melodically. That pretty much goes without saying that more people will have more of a percussive approach to melodic instruments.

DL. Did Tony demonstrate different styles of jazz sax playing? He's good at imitating earlier styles.

Clarence. Yeah, that came more throughout the private lessons when I got to Loyola. We started to sit down in a lesson and he introduced me to a lot of alternative styles, alternative saxophone techniques, different styles that people were playing, especially the avant-garde.

DL. Did he play recordings, or did he demonstrate the styles himself?

Clarence. You know, the great thing about lessons with Tony: we would share things, he would play things for me, both on his horn and on record. Aside from that, the greatest lessons I remember having with Tony were where we really didn't do much playing at all. Him sharing his experiences: on the road, how music affected his life, his decisions in his life. Stories about the road, stories about having a business. And those were, I think, the things I benefitted most from in having lessons from Tony: just him sharing his experiences with me.

DL. Well, he certainly has a lot. He sees everything very positively, I'm sure.

Clarence. Right. Those guys—Astral Project: when you asked me to come and do the interview, it was without question, because as a young student/musician coming up here in New Orleans, those guys were one of the key groups and key circle of musicians that helped me, took me under their wing, helped me out, allowing me to sit in.

DL. So you sat in with them?

Clarence. Oh, yeah, helped me come up through the ranks with them. In many instances playing at Snug Harbor, or they used to do a lot of performances at The Columns Hotel. And Tony, Johnny, and all those guys would always say, "Bring your horn, bring your horn." They wanted me to sit in. That really helped me out a lot, just to get that momentum going.

DL. Sitting in is an important activity that has almost disappeared now.

Clarence. It's almost disappeared, unfortunately. But those guys really had it on as far as helping out young people, especially me. And that led to further working relationships with Tony: when he would be out of town, he would refer gigs to me. So it was a great help. And all those guys helped out in their own way.

DL. When you sat in, did you play standards, or did you know their tunes?

Clarence. On most occasions we'd just play standards. And on some occasions, where I was very familiar with their songs, I would play their songs, too.

DL. You just picked them up from listening to them?

Clarence. Yeah.

Notes

1. Larry Englund, interview with Tony Dagradi, 3 October 2009; available from http://tonydagradi.com/interviewwtd.cfm; accessed 2 October 2013.

2. Astral Project clinic, Indiana University, 8 October 2003.

3. *Essential Scale Studies for Improvisation: A Comprehensive Approach for All Instruments* (Delevan, NY: Kendor Music, 2000).

4. *Scale Studies for Improvisation*, *Saxophone Journal* CD (Medfield, MA: Dorn Publications, 1994); study lead sheets appear in *Saxophone Journal* 19, no. 3 (November–December 1994): 3–7.

5. Tony Dagradi, "Saxophone Solis by Thad Jones," *Saxophone Journal* 15, no. 2 (September–October 1990): 44–45, 58; "Saxophone Solis by Thad Jones: 'Cherry Juice,'" 15, no. 4 (January–February 1991): 52–54.

6. Tony Dagradi, "Linear Compositional Styles of Jazz Artists," *Saxophone Journal* 16, no. 4 (January–February 1992): 54, 71; Linear Compositional Styles of Charlie Parker," 16, no. 6 (May–June 1992): 46–47.

7. Dagradi, "Linear Compositional Styles of Charlie Parker," 46.

8. Dagradi, "Linear Compositional Styles of Charlie Parker," 47.

9. Tony Dagradi, "Amazing Grace," *Saxophone Journal* 17, no. 6 (May–June 1993), 32–33.

10. Tony Dagradi, "Two & Three-Part Writing," *Saxophone Journal* 18, no. 2 (September–October 1993): 10–11; 18, no. 4 (January–February 1994): 46–47, 79; quotation from the first article, 11.

11. Tony Dagradi, "Back to Basics," *Saxophone Journal* 18, no. 6 (May–June 1994): 52–53; 19, no. 2 (September–October 1994): 14–15; quotation from first article, 52.

12. Tony Dagradi, "Reharmonization Techniques," *Saxophone Journal* 19, no. 4 (January–February 1995): 20–21.

13. Tony Dagradi, *Sax Solos over Jazz Standards: 12 Modern Etudes in Solo Form Based on Standard Changes which Explore Motivic Development, Chromaticism & Modal Techniques* (New Albany, IN: Jamey Aebersold Jazz, 2011).

14. Tony Dagradi, "Sax Solos over Jazz Standards," Woodshed/Master Class, *Down Beat* 79, no. 2 (February 2012): 86–87.

15. Tony Dagradi, "About the CD," in *Sax Solos over Jazz Standards*, iii.

16. David Demsey, review of *Sax Solos over Jazz Standards* in *Saxophone Journal* 37, no. 2

(November/December 2012): 51.

17. Paris: Alphonse Leduc, 1952, new impressions 1994 and 2004. Although the edition does not say so, it seems to be extracted from Bozza's *Douze études-caprices pour saxophone, Op. 60* (Paris: Alphonse Leduc, 1944), which has a preface by Marcel Mule.

Below: Tony Dagradi in performance with Astral Project, Jazz Fest, New Orleans, 3 May 2013; photograph by "Mr. B" (Brian Bennett), used by kind permission; see mrbsdomain.com

18. WHAT NOW?

Besides playing in Astral Project, with his own trio and quartet, and as a sideman, Tony has begun playing constructively with the new technology. On his website in March 2013, he described how:

> "Like many contemporary artists. I have set up a home studio so that I can work on recordings for myself and others. Some of the projects that I have completed recently include a play-along CD that accompanies my book *Sax Solos Over Jazz Standards* [see pp. 151–52], a 'smooth jazz' album, and another recording which features myself playing soprano, alto, tenor, and bari saxes in multi-layered arrangements.
>
> "Over the past few years I have also been working with several studios long distance. That is, they send me rhythm tracks (usually as an MP3 file) and I record sax solos, background riffs, and sometimes very elaborate arrangements. After recording my parts I send back CD-quality wave files, which can then be added and edited within the original session."[1]

His website has sound bites from two such recent albums. "'Hello Young Lovers' is from an album [*Sincerely Yours*] by Francis Dey, a great singer from Florida. I wrote the big band arrangement, produced the brass session, and played and recorded all the sax parts." The album, mp3s only, was released in December 2011.[2] "On 'Hey Lover' I added a background sax section and, of course, the tenor solo. This is from a new CD, *Let the Smoke Roll in*, by Kasie Lunsford" (released June 2012).[3]

In August 2013 he told me that "The smooth jazz CD is done, but I'm not sure what to do with it. Perhaps I'll just release it as a digital download." He has also "started a new project using virtual instruments and various plugins with live saxes, flute, clarinet, and bass clarinet on top. I'm really excited about it. Half of the pieces are new. The remaining pieces are some of my favorite older compositions, which I am revisiting in groove and orchestration."

Gemini Rising. TD (ss, as, ts, bs); Troy Davis, dr (2, 4, 11); Herlin Riley, dr (1, 3, 5, 8–9); John Vidacovich, dr (7, 10). Saxophones recorded at The Sanctuary, New Orleans, April 2011; drums recorded at Word of Mouth Studio, New Orleans, 15–17 May 2012. Astral Music AM 2014001, c2014. Available from www.tonydagradi.com. All compositions by TD unless otherwise stated.
1. The Wheel (4:37)
2. Sweet Faced Lie (5:01)
3. Mandela (4:23)
4. Sohana Sha Kirpal (3:47)
5. Gemini Rising (4:46)
6. Monk's Mood (Thelonious Monk) (3:51)
7. Spherical (4:45)
8. Sweet Remembrance (3:35)
9. Cannonball (4:17)
10. Tango (3:36)
11. Glory (4:48)

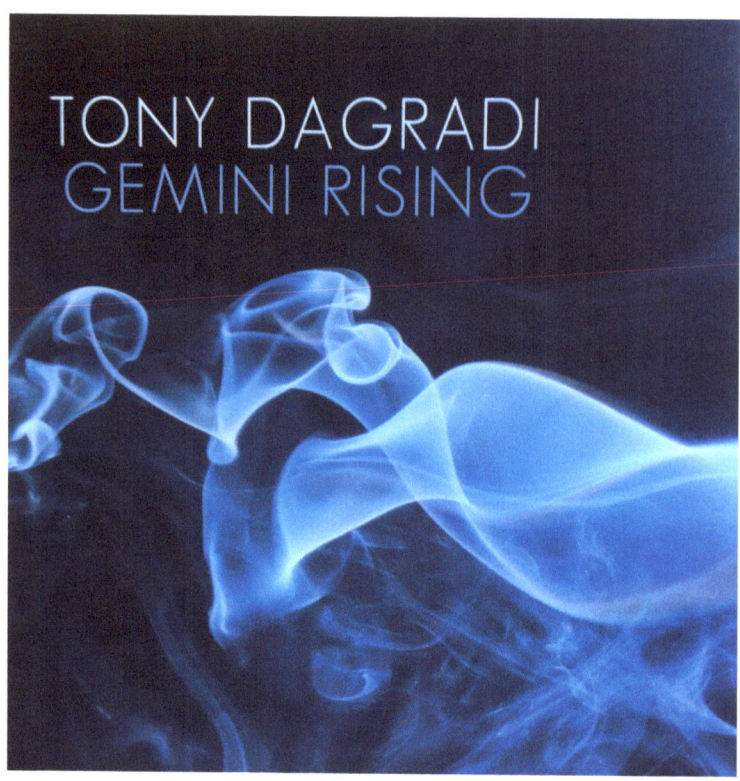

In 2014, Tony issued the CD referred to in the first paragraph above, *Gemini Rising*, in which he uses multiple tracking to play his own saxophone arrangements of his own tunes (and one by Monk), with drums added after the fact (not on "Monk's Mood"). The liner notes explain the concept:

"All the compositions on this recording were originally designed to be performed with the support of a conventional rhythm section. In adapting the pieces for saxophone quartet, my goal was to create aural landscapes with rhythmic and harmonic twists which would then serve as engaging backdrops for improvised solos.

"Those familiar with saxophone quartet literature will notice that certain arrangements employ a somewhat atypical instrumentation. While a traditional soprano–alto–tenor–baritone line-up is utilized on 'Tango,' 'Gemini Rising,' and 'Spherical,' the remaining quartet numbers, 'Sweet Remembrance,' 'Glory,' 'Monk's Mood,' 'The Wheel,' and 'Sweet Faced Lie,' feature alto, two tenors, and baritone. The resonance of the two tenors adds a density to the overall group texture which I find powerful and appealing.

"Beyond the quartets, there are several larger ensemble pieces. 'Mandela,' 'Sohana Sha Kirpal,' and 'Cannonball' blissfully grew in size and scope as they evolved during the recording process. At various points up to ten voices can be heard.

"In choosing to play all the saxophone parts myself, I was particularly influenced by the work of my friend Bobby McFerrin. His incredible vocal technique used in the realization of elegant and uplifting multi-layered creations inspired me to experiment with a similar concept using my own 'voice.' Recording the various parts, and assembling each tune layer by layer, was an exciting, challenging, and ultimately very gratifying experience.

"To complete the process, I invited three of my favorite drummers, John Vidacovich, Herlin Riley, and Troy Davis, to add their groove and genius to the finished sax tracks. Each brought distinctive flourishes and tremendous energy to every cut they played on."

Seven of Tony's pieces had already been recorded commercially: "Cannonball" on Astral Project's *Blue Streak*; "Gemini Rising" by the New Orleans Saxophone Ensemble and the Dirty Dozen Brass Band; "Sohana Sha Kirpal" and "Sweet Remembrance" on Tony's *Sweet Remembrance*; "Spherical" on Astral Project's *Big Shot*; and "The Wheel" (under the name "Too Close for Comfort") on Astral Project's *The Legend of Cowboy Bill* and Astral Project *Live in New Orleans*. "Glory" (as "Gloryland") and "Sweet Faced Lie" appear on a private recording of a live Astral Project performance in 1981, but they had not been recorded commercially before. Tony told me that the tune "Gloryland" was intended for his album *Lunar Eclipse* (1982), but he ended up rejecting the track. He changed the name of the tune "to avoid confusion with the New Orleans standard 'Gloryland' (which I didn't know about when I originally named it)." Two of the tunes on *Gemini Rising* are new to recording: "Mandela" and "Tango." Tony told me that "Mandela" was probably written in the early 1980s. "Tango" won a prize in a composition competition in a performance by the New Orleans Saxophone Ensemble in 1990 (see p. 91).

This is a wonderful CD, a culmination, even apotheosis, of Tony's work with NOSE for over thirty years as composer, arranger, leader, and performer, as well as a celebration of his mastery of new technology and his work ethic. It's full of exuberant energy, and far more varied than one might expect from saxophones played by the same player. It's also an astonishing achievement to produce such polished peformances through multi-tracking. I don't believe Tony has recorded more than once on alto and baritone saxes before, but you wouldn't know it from his mastery of the instruments here. On alto he sounds amazingly like himself on tenor, just a little higher in range. He takes the lead well in the A2TB arrangements, and solos fluently in hard bop, R&B, and gospel styles on "Cannonball," "Glory," and "The Wheel," respectively. He doesn't solo on baritone, but he was clearly in good form from playing with Baritone Bliss (see p. 142), and the instrument's growly and joyous tone is prominent in the bass-line riffs, countermelodies, and ensembles. The arrangements are full of the unexpected, including riffs in several styles, contrasting contrapuntal lines, altered harmonies, shout choruses, and variants of the head; and they are played with relish and accurate intonation. Tony also achieves variety by switching the solo instrument: alto (twice), soprano (twice), tenor (four times), alto then tenor, tenor then soprano, and soprano then tenor. Adding drums after the saxophones had been recorded generally works well, although I couldn't help wondering whether Tony wouldn't have been even more inspired in his soloing by a live encounter with any of these drummers.

"Gemini Rising" has an arrangement similar to that recorded by Tony with NOSE in 1985 (see p. 33), but much better played here. "Cannonball," Tony's tribute to the alto-playing member of the Adderley family, benefits from having an alto sax to take the lead in the snappy tune and the gloriously dense arrangement. "Monk's Mood," the only track without drums, is taken a little faster than Monk did, and kept moving right along. I love the way the voices shift on the arrangement of the head and the fullness of the A2TB saxophone sound, in which Tony wallows. "Spherical," Tony's funky NOLA blues inspired by "Blue Monk," benefits from Johnny V's greasy street beat, and has a soprano solo that begins judiciously and builds to an exuberant climax against the jubilant AT riffing. Yeah!

Of the two newly recorded pieces, "Mandela" is like a smooth-jazz calypso, on which Tony's tenor solo takes a bow to Sonny Rollins' calypso style, and later the soprano is intertwined with it in counter-solos. "Tango," especially its shout chorus, reminds me of Carla Bley's "Reactionary

Tango"; Tony recalls that he "played it a lot, so I'm sure some of that sank in." It features a danceable baritone riff, Johnny V's funky tango beat, and a poignant soprano solo, ending with a tag from "Hernando's Hideaway."

Geraldine Wyckoff in *OffBeat* lauded Tony's prowess on the bari sax but didn't seem to understand that the drum parts were added later, even professing surprise that "there are no drum solos on the album."[4] She concluded that *Gemini Rising* "looks back to the past for inspiration and forward ... for new ways to hear and explore jazz." Clearly, that was true even more for Tony than for the fortunate listener.

In 2017, Tony issued another CD with a similar concept, *Oneness*, on which he plays not only four sizes of saxophone but also flute, clarinet, bass clarinet, and even keyboards. Five of the tracks had already been recorded commercially: "Heart to Heart" on Tony's *Lunar Eclipse* and *Live at The Columns* as well as Phillip Manuel's *Heart to Heart* with Tony and James Singleton; both "Heart of the Matter" and "Hymn" on Astral Project's *Big Shot*; "Oneness" on *Astral Project New Orleans LA* and Manuel's *Heart to Heart*; and "Too Soon" (as "Too Soon to Tell") on Astral Project's *Elevado*. "Give and Take" goes back to a live Astral Project performance of 2001 and "Shimmer" to another live performance by the group in 2014.

Three compositions are recorded commercially for the first time. "The Big Tees" (2009), a punning tribute to the late Turbinton brothers, the saxophonist Earl Jr. and the keyboardist Willie Tee, is reminiscent of Thelonious Monk with funk. "Waltz for Joan," an early composition dedicated to Tony's wife, has a flowing, dance-like tune against straighter bass and drums. Tony's solo moves into double-timing, perhaps Viennese waltz? Tony writes that the composition has "a very interesting and demanding form. In the past, I always tried to solo over the entire form. For the recording, I created a shorter blowing section and added an ending vamp."[5] "The Mantra" bears a quotation from Mahatma Ghandi: "The mantra becomes one's staff of life and carries one through every ordeal. Each repetition has a new meaning, carrying you nearer and nearer to God." The mantra is depicted musically by a constant funky bass vamp, over which Tony starts soloing almost immediately, without a head.

Trumpet and trombone are mixed with saxophones and keyboards on half the tracks, to play riffs or the tunes in the background. Tony notes: "Whenever the trumpet and trombone are added, they are playing three or four parts each. Similarly, whenever you hear the brass, I am playing all five parts of a sax section. On 'Oneness,' I played two flute and two clarinet parts. On 'Give and Take,' I play the five voices of the sax section and an additional flute doubling the lead trumpet. All the varied orchestrations were chosen to make the setting as interesting as possible, but for me the soloing is the main event."

Tony plays sonorous tenor sax solos on eight tracks, switching effectively to soprano sax on "Hymn" and "The Mantra" with his beautiful vocal tone and heart-rending "cry." The head of "Heart of the Matter" is stated particularly evocatively with bass clarinet an octave under the tenor, inspiring a haunting solo. Steve Masakowski, Tony's Astral Project colleague, takes characteristic solos on four tracks ("The Big Tees," "Give and Take," "Shimmer," and "Heart to Heart") and adds to the statements of the heads. Ricky Sebastian on drums was recorded separately. Tony observes: "he was the last to record and did a masterful job in the studio. He had learned all the music and made it sound as if everyone was listing to him." As if in response to Geraldine Wyckoff, Sebastian is given short solos on "Give and Take" and "The Mantra." The pleasant surprise of the recording for me is Tony's highly accomplished, strongly rhythmic keyboard solos on "Oneness," "Hymn," and "Waltz for Joan," as well as keyboard intros on "Shimmer" and "Heart to Heart."

Tony plans to continue working at Loyola "for the foreseeable future. Retirement is a question mark." He still loves playing with Astral Project, "but in general I am accepting very few gigs these days. Basically, I am refusing anything that's in a bar! For the moment, Snug Harbor is the lone exception."

He has also been doing "a good bit" of studio work, including recordings by the singer Stephanie Jordan and the trumpeters Mark Braud, Bobby Campo, and Jamil Sharif, as well as movie soundtracks and commercials. "I really enjoy working in the studio environment; wish there was more to do."

And a surprising new development....

Tony Dagradi: *Books Transposed*
26 February–30 March 2018
JONATHAN FERRARA GALLERY is pleased to present the debut solo exhibition of New Orleans artist Tony Dagradi entitled *Books Transposed*. Perhaps best known for his musical talents as a Grammy-award winning jazz saxophonist, Dagradi began to apply his methodologies of jazz composition to visual creations in 2015 using his collection of antique books. The final products are sculptural collages, which act as a sort of visual summary of the book-in-question's contents. The exhibition will be on view from 26 February through 30 March 2018 with an opening reception on Saturday 3 March at 6:00–9:00 pm in conjunction with the Arts District New Orleans (ADNO)'s First Saturday Gallery Openings. There will a special performance by Astral Project during the opening on Saturday at 7:00–8:00 pm.

The artist elaborates on the correlation between his music and visual artwork:

"My decades-long career in contemporary jazz directly informs my work as a visual artist.

Music, for me, has always had a visual component, with the diverse elements suggesting colors, shapes, and textures. The juxtaposition of abstract shapes that come together as I work on a book is very much how I perceive the interplay of melody, harmony, and rhythm.

"Improvisation is also key to my approach in both genres. Within a jazz ensemble, each player is responsible for an individual part, which must support and inspire the other musicians. In the heat of the moment, unexpected phrases or motivic ideas can effect surprising new directions for the ensemble. Similarly, the tension and harmony that naturally occur as I uncover each new image unfailingly impact the whole and often shift the form and concept of the emerging composition.

"Cutting through each book page by page to expose selected subject matter is primarily a subtractive process. However, I often choose to reserve certain images for later use. This, too, is comparable to the open-ended conversation on the bandstand, and provides me with greater control over the development of each piece.

"I prefer working with vintage books and encyclopedias. The eclectic photos and illustrations represent material that is long out of date, yet offers a fascinating window into our past. Ultimately, I hope to provide a perspective on the transitory nature of what earlier generations understood to be factual, and offer insight into the way ever-evolving media have shaped contemporary perspectives."

The life of a jazz musician, especially a spiritually oriented one, is ever-flowing. For Tony "I never waste time" is true on several levels. It means finding new avenues for playing and renewing old ones, reaching an ever-changing audience, being creative with teaching, and investigating the latest technology, all the while keeping up practicing and interacting with a city that is still recovering from a devastating hurricane and learning to appreciate its precious musical heritage. The young man who was drawn early to the jazz path and the saxophone; the young man who apprenticed with soul and rhythm-and-blues bands, developing a strong sense of musical time as well as a love of the "energy" in music; the young man who found a spiritual path through his life partner, exploring eternity in meditation; the young man who gave New Orleans a try, finding compatible musical and spiritual colleagues there with whom he could share time indefinitely—all these strands have interwoven for four decades into the complex braid we have examined together in this book. And now visual art?! Stay tuned....

Notes

1. http://www.tonydagradi.com/recording.cfm; accessed 18 March 2013.

2. Infrared Records, Little Rock, AR.

3. Infrared Records, Little Rock, AR.

4. Geraldine Wyckoff, review in *OffBeat* 27, no. 6 (June 2014): 58.

5. Tony Dagradi, e-mail message to the author, 15 February 2018.

DISCOGRAPHY

For all performances under Astral Project's name, see Lasocki, *A Higher Fusion*.

Abbreviations
AP = Astral Project
as = alto saxophone
b = bass
bcl = bass clarinet
bs = baritone saxophone
cl = clarinet
d = drums
DT = David Torkanowsky
fl = flute
g = guitar
JS = James Singleton
JV = John Vidacovich
kbds = keyboards
p = piano
perc = percussion
perf. = performed
rec. = recorded
SM = Steve Masakowski
ss = soprano saxophone
7-s el-g = seven-string electric guitar
7-s g = seven-string guitar
TD = Tony Dagradi
tb = trombone
tpt = trumpet
ts = tenor saxophone
v = voice

As Leader
Oasis. TD, ss (3), ts (1–2, 4–7); Gary Valente, trombone; James Harvey aka Snake, p (4, 7); Kenny Werner, p (1–3, 5–6); Ed Schuller, b; D. Sharpe, d. Recorded at Grog Kill Studios, Woodstock, NY, March 1980. Gramavision GR 8001, 1980.
1. Urban Disturbance (TD) (5:18)
2. Oasis (TD) (5:23)
3. Juanita (TD) (5:54)
4. Ghana Folk Song (James Harvey) (4:33)
5. Radiation (TD) (8:31)
6. Esther (D. Sharpe) (7:06)
7. Green Jacket (James Harvey) (5:40)
   Reviewed by Kevin Whitehead in *Cadence* 7, no. 3 (March 1981): 78–79; Chris Sheridan in *Jazz Journal International* 34, no. 8 (August 1981): 30; Michael G. Nastos on http://www.allmusic.com; accessed 23 December 2004.

Lunar Eclipse. TD, ts (1–5); ss, bcl, fl (all on 4); DT, kbds; JS, b; JV, d; Mark Sanders, Brazilian perc, congas. Recorded at Studio in the Country, Bogalusa, Louisiana, 1981. Gramavision GR 8103, c1982. All compositions by TD.
1. Les deux couleurs (7:00)
2. Heart to Heart (8:20)
3. Duplicity (4:45)
4. Lunar Eclipse (11:10)
5. Whirl (5:30)

"Les deux couleurs" reissued on *Re: Source Masters from Gramavision* (Gramavision GR 8302, 1983) and *Gramavision 10th Anniversary Sampler* (Gramavision R2–79461, 1990).

Reviewed by Vincent Fumar in *Times–Picayune*, 6 August 1982, section Lagniappe, 10; James V. Murray, Knight–Ridder News Service, in *Times–Picayune*, 3 September 1982, section Lagniappe, 4; Richard B. Kamins in *Cadence* 8, no. 9 (September 1982): 74–75; Bill Shoemaker in *Down Beat* 49, no. 11 (November 1982): 36; Sam Sutherland in *High Fidelity/Musical America Edition* 32, no. 11 (November 1982): 91; in Richard Cook and Brian Morton, *The Penguin Guide to Jazz on CD, LP and Cassette* (Harmondsworth, Middlesex: Penguin Books, 1992), 253; Ron Wynn on http://www.allmusic.com; accessed 23 December 2004.

The New New Orleans Music: New Music Jazz. The New Orleans Saxophone Ensemble: TD, ts, leader; Earl Turbinton, Jr., ss, as; Fred Kemp, ts; Roger Lewis, bs. Recorded at Ultrasonic Studios, New Orleans, Louisiana, 21 October 1985. UPC 011661206625. Rounder CD 2066, cp1988.
1. NOSE Blues (TD) (5:12)
2. In a Sentimental Mood (lyrics, Manny Kurtz; music, Duke Ellington) (4:28)
3. Amazing Grace (trad.) (5:55)
4. Gemini Rising (TD) (4:25)
5. Radiation (TD) (7:30)

Coupled with: The Improvisational Arts Quintet (Edward "Kidd" Jordan, ss, ts; Kent Jordan, fl, piccolo; Clyde Kerr, Jr., tpt; Darryl Levine [i.e., Darrell Lavigne], p; Elton Heron, b; Alvin Fielder, d; Johnathan Bloom, perc [6]): 6. River Niger; 7. New Found Love; 8. Blues for A.T.

"Gemini Rising" reissued on *Modern New Orleans Masters* (Rounder 2072, 1990).

"NOSE Blues" reissued on *That's Core Jazz*, Vol. 2 (Line COCD 9.01125, 1991).

Reviewed by Vincent Fumar in *Times–Picayune*, 2 December 1988, section Lagniappe, 14; Lloyd Sachs in *Chicago Sun–Times*, 5 January 1989, section 2, Features, 40; Mike Joyce in *Washington Post*, 22 January 1989, g.02; Milo Fine in *Cadence* 15, no. 5 (May 1989): 81–82.

Images from the Floating World. The Tony Dagradi Trio: TD, ss (4), ts (1–3, 5–7); JS, b; JV, d, p. Recorded at Composers Recording Studio, New Orleans, Louisiana. UPC 4036290072768. Line/Core Records COCD 9.00727 0, c1986.
1. Parading (TD) (5:15)
2. A Flower is a Lovesome Thing (Billy Strayhorn) (7:12)
3. O. F. O. (TD) (6:08)
4. Images from the Floating World (TD) (8:40)
5. Code Blue (TD) (3:58)
6. When Your Own Heart Asks (TD) (9:32)
7. Guru Kirpal Ji Tera Saharah (TD) (6:00)

Re-released under the title *Parading* (Mirliton 0203, 2002).

"Guru Kirpal Ji Tera Saharah" reissued on *That's Core Jazz*, Vol. 2 (Line COCD 9.01125, 1991).

"Code Blue," "Guru Kirpal Ji Tera Saharah," and "Parading" reissued on *JazzSouth Program 6* (Southern Arts Federation SAF #6, 1993).

Reviewed in Richard Cook and Brian Morton, *The Penguin Guide to Jazz on CD, LP and Cassette* (Harmondsworth, Middlesex: Penguin Books, 1992), 253–54; also in *The Penguin Guide to Jazz on Compact Disc*, 3rd ed. (London: Penguin Books, 1996), 313; Keith Spera in *Times-Picayune*, 18 July 2003, section Lagniappe, 27.

Sweet Remembrance. TD, ss, ts; Fred Hersch, p; Harvie Swartz, b; Bob Moses, d; Lee Torchia, tambourine [i.e. tanputa]; Ray Spiegel, tabla. Recorded at Sorcerer Sound, 7–8 March 1987. UPC 051518870722. Gramavision 18–8707–2, p1987.
1. Sat Guru Sawan Sha (Invocation) (arr. TD) (4:21)
2. Chelo Ni Saiyo Sirsa (The Journey) (arr. TD) (6:58)
3. Sohana Sha Kirpal Pyara (Ocean of Love) (arr. TD) (5:21)
4. Tu Mera Pita (Our Father) (arr. TD) (4:31)
5. Mayro Mana Kyon Na Su Nay Dhuna Nama (Unstruck Sound) (arr. TD) (1:34)
6. Sweet Remembrance (TD) (7:20)
7. Tati Vao Na Laga Di Ji (The Protecting Circle) (arr. TD) (5:03)
8. Ute Jag Musaphir Bhor Bhai (Awakening) (arr. TD) (5:19)
9. Sant Satguru Satta Swaroopa (O Transcendental Lord) (arr. TD) (6:01)

Reviewed by Will Smith in *Omaha World–Herald*, 13 December 1987; Scott Yanow in *Cadence* 14, no. 2 (February 1988): 79; Russ Summers in *Option Magazine* (details unknown); Norman Provizer in *Jazziz*, February/March 1988.

Tony Dagradi and Astral Project, *Dreams of Love*. TD, ss (3), ts (1–2, 4–7); DT, p; SM, 7-s g, 7-s el-g; JS, b; JV, d, perc. Recorded at Southlake Recording Studio, Metairie, Louisiana, September 1987, January 1988. UPC 011661207127. Rounder CD 2071, p1988.
1. Child's Play (TD) (5:42)
2. Prayer (TD) (8:39)
3. Morning Star (TD) (8:54)
4. The Call (TD) (5:08)
5. Dreams of Love (TD) (7:27)
6. Parading (TD) (5:09)
7. I Cover the Waterfront (lyrics, Edward Heyman; music, Johnny Green) (5:47)

Reviewed by Lloyd Sachs in *Chicago Sun–Times*, 5 January 1989, 40; David Franklin in *Cadence* 15, no. 5 (May 1989): 71; Tim Price in *Saxophone Journal* 14, no. 2 (September/October 1989): 58–59; in Richard Cook and Brian Morton, *The Penguin Guide to Jazz on CD, LP and Cassette* (Harmondsworth, Middlesex: Penguin Books, 1992), 253; slightly different text in *The Penguin Guide to Jazz on Compact Disc*, 3rd ed. (London: Penguin Books, 1996), 313; Ron Wynn on http://www.allmusic.com; accessed 23 December 2004.

Live at The Columns. Tony Dagradi Trio: TD, ts; JS, b; JV, perc; with SM, g (6, 8). Recorded at The Columns Hotel, New Orleans, Louisiana, April–November 1993. UPC 783287940925. Turnipseed Music TMCD.07, p1994.
1. Meditations (Antonio Carlos Jobim) (7:59)
2. Heart to Heart (TD) (7:05)

3. Limbo Jazz (Duke Ellington) (8:00)
4. Urban Disturbance (TD) (5:57)
5. New Day (JV) (11:05)
6. Body and Soul (lyrics, Edward Heyman, Robert Sauer, Frank Eyton; music, Johnny Green) (5:22)
7. Fall Out (TD) (8:40)
8. Blue Monk (Thelonious Monk) (7:50)

"Body and Soul" reissued on *What's in the Fridge? The Musical Spices of Louisiana* (Louisiana Film Commission, 1995).

Reviewed by Geraldine Wyckoff in *OffBeat* 7, no. 6 (May 1994) and *JazzTimes* 25, no. 3 (March 1995): 100; Michael Ullman in *Stereophile* 18, no. 4 (April 1995); David Kuner in *Cadence* 21, no. 10 (October 1995): 109–10; Paul Evoskevich in *Saxophone Journal* 21, no. 1 (July–August 1996): 76–77; in Richard Cook and Brian Morton, *The Penguin Guide to Jazz on Compact Disc*, 3rd ed. (London: Penguin Books, 1996), 313; Jason Staczek on http://www.jellyroll.com/05/tonydagradi.html; accessed 5 December 2004.

Scale Studies for Improvisation. TD, s; JS, b. *Saxophone Journal* CD. Medfield, MA: Dorn Publications, 1994.
1. Introduction (3:55)
2. Long Tones (2:00)
3. Major Scales (5:00)
4. Diatonic Sevenths (1:54)
5. Inversions of Sevenths (2:30)
6. Pentatonic Scales (5:55)
7. Fourths (3:02)
8. Circle of Fifths (2:15)
9. ii/V/I Patterns (2:15)
10. Diminished Scale (2:39)
11. Whole-tone Scale (2:00)
12. Altered Dominant Scales (5:42)
13. Conclusion (2:35)

Includes excerpts from *Dreams of Love*.

Study lead sheets in *Saxophone Journal* 19, no. 3 (November–December 1994): 3–7.

Sax Solos over Jazz Standards: 12 Modern Etudes in Solo Form Based on Standard Chord Changes Which Explore Motivic Development, Chromaticism & Modal Techniques. TD, ts; with his own synthesized rhythm section. New Albany, IN: Jamey Aebersold Jazz, 2011.
1. Yellow Dawn (based on the chord changes of "Softly, As in a Morning Sunrise")
2. Silver Lining (based on "In Your Own Sweet Way")
3. Caught Red-Handed (based on "I've Got Rhythm")
4. White Hot (Blues in F Concert)
5. Brown Out (based on "Stella by Starlight")
6. Blue Plate Special (based on "Solar Flair")
7. Flesh Tones (based on "What Is This Thing Called Love")
8. Tickled Pink (based on "Alone Together")
9. Scarlet Letters (based on "Nica's Dream")
10. Totally Golden (based on "Impressions")

11. In the Black (Blues in Bb Concert)
12. Crimson Joy (based on "Poinciana")
   Reviewed by David Demsey in *Saxophone Journal* 37, no. 2 (November/December 2012): 51.

Gemini Rising. TD (ss, as, ts, bs); Troy Davis, dr (2, 4, 11); Herlin Riley, dr (1, 3, 5, 8–9); John Vidacovich, dr (7, 10). Saxophones recorded at The Sanctuary, New Orleans, April 2011; drums recorded at Word of Mouth Studio, New Orleans, 15–17 May 2012. Astral Music AM 2014001, c2014. Available from www.tonydagradi.com. All compositions by TD unless otherwise stated.
1. The Wheel (4:37)
2. Sweet Faced Lie (5:01)
3. Mandela (4:23)
4. Sohana Sha Kirpal (3:47)
5. Gemini Rising (4:46)
6. Monk's Mood (Thelonious Monk) (3:51)
7. Spherical (4:45)
8. Sweet Remembrance (3:35)
9. Cannonball (4:17)
10. Tango (3:36)
11. Glory (4:48)
   Reviewed by Geraldine Wyckoff in *OffBeat* 27, no. 6 (June 2014): 58

Oneness. TD (ss, as, ts, bs, fl, cl, bcl, kbds); Steve Masakowski, g (2, 4, 7, 9); Barney Floyd, tpt (1, 4); Jamil Sharif, tpt (2, 6, 10); Rick Trolsen, tb (1, 4, 6, 10); Roland Guerin, b (2, 5–6, 8, 10); Chris Severin, b (1, 3–4, 7, 9); Ricky Sebastian, d. Saxophones and woodwinds recorded at The Sanctuary, New Orleans, May 2015; drums recorded at Word of Mouth Studio, New Orleans, June 2015. Available from www.tonydagradi.com. Astral Music AM2017001, c2017. All compositions by TD.
1. Oneness (6:28)
2. The Big Tees (4:54)
3. Too Soon (4:54)
4. Give and Take (4:53)
5. Heart of the Matter (5:41)
6. Hymn (4:55)
7. Shimmer (4:40)
8. Waltz for Joan (5:52)
9. Heart to Heart (6:23)
10. The Mantra (4:03)
   Reviewed by Geraldine Wyckoff in *OffBeat*, 30 August 2017.

As Co-Leader
Ramsey McLean and Tony Dagradi, *The Long View*. McLean, cello, b, mburu [i.e. mbira] (5), Tibetan bells; TD, ss (1), ts (3, 6–7), fl (2), bcl (4). Recorded in the Playhouse of Longue Vue Gardens, New Orleans, Lousiana, January 1983. Prescription Records Pres. 4, c1983.
1. Swan Song (McLean) (7:20)
2. The Dark Horse (McLean) (4:47)
3. Without (McLean) (7:55)

4. Resurrection (For the Living) (McLean) (6:43)
5. Say "Good Night" (McLean) (0:36)
6. Purloin (McLean) (4:52)
7. High Pressure Zone (McLean, TD) (4:55)

Reviewed by Vincent Fumar in *Times–Picayune*, 6 April 1984, section Lagniappe, 15; Rhodes Spedale in *Jazz Times* 15, no. 2 (February 1985): 17; Ed Hazell in *Coda*, no. 204 (October–November 1985): 27.

As Sideman

For details of tracks and instruments, see the relevant chapters.

Sea Level, *Long Walk on a Short Pier* (Capricorn Records CPN 0227, 1979); ts
Ron Cuccia, *Music from the Big Tomato* (Oblique Records PB–002, 1980); bcl, fl, ss
Professor Longhair, *Crawfish Fiesta* (Alligator ALCD 4718, 1980); ts
Carla Bley, *Social Studies* (Watt/11 78118–23111-2, 1981); cl, ts
Ramsey McLean and The Lifers, *History's Made Every Moment: New Orleans Now* (Prescription Records RM–1981, c1981); bcl, ss, ts
Carla Bley, *Carla Bley Live!* (Watt Works 815730-2, 1982); ts
Professor Longhair, *The Last Mardi Gras* (Atlantic Deluxe SD 2–4001, pc1982); ts
Carla Bley, *Extraits de la bande originale du film* Mortelle randonnée [movie soundtrack] (Watt Works 812 097–1, 1983); ts
Carla Bley, *I Hate to Sing* (Watt Works 78118–20125-2, 1984); ts
Woodenhead, *Woodenhead Live* (Broken Records JR 3685, 1984); ss, ts
Patrice Fisher, *Singers* (Broken Records JR–3585, 1985); fl
Scott Goudeau, *The Secret Life of Children* (Broken Records, 1985)
Lawrence Sieberth, *Shadowlove* (Broken Records JR–3885, 1985); ts.
Jasmine, Sounds of Brazil, Patrice Fisher, *Foreign Affairs* (Broken Records JR–1086, 1986); ss, ts
Patrice Fisher, *Softly Strong* (Broken Records JT1087, 1987).
Scott Goudeau, *In the Nick of Time* (Broken Records BR–1186, 1987); ts
Damon Short, *Penguin Shuffle* (Blue Room 004, 1987); bcl, ss, ts
Patrice Fisher with Ensamble Acustico, *New Orleans Project* (Broken Records, JR388, 1988).
For Taylor Storer (TS 001; TS Records, 1988); ts
Scott Goudeau, *The Promise* (Broken Records BR–1288, 1988); ts
Mose Allison, *My Backyard* (Blue Note CDP 7 93840 2, cp1990); ts
I Migliori, *Live at Gino's* (Chromatose Productions, [1990]); ts
George Porter, Jr., *Runnin' Partner* (Rounder CD 2099, 1990); ss, ts
Sally Townes, *Just Want Some More* (Rabadash CD80191, 1990); ss
Robbie Robertson, *Storyville* (Geffen GEFD–24303, 1991); ss
Phillip Manuel, *A Time for Love* (All For One AFO 92–1128-20, cp1992); ss, ts.
Johnny Adams, *Good Morning Heartache* (Rounder CD 2125, 1993); ts
Professor Longhair, *Big Chief* (Rhino R2 71446 [1993]); ts.
Professor Longhair, *Rum and Coke* (Rhino R2 71447, 1993; Tomato TOM–2041, pc2002); ts.
John Vidacovich, *Street Beats: Modern Applications, New Orleans Drumming*; videotape; interviewer: Dan Thress ([Miami?]: DCI Music Video, 1993); reissued as part of the DVD *New Orleans Drumming* (Miami: Warner Brothers 905772, 2004); ts
Solomon Burke, *Live at The House of Blues* (Black Top CDBT–1108, 1994); ts

Johnny Adams, *The Verdict* (Rounder CD 2135, 1995); ss
Ellis Marsalis, *A Night at Snug Harbor, New Orleans* (Evidence Music ECD 22129, p1989, c1995); ts.
Phillip Manuel, *Heart to Heart* (Turnipseed Music TMCD.10, p1995); ss, ts
Better Than Ezra, *Friction, Baby* (Elektra 61944–2, 1996); cl, fl, ts
Tommy Ridgley, *Since the Blues Began* (Black Top BT–1115, 1995); ts.
Tim Laughlin, *Blue Orleans* (Good Time Jazz GTJCD–15004–2, 1996); ts
John Vidacovich, *Banks Street* (Record Chebasco RC1496, cp1996); ss, ts
The New Orleans C.A.C. Jazz Orchestra, *Mood Indigo* (Rounder CD 2145, 1997); cl, fl, ts
Clarence Gatemouth Brown, *Gate Swings* (Verve/Polygram 314 537 617–2, 1997); ts.
Michael Pellera, *Cloud 9* (Pajacis Music PAJ–001, pc1997); ss, ts
Better Than Ezra, *How Does Your Garden Grow?* (Elektra 62247–2, 1998); fl
Al Grey, *Echoes of New Orleans* (Progressive PCD–7108, pc1998); ts
Denise Mangiardi, *A River of My Own* (Crow Hill CHP–011298, 1998); ss, ts
Clarence Gatemouth Brown, *American Music, Texas Style* (Verve/Blue Thumb 314 547 536–2, 1999); ts
Professor Longhair, *Byrd Lives!* (Night Train International NTI CD 2002, pc1998); ts.
Al Arthur, *Mantis* (DM102000, 2000); ss, ts
¡Cubanismo!, *¡Cubanismo! in New Orleans: Mardi Gras Mambo* (Hannibal HNCD 1441, 2000); bs
Kevin Clark and the Crescent City Moonlighters, *Big Band Music* (KC0001, 2001).
John Mahoney Big Band, *In from Somewhere* (New Orleans Music Group, 2001); ts
Wayne Maureau, *Sidewalk Safari* (c2001); ts
Michael Pellera, *Son of Sky* (Pajacis paj–002, c2001); ss, ts
Wardell Quezergue, *A Creole Mass* (Creole CR 01000, 2001); as, ts, fl
Snooks Eaglin, *The Way It Is* (Money Pit Records 1111, 2002); ts
Kim Prevost, *Talk to Me* (STR Digital 1005, 2002); ts
John Vidacovich, *Vidacovich* (PawMaw Music 02, cp2002); bcl, ss, ts
Jay Weigel, *River May Cry* [movie soundtrack] (Floating City 101, 2004); ts
Jim McNeil, *Give me my Wings* (privately produced, AL–20051, 2005); ts
Phillip Manuel, *PM* (II Records, 2007); ts
Francis Dey, *Sincerely Yours* (Little Rock, AR: Infrared Records, 2011)
Kasie Lunsford, *Let The Smoke Roll In* (Little Rock, AR: Infrared Records, 2012)

Not traced:
Scott Goudeau, *Stereo Lounge*

Composition on Recording by Another Group
The Dirty Dozen Brass Band, *Voodoo* (Columbia CK 45042, 1989). Includes "Gemini Rising." Reissued on Dirty Dozen Jazz Band, *This is Jazz*, Vol. 30 (Columbia/Legacy CK 65046, 1997).

Index of Tony's Compositions
Angel Song: AP, *Blue Streak* (rec. 2007)
Astral Elevado: AP, *Acoustic Fusion* (1994); AP, *Elevado* (rec. 1997)
Awakening: see Ute Jag Musaphir Bhor Bhai
The Big Tees: ©2009; TD, *Oneness* (rec. 2015)

Blue Streak: AP, *Blue Streak* (rec. 2007)
Burning Instructions for Angel Wings (with Fielder, Sieberth, McLean): Ramsey McLean and The Lifers, *History's Made Every Moment* (1983)
The Call: TD, *Dreams of Love* (rec. 1987–88); Marsalis, *A Night at Snug Harbor, New Orleans* (rec. 1989); AP, *Acoustic Fusion* (1994)
Cannonball: AP, *Blue Streak* (rec. 2007); TD, *Gemini Rising* (rec. 2011)
Chelo Ni Saiyo Sirsa (The Journey): TD, *Sweet Remembrance* (rec. 1987)
Child's Play: TD, *Dreams of Love* (rec. 1987–88); AP, *Acoustic Fusion* (1994)
Ciao Bella (with Pellera, Vidacovich, Anderson): Pellera, *Son of Sky* (2001)
Cobalt Dreams: AP, *Blue Streak* (rec. 2007)
Code Blue: TD, *Images from the Floating World* (1986)
Delicately: AP, *The Legend of Cowboy Bill* (rec. 2004); *Astral Project Live in New Orleans* (rec. 2005)
Les deux couleurs: TD, *Lunar Eclipse* (rec. 1981)
Double Helix: AP, *Blue Streak* (rec. 2007)
Down Time: AP, *The Legend of Cowboy Bill* (rec. 2004)
Dreams of Love: TD, *Dreams of Love* (rec. 1987–88)
Duplicity: TD, *Lunar Eclipse* (rec. 1981)
Emperor of Love: AP, *Acoustic Fusion* (1994)
Fallen: AP, *Blue Streak* (rec. 2007), originally called Fallen Angel
Fallout [Fall Out]: live 1982; TD, *Live at The Columns* (rec. 1993); AP, *Voodoobop* (rec. 1998)
Free Fall: live 2013
Gemini Rising: New Orleans Saxophone Ensemble, *The New New Orleans Music: New Music Jazz* (rec. 1985); Dirty Dozen Brass Band, *Voodoo* (1989); TD, *Gemini Rising* (rec. 2011)
Get It Right: live 1983
Give and Take: live 2001; TD, *Oneness* (rec. 2015)
Glory: see Gloryland
Gloryland: live 1981; as Glory, TD, *Gemini Rising* (rec. 2011)
Guru Dev (from *Portraits and Sketches*): live 1982
Guru Kirpal Ji Tera Saharah: TD, *Images from the Floating World* (1986); *Astral Project New Orleans LA* (rec. 1990)
Heart of the Matter: AP, *Big Shot* (rec. 2002); TD, *Oneness* (rec. 2017)
Heart to Heart: TD, *Lunar Eclipse* (rec. 1981); TD, *Live at The Columns* (rec. 1993); Manuel, *Heart to Heart* (rec. 1995); TD, *Oneness* (rec. 2015)
High Pressure Zone (with Ramsey McLean): McLean and TD, *The Long View* (1983)
Hymn: AP, *Big Shot* (rec. 2002); TD, *Oneness* (rec. 2015)
Images from the Floating World: TD, *Images from the Floating World* (1986)
Indian Folk Song: see Guru Kirpal Ji Tera Saharah
Invocation: see Sat Guru Sawan Sha
The Journey: see Chelo Ni Saiyo Sirsa
Juanita: TD, *Oasis* (rec. 1980)
Lavender Sleep: AP, *Blue Streak* (rec. 2007)
Lunar Eclipse: TD, *Lunar Eclipse* (rec. 1981)
Mandela: *ca.* 1984–89; TD, *Gemini Rising* (rec. 2011)
The Mantra: TD, *Oneness* (rec. 2015)
Mayro Mana Kyon Na Su Nay Dhuna Nama (Unstruck Sound): TD, *Sweet Remembrance* (rec. 1987)

Mess o' Fess: live *ca*. 1980
Miles: *Astral Project New Orleans LA* (rec. 1990); AP, *Acoustic Fusion* (1994)
Moon in Scorpio: live 2000
Morning Star: TD, *Dreams of Love* (rec. 1987–88); AP, *Acoustic Fusion* (1994)
N. O. Goodbyes: written 1988; AP, *Elevado* (rec. 1997)
Nowhere to Hide: AP, *The Legend of Cowboy Bill* (rec. 2004)
Nose Blues: The New Orleans Saxophone Ensemble, *The <u>New</u> New Orleans Music: New Muisc Jazz* (rec. 1985)
Nose Dive: AP, *Elevado* (rec. 1997)
O Transcendental Lord: see Sant Satguru Satta Swaroopa
O. F. O. [One for Ornette]: TD, *Images from the Floating World* (1986); AP, *Elevado* (rec. 1997)
Oasis: TD, *Oasis* (rec. 1980)
Ocean of Love: see Sohana Sha Kirpal Pyara
Oneness: *Astral Project New Orleans LA* (rec. 1994); Manuel, *Heart to Heart* (rec. 1995); TD, *Oneness* (rec. 2015)
Our Father: see Tu Mera Pita
Parading: TD, *Images from the Floating World* (1986); TD, *Dreams of Love* (rec. 1987–88)
Prayer: TD, *Dreams of Love* (rec. 1987–88)
The Protecting Circle: see Tati Vao Na Laga Di Ji
Radiation: TD, *Oasis* (rec. 1980); New Orleans Saxophone Ensemble, *The <u>New</u> New Orleans Music: New Music Jazz* (rec. 1985)
Return: live 1990
Retro-Active: AP, *Big Shot* (rec. 2002)
Salutations (from *Portraits and Sketches*): live 1982
Sant Satguru Satta Swaroopa (O Transcendental Lord): TD, *Sweet Remembrance* (rec. 1987)
Sat Guru Sawan Sha (Invocation): TD, *Sweet Remembrance* (rec. 1987)
Second Thoughts: AP, *The Legend of Cowboy Bill* (rec. 2004)
Secret Sky: live 2009
Shimmer: live 2014; TD, *Oneness* (rec. 2015)
Sling Slang: live 1984
Smoke and Mirrors: AP, *Voodoobop* (rec. 1998)
Sohana Sha Kirpal Pyara (Ocean of Love): TD, *Sweet Remembrance* (rec. 1987); TD, *Gemini Rising* (rec. 2011)
South by Southwest: live 2000
Spherical: AP, *Big Shot* (rec. 2002); *Astral Project Live in New Orleans* (rec. 2005); TD, *Gemini Rising* (rec. 2011)
Supersonic Hawk: *Astral Project New Orleans LA* (rec. 1994)
Sweet Faced Lie: live 1981; TD, *Gemini Rising* (rec. 2011)
Sweet Remembrance: TD, *Sweet Remembrance* (rec. 1987); TD, *Gemini Rising* (rec. 2011)
Tango: live 1990; TD, *Gemini Rising* (rec. 2011)
Tati Vao Na Laga Di Ji (The Protecting Circle): TD, *Images from the Floating World* (1986); AP, *Voodoobop* (rec. 1998)
Too Close for Comfort: AP, *The Legend of Cowboy Bill* (rec. 2004); *Astral Project Live in New Orleans* (rec. 2005); as The Wheel, TD, *Gemini Rising* (rec. 2011)
Too Soon to Tell: AP, *Elevado* (rec. 1997); as Too Soon, TD, *Oneness* (rec. 2017)
The Two Colors: see Les deux couleurs
2 People (with Pellera, JV, Anderson): Pellera, *Son of Sky* (2001)

Tu Mera Pita (Our Father): TD, *Sweet Remembrance* (rec. 1987)
Unstruck Sound: see Mayro Mana Kyon Na Su Nay Dhuna Nama
Up, Over & Gone: live 1995
Urban Disturbance: TD, *Oasis* (rec. 1980); TD, *Live at The Columns* (rec. 1993)
Ute Jag Musaphir Bhor Bhai (Awakening): TD, *Sweet Remembrance* (rec. 1987)
The Wheel: see Too Close for Comfort
Waltz for Joan: TD, *Oneness* (rec. 2015)
When Your Own Heart Asks: TD, *Images from the Floating World* (1986)
Whirl: TD, *Lunar Eclipse* (rec. 1981)
The Whole Truth: AP, *Voodoobop* (rec. 1998); *Astral Project Live in New Orleans* (rec. 2005)
X-Ray Vision: ©1996; AP, *Big Shot* (rec. 2002)
Yeah You Right!: live 2001

In chronological order:
Juanita (rec. 1980)
Mess o' Fess (live *ca.* 1980)
Oasis (rec. 1980)
Prayer (live *ca.* 1980)
Radiation (rec. 1980)
Urban Disturbance (rec. 1980)
Les deux couleurs (rec. 1981)
Duplicity (rec. 1981)
Gloryland (live 1981), later renamed Glory (rec. 2011)
Heart to Heart (rec. 1981)
Lunar Eclipse (rec. 1981)
Morning Star (live 1981)
Sweet Faced Lie (live 1981)
Whirl (rec. 1981)
Fallout [Fall Out] (live 1982)
Guru Kirpal Ji Tera Saharah (live 1982)
Nose Dive (live 1982)
O. F. O. [One for Ornette] (written 1982?; rec. 1986)
Sweet Remembrance (live 1982)
Mandela (probably early 1980s)
Burning Instructions for Angel Wings (rec. 1983)
Get It Right (live 1983)
High Pressure Zone (with Ramsey McLean) (rec. 1983)
Sling Slang (live 1984)
Supersonic Hawk (live 1984)
Gemini Rising (rec. 1985)
Nose Blues (rec. 1985)
Code Blue (rec. 1986)
Images from the Floating World (rec. 1986)
Parading (rec. 1986)
Tati Vao Na Laga Di Ji (The Protecting Circle) (rec. 1986)
When Your Own Heart Asks (rec. 1986)
The Call (live 1987)

Chelo Ni Saiyo Sirsa (The Journey) (rec. 1987)
Mayro Mana Kyon Na Su Nay Dhuna Nama (Unstruck Sound) (rec. 1987)
Sant Satguru Satta Swaroopa (O Transcendental Lord) (rec. 1987)
Sat Guru Sawan Sha (Invocation) (rec. 1987)
Sohana Sha Kirpal Pyara (Ocean of Love) (rec. 1987)
Tu Mera Pita (Our Father) (rec. 1987)
Ute Jag Musaphir Bhor Bhai (Awakening) (rec. 1987)
Child's Play (rec. 1987–88)
Dreams of Love (rec. 1987–88)
N. O. Goodbyes (written 1988)
Miles (rec. 1990)
Return (live 1990)
Tango (live 1990; rec. 2011)
Emperor of Love (live 1991)
Astral Elevado (rec. 1994)
Oneness (rec. 1994)
Too Soon to Tell (live 1995)
Up, Over & Gone (live 1995)
X-Ray Vision (©1996, rec. 2002)
Smoke and Mirrors (rec. 1998)
The Whole Truth (rec. 1998)
Moon in Scorpio (live 2000)
Retro-Active (live 2000)
South by Southwest (live 2000)
Ciao Bella (with Pellera, JV, Anderson) (rec. 2001)
Give and Take (live 2001)
Heart of the Matter (live 2001)
Hymn (live 2001; written 20 years earlier?)
Spherical (live 2001)
2 People (with Pellera, JV, Anderson) (rec. 2001)
Yeah You Right! (live 2001)
Second Thoughts (live 2002)
Delicately (live 2003)
Down Time (live 2003)
Nowhere to Hide (rec. 2004)
Too Close for Comfort (rec. 2004), later renamed The Wheel (rec. 2011)
Fallen (live 2005), originally called Fallen Angel
Blue Streak (live 2006)
Cannonball (live 2006)
Cobalt Dreams (live 2006)
Lavender Sleep (live 2006)
Double Helix (rec. 2007)
The Big Tees (2009)
Secret Sky (live 2009)
Free Fall (live 2013)
Shimmer (live 2014)
The Mantra (rec. 2015)

Waltz for Joan (rec. 2015)

BIBLIOGRAPHY

Note: This bibliography does not include reviews of recordings, unless they are in named articles.

Aiges, Scott. "Astral Project Lands a Heavenly Award." *Times–Picayune*, 20 November 1992, section Lagniappe, L7.

———. "Best Bets at the Clubs." *Times–Picayune*, 9 July 1993, section Lagniappe, L10.

———. "Happy Times with David Byrne." *Times–Picayune*, 2 October 1992, section Lagniappe, L7.

———. "Heaven Sent: Members of Astral Project Cultivate a Spiritual Union that Sends the Group's Music into the Stratosphere." *Times–Picayune*, 2 May 1993, section Living, D1–D2.

———. "Hot Pix." *Times–Picayune*, 26 October 1990, section Lagniappe, L8.

[———]. "In the Key of Jazz." *Times–Picayune*, 15 April 1994, section Lagniappe, L8.

[———]. "Jazz." *Times–Picayune*, 28 April 1995, section Lagniappe, L12.

———. "Jazz Month Gets into Swing with Tribute to Basie." *Times–Picayune*, 27 September 1991, section Lagniappe, L7.

———. "A Jazzy Salute." *Times–Picayune*, 25 September 1992, section Lagniappe, L8.

———. "Just Call him Mister Medley." *Times–Picayune*, 2 April 1993, section Lagniappe, L9.

[———]. "Let Jazz Add Some Pizzazz to Your Weekend." *Times–Picayune*, 1 September 1995, Lagniappe, L6.

———. "Lifestyles of the Young and Funky Set to Music." *Times–Picayune*, 10 December 1993, section Lagniappe, L8.

———. "Sass, Sophistication in the Blood Lines." *Times-Picayune*, 9 June 1995, section Lagniappe, L6.

———. "Testing Boundaries with a Jazz Sax." *Times–Picayune*, 4 February 1994, section Lagniappe, L11.

———. "Three Pillars of Jazz." *Times–Picayune*, 13 January 1995, section Lagniappe, L9.

———. "What a Big Band Should Be." *Times–Picayune*, 22 January 1993, section Lagniappe, L6.

Anding, Jill T. "A Tale of Two Houses." *Times–Picayune*, 11 August 1989, section Lagniappe,

7. "Arts and Leisure Guide." *New York Times*, 13 May 1979, D35.

"The Arts Corner." *The State Journal–Register* (Springfield, IL), 20 November 1986, section Lifestyle, 20.

Astral Project. *"Big Shot": Lead Sheets and Transcriptions from the Latest Album by New Orleans' Top Modern Jazz Group*. Privately printed, 2002.
As well as all the compositions, includes Tony Dagradi's solo on "Retro-Active."

Bacon, Peter. "A Beacon of Great Jazz." Peter Bacon's Jazz Diary. *Birmingham Post* (England), 11 August 2004.

Barry, John M. "After the Deluge, Some Questions." *New York Times*, 13 October 2005, Late Edition—Final, Section A, 27.

Berry, Jason. "Turbinton Helps Keep the Coltrane Sax Spirit Alive." *Times–Picayune*, 8 February 1985, section Lagniappe, 20.

———. "Tyler's Fate not an Open and Shut Case." *Times–Picayune*, 22 January 1989, section JJ, J3.

———, Jonathan Foose, and Tad Jones. *Up from the Cradle of Jazz: New Orleans Music since World War II*. Athens, GA: University of Georgia Press, 1986; reprint, New York: Da Capo Press, 1992.

Booth, Philip. "Fresh Gumbo." *Jazziz* 17, no. 5 (May 2002): 39.

———. "Future Jazz: A Report from the IAJE in New Orleans." Available from http://citypaper.net/articles/020300/mus.jazz.shtml; accessed 27 September 2006.

———. "Music, Tragically, is Missing." *Sarasota Herald-Tribune* (Florida), 8 September 2005, section Florida West, E1.

Breeding, Lucinda. "Help for Back Home." *Denton Record–Chronicle* (Texas), 29 September 2005, section Denton Time, 6.

Brown, Bill. "Jazz Goes Underground: Music Series Takes over Danna Center Basement." *The Maroon* (Loyola University, New Orleans), 6 December 2002. Available from http://maroon.loyno.edu/media/paper542/news/2002/12/06/News/Jazz-Goes.Underground-338020.shtml; accessed 29 June 2005.

Burns, Mick. *Keeping the Beat on the Street: the New Orleans Brass Band Renaissance*. Baton Rouge: Louisiana State University Press, 2006.

Ciccone, Kristin. "Astral Project Celestially Showers the States with Stellar Grooves." Available from http://www.jambase.com/headsup.asp?storyID=656; accessed 2 January 2005.

Citron, Alan. "Musicians Help Themselves." *Times–Picayune*, 19 February 1978, section 2, 5.

Clark, Anthony. "Jazzcats." *OffBeat* 4, no. 5 (May 1991): 32–38.

Cook, Richard, and Brian Morton. *The Penguin Guide to Jazz on CD*, 7th ed. London: Penguin Books, 2004.

———. *The Penguin Guide to Jazz on CD, LP and Cassette*. Harmondsworth, Middlesex: Penguin Books, 1992.

———. *The Penguin Guide to Jazz on Compact Disc*, 3rd ed. London: Penguin Books, 1996.

———. *The Penguin Guide to Jazz Recordings*, 9th ed. London: Penguin, 2008.

Cook, Richard J., Sr. *The Twentieth Century Limited, 1938–1967*. Lynchburg, VA: TLC Publishing, 1993.

"Dagradi Gets Plugged In." *Times-Picayune*, 13 March 1998, section Third, L9.

"Dagradi to Perform." *The Baton Rouge Sunday Advocate*, 22 October 1989, section News, 5-B.

Dagradi, Tony. "Amazing Grace." Writing for Saxophones. *Saxophone Journal* 17, no. 6 (May–June 1993), 32–33.

———. "Back to Basics." Writing for Saxophones. *Saxophone Journal* 18, no. 6 (May–June 1994): 52–53; 19, no. 2 (September–October 1994): 14–15.

———. "*Down in Front*: David Dempsey's Tenor Solo from Neo-Bop Jazz Player Play-Along CD: Transcription & Analysis." *Jazz Player* 1, no. 3 (April–May 1994): 47–51.

———. "The Ellington Effect." Writing for Saxophones. *Saxophone Journal* 17, no. 2 (September–October 1992): 52–53; 17, no. 4 (January–February 1993): 38–39, 79.

———. *Essential Scale Studies for Improvisation: A Comprehensive Approach for All Instruments*. Delevan, NY: Kendor Music, 2000.
Listed in *Jazz Times* 30, no. 6 (August 2000): 20.

———. "Gary Campbell's Tenor Solo on *Spanglish* [from his Miami Quartet's] *Jazz Player* Play-Along CD: Transcription & Analysis." *Jazz Player* 2, no. 3 (April 1995): 43–48.

———. "Greg Yasinitsky's Tenor Solo on *A Mode for Miles* [from his Crosscurrent Quintet's] *Jazz Player* Play-Along CD: Transcription & Analysis." *Jazz Player* 2, no. 2 (February–March 1995): 56–58, 79–80.

———. "Linear Compositional Styles of Charlie Parker." Writing for Saxophones. *Saxophone Journal* 16, no. 6 (May–June 1992): 46–47.

———. "Linear Compositional Styles of Jazz Artists." *Saxophone Journal* 16, no. 4 (January–February 1992): 54, 71.

———. "*Lisa's Da Bossa*: Miles Osland's Flute/Soprano Solo from Latin Jazz *Jazz Player* Play-Along CD: Transcription & Analysis." *Jazz Player* 1, no. 6 (October–November 1994): 44–48, 79.

———. "*Longhorn*: Mel Martin's Solo from Bebop & Beyond *Jazz Player* Play-Along CD: Transcription and Analysis." *Jazz Player* 1, no. 1 (December 1993): 54–57, 77. Also available from http://www.melmartin.com/html_pages/ana.html. Accessed 14 December 2004.

———. "*Morning Star*: Tony Dagradi's Soprano Solo from the Astral Project *Jazz Player* Play-Along CD: Transcription & Analysis." *Jazz Player* 1, no. 4 (June–July 1994): 53–57.

———. "*P's Rough House*: Greg Abate's Alto Solo from Rhythm & Blues *Jazz Player* Play-Along CD: Transcription & Analysis." *Jazz Player* 1, no. 2 (February–March 1994): 54–58.

———. "*Parker House Stomp*: Jeff Holmes' Trumpet Solo Jeff Holmes' Quintet Jazz Variety 5-Pak *Jazz Player* Play-Along CD: Transcription & Analysis." *Jazz Player* 2, no. 1 (December 1994–January 1995): 57–59, 79.

———. "Reharmonization Techniques." Writing for Saxophones. *Saxophone Journal* 19, no. 4 (January–February 1995): 20–21.

———. "Sax Solos over Jazz Standards," Woodshed/Master Class. *Down Beat* 79, no. 2 (February 2012): 86–87.

———. *Sax Solos over Jazz Standards: 12 Modern Etudes in Solo Form Based on Standard Changes which Explore Motivic Development, Chromaticism & Modal Techniques*. New Albany, IN: Jamey Aebersold Jazz, 2011.

———. "Saxophone Solis by Thad Jones." Writing for Saxophone. *Saxophone Journal* 15, no. 2 (September–October 1990): 44–45, 58.

———. "Saxophone Solis by Thad Jones: 'Cherry Juice.'" *Saxophone Journal* 15, no. 4 (January–February 1991): 52–54.

———. "*Shorty (D's Tune)*: Jon Metzger's Vibraphone Solo from The Frank Bongiorno Septet *Jazz Player* Play-Along CD: Transcription & Analysis." *Jazz Player* 1, no. 5 (August–September 1994): 51–53.

———. "Two & Three-Part Writing." *Saxophone Journal* 18, no. 2 (September–October 1993): 10–11; 18, no. 4 (January–February 1994): 46–47, 79.

Dictionnaire du jazz. [Sous la direction de] Philippe Carles, André Clergeat, et Jean-Louis Comolli. Paris: Robert Laffont, 1988; nouvelle édition, augmentée, 1994. S.v. "Dagradi, Anthony Tony [sic]," par Pascale Barithel and Christian Gauffre. In Spanish as *Diccionario del jazz*, traducido por Carlos Sampayo. Madrid: Anaya & Mario Muchnik, 1995.

Dreher, Rod. "After 10 Years, Mose Returns." *The Advocate* (Baton Rouge, LA), 17 April 1992, section Fun, 10–Fun.

Elson, Martha. "Touring Jazz Group Really on the Road." *The Courier–Journal* (Louisville, KY), 30 September 2005, edition Metro, section News, 03B.

Enright, Ed. "On the Road with Bobby McFerrin & Astral Project." *Down Beat* 66, no. 11 (November 1999): 32–34, 36–37.

Freeman, Wanda. "Gramavision Label Signs Up Saxophonist Dagradi." *Billboard* 91 (18 April 1981): 71.

Fumar, Vincent. "Bobby McFerrin Solos with Unusual Jazz Style." *Times–Picayune*, 20 May 1988, section Lagniappe, 6.

———. "The Busy Man from the Dirty Dozen." *Times–Picayune*, 21 October 1983, section Lagniappe, 9.

———. "The Do-it-yourself Way to Discs." *Times–Picayune*, 12 June 1982, section Lagniappe, 9.

———. "'Happy Birthday' Sung to WWOZ with N.O. Accent." *Times–Picayune*, 18 December 1981, section Lagniappe, 13.

———. "He'll be Drumming up his Own Jobs Now." *Times–Picayune*, 1 April 1988, section Lagniappe, 14.

———. "Henry Butler Shows off a New Sound." *Times–Picayune*, 21 July 1989, section Lagniappe, L7.

———. "In Search of Modern Jazz." *Times–Picayune*, 13 October 1989, section Lagniappe, L6.

———. "Lacinak on a Winning Jazz Track." *Times–Picayune*, 21 April 1989, section Lagniappe, L6.

———. "Listening to Albums by Two Local Trios." *Times–Picayune*, 15 May 1987, section Lagniappe, 10.

———. "Making Radio More Aware of Jazz." *Times–Picayune*, 25 September 1987, section Lagniappe, 21.

———. "Memories of a Mardi Gras Past." *Times–Picayune*, 25 June 1982, section Lagniappe, 8.

———. "N.O. Guitarist Makes a Record His Way." *Times–Picayune*, 3 April 1987, section Lagniappe, 9.

———. "N.O.'s Musical Roots Run Deep." *Times–Picayune*, 4 May 1986, section A, 25.

———. "Sax Man Uses his Music for Healing." *Times–Picayune*, 4 October 1985, section Lagniappe, 9.

———. "A Summit of the Saxes." *Times–Picayune*, 19 April 1985, section Lagniappe, 12.

———. "Variety in Pop Music." *Times–Picayune*, 11 September 1987, section Lagniappe, 9;

———. "Woodenhead Fuses its Sound on Record." *Times–Picayune*, 24 May 1985, section Lagniappe, 20.

Gagnard, Frank. "Sound of New Music Draws a Crowd to CAC." *Times–Picayune*, 27 November 1990, section Living, D6.

Garcia, Antonio J. "Jazz Education in New Orleans, Post-Katrina." *Jazz Education Journal* 39, no. 3 ([December 2006]): 50–59.

Giddins, Gary. *Riding on a Blue Note: American Jazz and Pop*. New York: Oxford University Press, 1981.

Gilbert, Calvin. "Jazz at Gino's is Recorded for Takeout Orders." *The Advocate* (Baton Rouge, LA), 26 July 1991, section Fun, 8–Fun.

———. "Saxophone Series." *The Advocate* (Baton Rouge, LA), 25 November 1988, section Fun, 4–Fun.

Goodwin, Michael. "Goodbye Professor, Goodbye Professor." *The Village Voice* 25 (3 March 1980): 59.

Grove Music Online. Available from http://www.grovemusic.com by subscription. S.v. "Dagradi, Tony," by Gary W. Kennedy.

Guillaud, Betty. "Back Here Playing Jazz and Pulling 'Heartstrings' Here," *Times–Picayune*, 5 July 1994, section Living, D3.

———. "Fire is a Word that Really Rings a Bell with Warren." *Times–Picayune*, 26 August 1994, section Living, E2.

"Indian Music." *Times–Picayune*, 17 October 2003, section Lagniappe, 30

Iwaski, Scott. "Astral Project Bringing Eclectic Sound to S.L." *Deseret News*, 28 July 2000, W03.

"Jazz." *Times–Picayune*, 28 April 2000, section Lagniappe, L22.

The Jazz & Heritage Festival Crossword. *Times–Picayune*, 8 May 1981, section Lagniappe, 4–5.

Jones, Max. "I'm a Little Rowdy with my Playing: Professor Longhair Talks to Max Jones." *Melody Maker*, 1 April 1978, 44.

Joyce, Mike. "Professor Longhair." *Washington Post*, 14 May 1979, section Performing Arts, B13.

Kernfeld, Barry. *The Blackwell Guide to Recorded Jazz*, 2nd ed. Oxford and Cambridge, MA: Blackwell, 1995.

Kinzer, Charlie. "The Astral Perspective: A Conversation with Tony Dagradi." *Jazz Society* (Baton Rouge, LA) 2, no. 6 (June 1990).

Knight, Brian L. "New Orleans 2000—A Hazy Recap." *The Vermont Review* (2000). Available from http://vermontreview.tripod.com/Concert%20reviews/nawlins00.htm; accessed 11 December 2006.

Koransky, Jason. "Backstage with ... Astral Project." *Down Beat* 69, no. 7 (July 2002): 12.

Lane, Richard. *Images from the Floating World: The Japanese Print; Including an Illustrated Dictionary of Ukiyo-e*. Old Saybrook, CT: Konecky & Konecky, 1978.

Lasocki, David. *A Higher Fusion: The New Orleans Modern-Jazz Group Astral Project at 34*. Portland, OR: Instant Harmony, 2012.

———. *James Singleton, Rhythm Crusader: The Life and Work of the New Orleans Jazz Bassist and Bandleader*. Bloomington, IN: Instant Harmony, 2010.

———. *Steve Masakowski, Big Easy Innovator: The Life and Work of the New Orleans Jazz Guitarist and Educator*. Portland, OR: Instant Harmony, 2014.

Lichtenstein, Grace, and Laura Dankner. *Musical Gumbo: The Music of New Orleans*. New York: W. W. Norton, 1993.

"Local Rock." *Times–Picayune*, 7 November 1997, section Lagniappe, L8.

Lynch, Kevin. "Sending out Big Easy Spirit: Astral Project Finds Solace in New Orleans Jazz." *Wisconsin State Journal*, 29 September 2005. Available from http://www.madison.com/archives/read.php?ref=/wsj/2005/09/29/0509280421.php; accessed 15 November 2006.

Mahne, Theodore P. "New Concerto is Jazzy Smash." *Times–Picayune*, 21 November 1995, section Living, D14.

———. "Singer Crosses Musical Boundaries." *Times–Picayune*, 6 April 1995, section Living, E1.

Margasak, Peter. "Post No Bills: Damon Short Tries it at Home." *Chicago Reader* 31, no. 9 (30 November 2001): 1, S–3.

Merli, Melissa. "Next Wall to Wall Already in Works." *The News–Gazette* (Champaign, IL), 2 October 2005, F.

M[iller], M[ark]. "Carla Bley's Many Faces: Mistress of Deception." *Globe and Mail* (Edmonton, Alberta), 23 August 1982, P14.

The Mysticism of Sound and Music: The Sufi Teaching of Hazrat Inayat Khan, rev. ed. (Boston: Shambhala, 1996).

"Nontraditional Path to Trad Jazz." *Times–Picayune*, 9 July 1999, section Lagniappe, L9.

"November Cultural Calendar." *The Advocate* (Baton Rouge, LA), 26 October 1997, section MAG, 11–MAG.

Palmer, Don. "Carla Bley Returns to Form." *New York Times*, 10 February 1985, 97.

Palmer, Robert. "Prof. Longhair is Swinging at the Gate." *New York Times*, 18 May 1979, C13.

———. "Professor Longhair: Deep South Piano and the Barrelhouse Blues." In Pete Welding and Toby Byron, ed. *Bluesland: Portraits of Twelve Major American Blues Masters*, 158–75. New York: Dutton, 1991.

Parikh, Arvindkumar. "N.O. Man Fuses Jazz with Music of India." *Times–Picayune*, 28 May 1998, section Picayune, 3A1.

Patton, Kevin. "Astral Project." *The New Orleans Art Review* 11, no. 2 (September–October 1992): 30–31.

Pope, John. "Music Manager, JazzFest Pioneer Allison Miner Dies." *Times–Picayune*, 24 December 1995, section Metro, B5.

Provizer, Norman. "Mix of Sounds Works Well at Winter Park Jazz Fest." *Rocky Mountain News*, 4 August 1993, section Entertainment/Weekend Spotlight, 18C.

———. "Tony Dagradi." *Jazziz* (February–March 1988).

Ramsey, Doug. *Take Five: The Public and Private Lives of Paul Desmond*. Seattle: Parkside Publications, 2005.

Ramsey, Jan. "What Will Happen to New Orleans Music?" *OffBeat Weekly Beat Newsletter*, mislabeled 3, no. 33 (25 August 2005); in fact issued on 12 September 2005.

Rawls, Alex. "Let's Stay Together. How Does a Band Last 30 Years? Ask Astral Project." *OffBeat* 21, no. 5 (May 2008): 64–68.

Reich, Howard. "Astral Project Blows its Blues away." *Chicago Tribune*, 26 September 2005, section Tempo, 1.

———. "Astral Takes Distinctive, Jazzy Sound on the Road." *Chicago Tribune*, 23 September 2005, edition Chicago Final, section On The Town, 11.

———. "Sabotaging the Moment." *Down Beat* 64, no. 10 (1 October 1997): 40.

———. "Shining Time: Astral Project just may Be New Orleans' Best." *Chicago Tribune*, 20 October 1996, section Arts & Entertainment, 9.

Reynolds, Paul. "In the Tradition." *Coda: The Journal of Jazz & Improvised Music*, no. 221 (August–September 1988): 12–14.

Sachs, Lloyd. "Arkestra Plays on as Founder Sun Ra Would Have Wanted; Astral Peaks." *Chicago Sun-Times*, 29 October 1996, section Features, Jazz, etc., 32.

Santusuosso, Ernie. "Jazz Drummer D. Sharpe is Mourned." *Boston Globe*, 23 January 1987, section Arts and Film, 55.

———. "Weekend: Two Clubs Revive Big-Band Nights." *Boston Globe*, 8 February 1980, section Arts/Films.

Shipton, Alyn. "Brecon '99, Powys." *The Times* (London), 17 August 1999, Features, 37.

———. *A New History of Jazz*. London & New York: Continuum, 2001.

"Sittin' in with Tony Dagradi and Astral Project." *Jazz Player* 1, no. 4 (June–July 1994): 22–23 (with lead sheets by TD on pp. 24–34).

Simpson, Joel. "Tony Dagradi: From the Crescent City to the Crowned Heads of Europe, Saxist Tony Dagradi has Moved from Second Line to Front Line." *Down Beat* 49, no. 7 (July 1982): 54.

Singleton, James. "Obituary: Charlie Brent, 1948–2006." *OffBeat*, January 2007, 44.

Smith, Tod. "Jazz Underground." Available from http://www.allaboutjazz.com/articles/newo0202.htm; accessed 29 June 2005.

Spedale, Rhodes, Jr. "Tony Dagradi: In the Forefront." *Jazz Times* 20, no. 12 (December 1990): 53.

Spera, Keith. "All-Star Band Pays Tribute to Armstrong." *Times-Picayune*, 6 October 2000, section Lagniappe, 25.

———. "Five nor [recte Now] Four." *Times–Picayune*, 25 May 2001, section Lagniappe, 25.

———. "Horns Aplenty in Inside Out." *Times–Picayune*, 21 January 2000, section Lagniappe, L9.

———. "Jazzed Up: Modern Jazz Musicians Finding More Clubs to Call Home." *Times–Picayune*, 31 May 1996, section Lagniappe, L18.

———. "Jazzin' up Christmas—Loyola University Professor John Mahoney Unleashes his Big-Band Sound on the Music of the Season." *Times-Picayune*, 1 December 2009, section Living, C 01.

———. "Spera's Spins." *Times–Picayune*, 8 May 2000, section National, A07.

———. "Willie Metcalf Jr., 74, Pianist, Jazz Mentor." *Times–Picayune*, 11 December 2004, section Metro, 04.

Spratt, Skip. "Lon Price." *Saxophone Journal* 30, no. 3 (January/February 2006): 30.

Tabak, Jonathan. "Astral Project at 20." *OffBeat* 12, no. 6 (June 1999). Available from http://www.offbeat.com/ob9906/astral_project.html; accessed 23 March 2004.

The Taper's Almanac Professor Longhair Discography. compiled by Bill DeBlonk. Available from http://www.geocities.com/tapersalmanac/fess.html, accessed 14 October 2005.

Tolleson, Robin. "Stroke of Genius: Artist Wears Many Hats—All Well." *Mountain Xpress* (Asheville, NC) 8, no. 6 (18 September 2001): 34.

Tsunetomo, Yamamoto. *Hagakure: The Book of the Samurai*, trans. William Scott Wilson. Tokyo & New York: Kodansha International, 1979.

Waddington, Chris. "Jazz Bandleader Carla Bley Is Full of Musical Surprises." *Star Tribune* (Minneapolis), 28 June 2003, section Variety, 1E.

Webster, Jill Anding. "A New Beat at The Columns." *Times–Picayune*, 5 March 1993, section Lagniappe, L18.

"What's Up." *San Antonio Express–News*, 6 August 2000, section S.A. Life, 2H.

Wilson, John S. "Carla Bley's Band at Seventh Avenue South." *New York Times*, 1 August 1981, section 1, 8.

———. "Carla Bley's Jazz Style Taps Many Roots." *New York Times*, 9 January 1983, section 2, 21.

Wirt. John. "Vidacovich Adds Life to his Sound with Hereditary New Orleans Beat." *The Advocate* (Baton Rouge, LA), 28 June 1996, section Fun, 17–Fun.

Wolff, Carlo. "McFerrin Happy to be Playing with Friends Again." *The Plain Dealer* (Cleveland, OH), Final/All Edition, 30 June 1999, Section: Entertainment, 1E.

Wyckoff, Geraldine. "Astral Project Blasts off Jazz Month." *Gambit Weekly*, 29 September 1992.

———. "The Project Comes Together." *Gambit Weekly*, probably January 1999.

http://tonydagradi.com/

INDEX OF NAMES

All the places are in New Orleans, unless otherwise stated.

Abate, Greg 150
Absolute Monster Gentlemen 126
Academy of Black Arts (Detroit) 18
Acoustic Fusion (Astral Project) 87
Adams, Johnny 92, 121–23
Adams, Patti 148
Adams, Pepper 6
Adams, Terry 32
Adderley, Julian "Cannonball" 4, 5, 38, 142
Adderley, Nat 29, 38, 87
Adjani, Isabelle 43
Aebersold, Jamey 151
Aiges, Scott 2, 84–85, 87, 92–95, 106–9, 132, 134
Albenga, Matilda: see Dagradi, Matilda
Albert, Jeff 115
Aless, Tony 5–7
Allen, Lee 23–24
Allen, Victor "Red" 125
Allison, Mose 67–68
American Institute of Music (Vienna, Austria) 89
American Music Texas Style (Gatemouth Brown) 123–24
Anderson, Jim 77
Anderson, Mark 115, 125
Anderson, Wes 117
Anderson Plating 141
Andersson, Theresa 132
Andrews, Troy 132
Ann Arbor (Michigan) 111
Archie Bell and The Drells 13–14
Arlen, Harold 103
Arlington (Virginia) 137
Armstrong, Louis 92, 95
Armstrong Park 83
Arnold, Chuck 116
Arthur, Al 126
Astral Orchestra 49, 91
Astral Project 1, 22, 25, 29, 35–40, 46, 48, 51, 65, 72, 74–78, 81–88, 91, 94–96, 101, 105, 107–14, 116–17, 121, 123, 131–35, 137–40, 143–45, 148, 156, 158, 160–61, 163
Astral Project Live in New Orleans 134
Astral Project, New Orleans LA 72, 87, 105, 107
Astrodome (Houston, Texas) 137
Atkins, Victor 116–17, 127, 141
Audubon Zoo 143
Austin (Texas) 138
Ayler, Albert 10, 72
Bach, Johann Sebastian 6, 142
Bacon, Peter 111
Baker, David N. 6
Baltimore 137
Banks Street (John Vidacovich) 121
Barber, Lynden 42
Barbieri, Gato 36, 45
Baritone Bliss (group) 142
Baritone Madness (group) 142
Baron, Art 47–48
Barry, Rebecca 2, 155–56
Bartholomew, Dave 83
Basie, Count 4, 92, 123–24
Batiste, Alvin 117
Baton Rouge (Louisiana) 68, 90, 138
Bayers, Randy 2
Bayou, The (Washington, DC) 23
Bazzle, Germaine 83, 92, 132
BBC (British Broadcasting Corporation) 111
Beatles, The 4, 127
Beastie Boys 126
Bechet, Troi 132
Beck 126
Belafonte, Harry 3
Bell, Archie: see Archie Bell and The Drells
Belletto, Al 2, 35, 47, 59
Belote, Doug 140
Bennett, Brian 160
Berger, Karl 126
Bering, Charlie 18, 86
Berklee School (now College) of Music (Boston) 7–8, 10, 30, 35, 63, 81, 150, 152
Berlin Jazz Festival 82
Better than Ezra 126
Big Chief (Professor Longhair) 80
Big Shot (Astral Project) 133–34
Bigard, Barney 42

Bitches Brew (Miles Davis) 7, 121
Black, James 17, 19, 25, 81, 122
Blackwell, Ed 31, 57
Blade, Brian 90, 116
Blakey, Art 67, 116, 131
Blanchard, Terence 18, 115
Bley, Carla 1, 18, 29–32, 36, 39, 41–47, 59, 63, 67, 73, 87, 126, 163
Blood, Sweat and Tears 8
Bloom, Jonathan 32, 47
Blue Note (New York) 109, 113
Blue Orleans (Tim Laughlin) 123
Blue Streak (Astral Project) 143
The Blues Project 35
Blues Saloon 38
Blues Scholars 23–25
Blumenthal, Bob 42
Bohm, David 85
Bohr, Niels 85
Bonnette, Sister Mary 17
Bonnie and Clyde 43
Booth, Philip 112, 138
Boston 7–10, 12–14, 17
Boston Club 13
Bou, Olivier 2
Boudreaux, Jeff 2, 89, 93–94
Bourgeois, Scott 115, 156
Bowens, Alonzo 115, 141
Boyd, Jesse 142
Bozza, Eugène 157
Bramblett, Randall 25
Braud, Mark 116, 164
Brecker, Michael 78, 143, 155
Brecon Festival (Wales) 111
Brent, Charlie 38
Brighter Days (Ghetto/Mysticism) 10
Brooks, Glenn 104, 106
Brooks, Mark 115
Brown, Charles 126
Brown, Clarence "Gatemouth" 29, 35
Brown, Gary 18
Brown, James 13, 35
Brunious, Wendell 47–48
Bultman Funeral Home Solarium 115
Burbank, Albert 59
Budnick, Dean 109
Burke, Solomon 122

Burris, Brad 90
Burton, Gary 8
Butler, Henry 36, 117
Byard, Jaki 6
Byers, Billy 7
Byrd, Henry: see Longhair, Professor
Byrd Lives! (Professor Longhair) 20
Cafe St. Charles 90
Café Edwige (Provincetown, MA) 11
Caliente (group) 81
Call, Tim 2
Campo, Bobby 164
Campbell, Gary 150
Cape Cod (Massachusetts) 8, 11–12
Cape School of Art (Provincetown, Massachusetts) 11
Capricorn Studios (Macon, Georgia) 25
Carla Bley Live!: see *Live!*
Carnegie Hall (New York) 6
Carnegie Mellon University (Pittsburgh) 137
Carney, Harry 59
Carroll, Dan 118
Carter, Ron 6
Castenell, Amadee 91
Castle Hotel (Brecon, Wales) 111
Chakrabarty, Pandit Ajoy 117
Chancy, Vincent 44
Chaplin, Chuck 140–41
Chapman, Topsy 132
Charity Hospital 19
Charlie B's 86
Chase, Leah 142
Le Chat Noir 132
Chaudhuri, Pandit Swapan 117
Chen, Lilin 1
Cherry, Don 31, 36, 57
Chicago 138
Chicago (band) 8
Chickie Wah Wah 142
Chopin, Frédéric 6
Christopher, Evan 117
Cleary, John 126
Clements, Cranston 126
Cleveland (Ohio) 111
Cloud 9 (Michael Pellera) 125
Club 300 Jazz Bistro 140–41
Cochran, Wayne 13

Cognac Hennessy Jazz Search 83, 86, 90
Cohen, Nerissa 117
Coker, Jerry 6
Cole, Nat King 105
Coleman, Ornette 31–32, 57, 66, 72–74
Coltrane, Alice 78
Coltrane, John 4–5, 8, 10–11, 23–24, 30–33, 53–55, 59, 65, 67–78, 73–74, 78–79, 85, 91, 94–95, 100, 103, 108, 112, 115–17, 121, 125, 141–42, 148, 156–57
Columbia University (New York) 23
Columns Hotel, The 87, 89–90, 93–96, 99–100, 104, 140, 155–58
Comiskey, Fran 65
Composers Recording Studio 71–72
Conference of the Birds (Dave Holland) 32
Contemporary Arts Center 46, 52, 91–92, 95–96, 115, 142
Contemporary Arts Center Big Band: see New Orleans C.A.C. Jazz Orchestra
Continental Airlines 3
Continental Drifters 107
Coogan, Brian 117
Cook, Junior 156
Cook, Richard 67–68, 102
Corea, Chick 5, 115
Cowherd, Jon 116
Crawfish Fiesta (Professor Longhair) 29
Creppel, Claire 94
Crescent City (radio show) 132, 134
Creston, Paul 7, 156
¡Cubanismo! 126
¡Cubanismo! *in New Orleans: Mardi Gras Mambo* 126
Cuccia, Ron 2, 5
Cullen, Thomas J., III 24
Curtis, King 24
Cyrus, Bernie 87
D'Addario, Joe 5
Dagradi, Arnold Anthony (father) 3
Dagradi, Dominic (son) 137
Dagradi, Joan, née Lissy (wife) 1, 11–14, 17–18, 72, 74, 81, 107, 137, 140
Dagradi, Matilda, née Albenga (mother) 3
Dagradi, Tony: see book
Dameron, Tadd 117
Davenport, Jeremy 132

Davenport, John: see Blackwell, Otis
David Letterman Show 9
Davis, Art 59
Davis, Clive 68
Davis, Miles 6–7, 10, 47, 83, 112, 115, 131, 142
Davis, Ocie 117
Davis, Quint 25
Davis, Stanton, Jr. 2, 10
Davis, Troy 142, 163
Debussy, Claude 60
DeJohnnette, Jack 54
Deluxe (Better than Ezra) 126
Demmer, Eric 124
Demsey, David 150, 152
Denton (Texas) 140
Desmond, Paul 9
Dew Drop Inn 124
Dey, Francis 161
DiFlorio, Mark 2, 115
Diliberto, John 42
Dirty Dozen Brass Band 33, 57, 42
Dr. John: see Rebennack, Mac
Dodds, Johnny 59
Dolphy, Eric 54, 59
Dominic, Benny 118
Domino, Fats 20, 24
Dorsey, Tommy 4
Dougay, Derek 116
Dream Palace 21
Dreams of Love (Tony Dagradi) 66, 72, 81, 87, 148
Drells, The: see Archie Bell and The Drells
Drew, James 2, 90
DuBois, John 57
Dubois, Pierre Max 156
Duncan Plaza 47
Dunn, Archer 25
Durta, Andy 2
Dutilleux, Henri 60
Eaglin, Snooks 122, 126
Easley, Dave 2, 155
Eastern Airlines 3
Echoes of New Orleans (Al Grey) 124
Edgewood College (Madison, Wisconsin) 134
8½ (Federico Fellini) 46
Elevado (Astral Project) 108, 121, 133

Ellington, Duke 4, 6, 32–33, 42, 44, 46, 91–92, 99, 102, 107, 115, 150
Ellis, John 92, 148
Enright, Ed 111
Ernest, Herman 121
Essenault, Mike 142
Essential Scale Studies (Tony Dagradi) 148
Europeans, The 29
Evans, Bill 112
Evans, Gil 115
Evoskevich, Paul 102
Ewing, Mary Jane 140–41
Farrell, Joe 6
Faubourg, The 38, 46, 51–53, 83
Fawkes, Guy 43
Fayetteville (Arkansas) 137
Fazola, Irving 59
Federal Emergency Management Agency (FEMA) 138
Feinstein, Sascha 2
Fellini, Federico 46
Fess: see Longhair, Professor
Fielder, Alvin 32, 53–54
Fig, Anton 8
Fine, Milo 34
Fisher, Patrice 2, 54, 65
Fletcher, Aaron 115–16
Focus (Stan Getz) 5
For Taylor Storer 44
Foreign Affairs (Patrice Fisher) 65, 154
Freeman, Wanda 29
French, George 92
Friction, Baby (Better than Ezra) 126
Frohnmayer, Phil 148
Fumar, Vincent 20, 25, 34, 53, 57–58, 63–65, 83
Funky Butt 95, 112, 115
Gagnard, Frank 91
Galerie Simonne Stern 86
Gambrell, Antonio 92
Gant, Cecil 24
Garbarek, Jan 78, 155
Garcia, Julian 115
Gardner, Jeff 142
Garrison, Jimmy 74
Gate Swings (Gatemouth Brown) 123
Gaye, Marvin 8
Germann, Jim 141
Gerard, David 126
Getz, Stan 5, 101
Giant Steps (John Coltrane) 5
Ghetto/Mysticism 10, 35
Gibbs, Lawrence 123
Giddins, Gary 23
Gilder, Rusty 17
Gillespie, Dizzy 116
Gillet, Helen 2
Gino's Restaurant and Bar (Baton Rouge, Louisiana) 90
Give me my Wings (Jim McNeil) 127
Glazounov, Alexandr 7
God 76, 78, 137
Goines, Victor 66, 91, 157
Gold, Sanford 6–7
Goldberg, Michael 24
Goode, Brad 140
Goodman, Benny 52
Goodwin, Michael 24
Gordillo, Bernard 2
Gordon, Earl 25
Goss, Bill 2
Goudeau, Scott 65–66, 115
Gourrier, Mike 83, 116
Governor Bradford Hotel (Provincetown, Massachusetts) 11
Green, Tim 2, 142
Green Mill (Chicago) 2, 107, 109, 111, 138
Gregory, Rex 142
Gretna Festival (Gretna, Louisiana) 143
Grey, Al 124–25
Grimes, Bill 91
Grog Kill Studios (Woodstock, New York) 30
Guerin, Roland 92, 116–17, 141–42
Haden, Charlie 31–32, 57, 77
Hadley, Frank-John 123
Hamlet (William Shakespeare) 43
Hampton, Lionel 123–24
Hancock, Herbie 5–6, 10
Hanna, Roland 6
Harrah's Casino 142
Harris, Peter 140
Harrison, Donald, Jr. 18, 67, 91, 132
Harrison, Kelvin 116, 157
Harvey, James aka Snake aka JJ 18, 30–32

Hawkins, Coleman 42, 72, 100–1, 124, 148, 155–56
Headhunters 36
Hear & Now (Don Cherry) 36
Heart to Heart (Phillip Manuel) 38, 96, 103–6
Heart-to-Heart Talks (Kirpal Singh) 104
Henderson, Joe 8, 117, 156–57
Henry, Frogman 18
Henry, Richard 2
Hersch, Fred 75, 77–78
Heritage (Alvin "Red" Tyler) 100
Heron, Elton 32
Hicks, Dylan 140
Higgins, Billy 46
High Life (Wayne Shorter) 143
A Higher Fusion (David Lasocki) 1, 38, 66, 72, 78, 81, 87, 108, 110, 133–34, 144
Highlands–Douglass Big Rock Jazz Fest (Louisville, Kentucky) 140
Hillman, Christopher 125
History's Made Every Moment: New Orleans Now! (Ramsey McLean) 52–54
Hock, Roger 8
Hodges, Johnny 33, 72, 101, 103, 123–24
Holiday, Billie 123
Holland, Dave 32
Holmes, Jeff 150
Holy Name of Jesus Church 142
House, Son 23
The House of Blues 122
Houston (Texas) 13–14, 137
How Does Your Garden Grow? (Better than Ezra) 126
Howlin' Wolf 115
Huntington, Bill 67–68, 82, 89, 91, 93, 96, 121, 125, 156–57
Huntley, Sherry 141
Hurricane Katrina 117, 132, 137–45, 155
Hyatt Regency Hotel 89
I Hate to Sing (Carla Bley) 43
I Love Bein' Here with You (Mary Jane Ewing) 140
Ice Cube Slim 21
Ignatius Saxophone Quartet 142
Images from the Floating World (Tony Dagradi) 71–74, 94
Images from the Floating World (Richard Lane) 72
Improvisational Arts Quintet 32
In the Nick of Time (Scott Goudeau) 65–66
Indiana University 2, 109, 134, 139
Indianapolis 111
Inner Visions 10–12, 30, 35, 38, 41
Inside Out 116
Iron Post (Urbana, Illinois) 139
JJ: see Harvey, James
J & M Studios 23
Jackson (Mississippi) 137
Jackson Square 14
Jacquet, Illinois 124
James, Boney 131
Jarreau, Al 106
Jarrett, Keith 53, 78
Jasmine 65, 154
Jazz at Lincoln Center Orchestra 66, 157
Jazz at the Philharmonic 125
Jazz City (Edmonton, Alberta) 45
Jazz Crusaders 32
Jazz Fest: see New Orleans Jazz and Heritage Festival
Jazz Jamboree (Warsaw, Poland) 42
Jazz Messengers 30, 67
Jazz Tage (Ingolstadt, Germany) 132
Jazz Underground (Loyola University) 116, 141–42
Jazzclub Allmend (Oberengstringen, Switzerland) 107
Jazzhaus (Copenhagen) 111
Jazzin' up Christmas (John Mahoney) 142
Jazztown (radio show) 66
Jed's 21
Jeff Fest (Metairie, Louisiana) 96
Jekabson, Erik 115
Jenkins, Leroy 115
Jimmy's 21, 65
Jobim, Antônio Carlos 100
Johnson, Calvin 142
Johnson, Clarence, III 2, 92, 116, 141, 155, 157
Johnson, Seán 118
Jolivet, André 60
Jones, Elvin 100
Jones, Leroy 132
Jones, Thad 6, 92, 150

Jordan, Edward "Kidd" 32, 47–48, 64, 91, 93
Jordan, Kent 32, 47–48, 82
Jordan, Stephanie 142, 164
Joseph, Kirk 52, 57
Joyce, Mike 23–24, 34
Jump Jazz (Ramsey McLean) 56
K-Doe, Ernie 25
Kabby's 94
Karlins, M. William 73
Kaslow, Andy 19–23, 25
Kemp, Fred 32–33
Kent, Luther 37–38
Kernfeld, Barry 42
Kerr, Clyde, Jr. 2, 32, 46–47, 82, 91
Khan, Hazrat Inayat 10
Khan, Ustad Ali Akbar 117
Kim, Marianne Weiss 2
Kim, Norman 2
Kind of Blue (Miles Davis) 142
King, Matt 90
Klein, Craig 92
Knight, Brian L. 112
Koransky, Jason 133
Koz, Dave 117
Krall, Diane 112
Krown, Joe 117
Kuner, David 102
Kurth, Wolfgang 2
Kurtz, Manny 32
Lacinak, Chris 90
Lackner, Tom 68
Lafayette (Lousiana) 138
Lake Pontchartrain 137
Landry, Dickie 52
Lane, Richard 72
Las Vegas 7
Lasocki, Lucien cover design, 1
Lasocki, Margaret 1
The Last Mardi Gras (Professor Longhair) 20
Laughlin, Tim 94, 123, 132
Lavigne, Darrell 115, 127, 132
Leavell, Chuck 25
Lee, David, Jr. 67
Lee, Khari Allen 141–42
Lee, Peggy 104
Lefcoski, Jonathan 115
The Legend of Cowboy Bill (Astral Project) 134

Let The Smoke Roll in (Kasie Lunsford) 161
Levy, Howard 111
Lewis, David 125
Lewis, George 59
Lewis, Lula Lowe 2
Lewis, Mel 6, 150
Lewis, Ramsey 29
Lewis, Roger 2, 17, 32–33, 52, 57, 142
Liberation Jazz Orchestra 31
Library of Congress (Washington, DC) 23
Liebman, Dave 81
Lifers, The 46, 51–53
Light of the Night (Randall Bramblett) 25
Lionel Hampton Jazz Club (Paris) 123
Lissy, Joan: see Dagradi, Joan
Live! (Carla Bley) 42
Live at Gino's (I migliori) 91
Live at The Columns (Tony Dagradi) 87, 99–102, 104
Live in Germany (Professor Longhair) 20
Lokumbe, Hanibal 92
Lomax, Alan 23
London (England) 43, 58
The Long View (Ramsey McLean and Tony Dagradi) 51–62
Long Walk on a Short Pier (Sea Level) 25
Longhair, Professor 1, 19–25, 41, 107, 112, 121, 158
Longue View Gardens 57–58
Lord, The: see God
Loreti, Joe 5
Los Angeles 14, 63, 138
Los Hombres Calientes 115
Lott, Simon 117, 140, 142
Louis Armstrong Archives (Queens College, New York) 92
Louisiana Music Commission 87
Louisiana Music Factory 133
Louisiana State Arts Council 19, 47
Louisiana State Jazz Composers Series 90
Louisiana State University Jazz Ensemble 143
Louisville (Kentucky) 140
A Love Supreme (John Coltrane) 78
Loyola University 1, 18, 35, 63–64, 90, 116, 137, 140, 142, 147–49, 151, 155–58, 164
Lu & Charlie's 17–19, 36, 51, 84
Lucero, Eric 92, 115

Lucia, Ingrid 132
Ludwig, Ted 2
Lumley, Les 35
Lunar Eclipse (Tony Dagradi) 38–39, 42, 63, 87, 100, 104, 163
Lunsford, Kasie 161
Lynch, Dave 25
Lynch, Kevin 139
McDermott, Tom 117
McFerrin, Bobby 36–38, 52, 96, 104, 110–12, 162
McGhee, Andy 7, 132
McGinley, Paul 64, 91
McLaughlin, John 66
McLean, Andrew 117–18
McLean, Ramsey 1–2, 19, 36, 46, 51–60
McNeil, Jim 127
McNerney, Kevin 132
Macintosh, Tommy 2
Mackie, Hank 94
Madison (Wisconsin) 139
Magnie, John 25
Mahne, Theodore P. 95
Mahoney, David 140
Mahoney, John 91, 140, 142, 148
Mancini, Henry 42
Mangiardi, Denise 123
Mantis (Al Arthur) 126
Mantler, Mike 30, 44
Manuel, Phillip 95–96, 104–6, 125, 132
Maple Leaf Bar 21, 94, 142
Margitza, Rick 67, 89
Mariano, Charlie 8
Mars (group) 81
Marsalis, Branford 1, 18
Marsalis, Ellis 17, 66–67, 91, 132
Marsalis, Jason 117, 132
Marsalis, Wynton 1, 18, 66, 82
Martin, Mel 150
Martin, Peter 92, 116–17
Masakowski, Steve 1, 66–68, 72, 81–82, 85–86, 89–91, 94–95, 99–100, 102, 108, 110–12, 125, 131–32, 134, 139–43, 156–57
Masakowski, Ulrike 1, 85, 91
Maureau, Wayne 127, 142
Mayfield, Irvin 117
Meditations (John Coltrane) 78

Melancon, Philip 94
Melbourne (Australia) 123
Mentel, Jim 24
Mercy, Mercy, Mercy (Cannonball Adderley) 5
Messiaen, Olivier 60
Metcalf, Willie, Jr. 18–19
Metzger, Jon 150
Meyer, Jeffrey 122
Michael's Pub (Boston) 13
Midtfyns Rock Festival (Ringe, Denmark) 112–13
Migliori, I 91
Milburn, Amos 24
Miller, Charlie 92
Miller, Claude 43
Miller, Glenn 4
Miner, Allison 19–20, 107
Mills, Irving 42
Mingledorff, Jason 141
Mingus, Charles 31–32, 47, 54, 115
Mr. B's 131
Monk, Thelonious 6, 31, 101, 115–16, 125, 162–63
Montreux Jazz Festival 123
Mooney, Davy 2
Moore, Ray 142
Moore, Stanton 2, 95, 117, 142
Mortelle randonnée (Carla Bley) 43
Morton, Brian 67–68, 102
Moses, Bob 75, 77–78
Motian, Paul 77
Mule, Marcel 157–58
Mullins, Mark 92, 115, 126, 132
Music from the Big Tomato (Ron Cuccia) 25
Musicians for Music 19
Museum of Modern Art (New York) 6
My Backyard (Mose Allison) 67–68
My Fair Lady 3
Mystery Street (John Vidacovich) 105
The Mysticism of Sound (Hazrat Inayat Khan) 10
Nagin, Ray 137
Nancy Jazz Pulsations (France) 132
Nashville (Tennessee) 138
Nastos, Michael G. 32
National Endowment for the Arts 19, 47
Neslort (group) 83

Nestico, Sammy 143
Neville, Charles 56
The Neville Brothers 56, 108
New Arrival (Chris Lacinack) 90
New England Conservatory (Boston) 8–10, 30
New Haven (Connecticut) 137
A New History of Jazz (Alyn Shipton) 111
New Music Jazz: see *The New New Orleans Music: New Music Jazz*
The New New Orleans Music: New Music Jazz (NOSE) 32–34
New Orleans Blues Septet 22
New Orleans C.A.C. Jazz Orchestra 92
New Orleans Jazz and Heritage Festival (Jazz Fest) 17, 19, 21, 25, 29, 36–38, 46–47, 52, 66–67, 76, 81, 92, 96, 108, 110, 112–13, 115, 131, 133–34, 142, 144, 160
New Orleans Jazz Historical Park Concerts 141
New Orleans Jazz Orchestra 142
New Orleans Museum of Modern Art 95
New Orleans Repertory Big Band 92
New Orleans Saxophone Ensemble (Quartet) (NOSE) 32–34, 66, 91, 115, 141, 150, 156, 163
New York 5–6, 14, 22, 41, 47, 52, 58, 65, 75–76, 79, 81, 113, 123, 141, 150
Newark (New Jersey) 3
NOCCA 131
North Sea Jazz Festival (The Hague, Netherlands) 113, 123
North Texas State University: see University of North Texas
Oasis (Tony Dagradi) 25, 29–32, 34, 38, 41, 100
O'Day, Kevin 142
Oestreicher, Dan 142
O'Farrill, Arturo 41
Ogden Museum of Southern Art 95, 141
Old Absinthe Bar 38
Old and New Dreams (Don Cherry) 31
Ole Man River's 21
Omar, Freddy 132
O'Neil, Brian 126
lOneness (Tony Dagradi) 164
Orpheum Theater 143
Orvieto festival 96

Osland, Miles 150
Oslo Jazz Festival 111
Pagnotta, Carlo 96
Palfi, Stevenson 21
Palmer, Don 44
Palmer, Earl 12
Palmer, Robert 22–24
Parading (Tony Dagradi): see *Images from the Floating World*
Parker, Charlie 9, 116, 126, 150
Parker, Robert 24
Pasqua, Alan 17
Patterson, Jason 124
Patton, Kevin 83
Pavarotti, Luciano 108
Payton, Nicholas 92
Payton, Walter 47–48
Pellera, Michael 2, 25, 66, 83, 108, 116, 121–22, 125–26, 131, 141–42, 156
Penguin Shuffle (Damon Short) 66
Perrilliat, Nat 59
Perrine, Matt 122
Perugia festival 96
The Pfister Sisters 132
Philadelphia 13
Phillips, Laurie 2
Picou, Alphonse 59
Pie in the Sky 94
Pink Panther 44
Pomeroy, Herb 7, 150
Porter, George, Jr. 123, 142
Portraits and Sketches (Tony Dagradi) 47–48, 91
Potter, Gary 2
Powell, Bud 5
Prevost, Kim 127
Price, Lon 20
Price, Tim 117
Proefrock, Stacia 43
The Promise (Scott Goudeau) 66
Prout's Club Alhambra 46
Provincetown (Massachusetts) 11, 73
Provizer, Norman 78
Prunka, Brian 142
Puzzullo, Frank 2, 18
Ra, Sun 10, 47
Radiators 20

Ramsey, Jan 137
Rawls, Alex 141
Rebennack, Mac (Dr. John) 24
Redman, Dewey 31, 36
Redmann, Alice 2
Reeks, John 142
Refugees, The 52
Reich, Howard 106–8, 138
Reisman, Carl 2
Return to Forever 36
Reynolds, Paul 66
Richardson, Rex 116
Rick's Café Américain (Baton Rouge, Louisiana) 68
Ridgley, Tommy 122–23
Riley, Herman 91, 121, 142, 163
A River of My Own (Denise Mangiardi) 123
Rivers, Sam 112
Roberts, Alfred "Uganda" 19–20
Robinson, Jimmy 64–65
Rollins, Sonny 6, 44, 100, 102, 117, 156, 163
Roma, Gene 11
Rome, Jonathan 25
Rose, Adonis 116–17
Rose, Earl 29
Rose, Jonathan F. P. 29–30, 76–77
Rosemont Studio 53
Rosy's Jazz Club 21, 143
Rothstein, Evan 2
Rouzan, Wanda 132
Royen, John 94
Rudd, Roswell 32, 41
Ruffins, Kermit 92, 132
Rum and Coke (Professor Longhair) 20
Russell, Richard 2
Ruth (band) 32
Rytmisk Musikkonservatorium (Copenhagen) 109
Sachs, Lloyd 34, 107
Saenger Theater 29
Sager, David 92
St. Albans Naval Hospital (Queens, New York) 3
Saint Paul Chamber Orchestra 110
Sample, Joe 112
Sampen, John 156
Sanborn, David 117
Sandbar, The 91
Sanders, Fred 140, 142
Sanders, Mark 2, 25, 35, 37–39, 48, 54, 65, 81, 131
Sant Mat (Surat Shabd Yoga) 12, 76
Sax Solos over Jazz Standards (Tony Dagradi) 151–52, 161
Sax Traxx 141
Scanlan, Reggie 20
Schuller, Ed 8, 18, 30
Sciple, Tommy 137
Sea Level 25
Sea-Saint Studio 25
Sears Corporation 57
Sebastian, Ricky 54, 65, 115
Serrault, Michel 43
Severin, Chris 115–17, 141
Shadowlove (Larry Sieberth) 65
Shapiro, Noah 24
Sharif, Jamil 115, 132, 164
Sharpe, D. 9, 11, 18–19, 29–32, 41
Sharpe, Nancy 9
Shaw, Connor 47
Sheppard, Bob 18
Sheridan, Chris 32
Shipton, Alyn 111
Short, Damon 66
Shorter, Wayne 6, 115, 117, 125, 143
Shostakovich, Dmitri 59
Shreveport (Louisiana) 137
Sidewalk Safari (Wayne Maureau) 127
Sieberth, Larry 2, 25, 46, 53–54, 65, 81, 90–91, 111, 115, 117, 126–27, 131, 142
Silver, Horace 116
Simeon, Omer 59
Simion, Nicolas 132
Simon, Ralph 29
Simpson, Joel 46–47
Since the Blues Began (Tommy Ridgley) 123
Sincerely Yours (Francis Dey) 151
Singers (Patrice Fisher) 65
Singh, Kirpal 12, 74
Singh, Sant Ajaib 12
Singleton, James 1, 13, 17, 19, 25, 35–39, 48, 66–67, 72–74, 81–82, 85–86, 90–96, 99–100, 102, 104–8, 110–11, 116, 121, 124, 132–34, 138–39, 144, 155, 157

Singleton, Jim (father) 2

Singleton, Marcela Lineiro 1
Singleton, Mary Anne 2
Sirker, Victor 25
Skinkus, Michael 127
Slagle, Steve 44–45
Slim, Ice Cube: see Ice Cube Slim
Slonimsky, Nicholas 7
Smith, Greg 140
Smith, Tod 116
Smith, Ward 142
Smith, Will 78
Smoak, Dale 1221
Smokey's 81
Snake: see Harvey, James
Snug Harbor 2, 51, 57, 66, 82–83, 86–87, 90, 95–96, 101, 108, 110, 112, 115, 117, 124, 131, 134–35, 140–42, 157–58, 164
Social Studies (Carla Bley) 29, 41
Softly Strong (Patrice Fisher) 65
Sohmer, Jack 67
Solley, Bill 127
Solo (Earl Rose) 29
Son of Sky (Michael Pellera) 125
Sosa, Byron 65
Sounds of Brazil 65
Southwest School of Art & Craft (San Antonio, Texas) 95
Spera, Keith 108, 112, 115
Spiegel, Ray 75, 79
Sprenger, Migo 87
Staczek, Jason 102
Staehle, Freddie 126
State Department of Culture, Recreation and Tourism (Louisiana) 19
Stephens, Rosanna Fidler 2
Stewart, Bob 44
Storer, Taylor 44
Storyville 17
Strayhorn, Billy 72, 139
Street Beats: Modern Applications (John Vidacovich) 121
Stradivari, Antonio 57
Summers, Bill 142
Summers, Russ 78
Summit (New Jersey) 3

Summit High School (New Jersey) 4
Superdome 21
Surat Shabd Yoga: see Sant Mat
Survivors, The 51
Swallow, Steve 41
Swartz, Harvie 75, 77–78
Sweet Rain (Stan Getz) 5
Sweet Remembrance (Tony Dagradi) 12, 71, 75–80, 142
Tabak, Jonathan 40
Talk to me (Kim Prevost) 127
A Tan Nightingale (Johnny Adams) 122
Taylor, Cecil 6, 31
Taylor, James 95
Temptations, The 143
Thesaurus of Scales and Intervals (Nicholas Slonimsky) 7
Theriot, Shane 122, 142
1369 (Boston) 13
3NOW4 155
Thress, Dan 121
Time Being (Ralph Simon) 29
A Time for Love (Phillip Manuel) 95
Timmons, Bobby 30
Tipaldi, Art 123
Tipitina's 19–21, 51, 57, 68, 72, 141
Torchia, Lee 25, 79
Torkanowsky, David 2, 17, 35–39, 47–48, 81–85, 87, 89, 91–92, 101, 108, 110–12, 121, 123, 131, 133–34, 142
Toussaint, Allen 90–91
Tower Records 133
Town Hall (New York) 6
Traub, Eric 105, 121, 123–24
Trick Bag 38
Trinity Episcopal Church 142
Triplett, Katie 2
Trolsen, Rick 83, 92, 116–17, 124, 142
Tropic Appetites (Carla Bley) 45
Trosclair, Angelle 2
TSU Tornados 13
Turbinton, Earl, Jr. 17, 32–34, 46, 67
Tulane University 64, 82, 93, 116, 148
Turner, Tina 107
Turrentine, Stanley 42, 58, 68
Twangorama 115
12 Modern Etudes (Tony Dagradi) 151

Twentieth Century Limited, The 8
Tyler, Alvin "Red" 23–24, 59, 82, 85, 90–91, 100, 117, 121
Tyler's Beer Garden 25, 38
Tyner, McCoy 5, 30, 112
Ullman, Michael 102
Ultrasonic Studios 32
University of Chicago 134
University of Connecticut (Storrs) 6
University of New Orleans 20, 63, 91, 148, 156–57
University of North Texas 35, 132, 140
Valente, Gary 6, 8, 11, 18, 29–32, 41, 44
The Verdict (Johnny Adams) 122
Victor Sirker & The Circuit Breakers 25
Vidacovich (John Vidacovich) 121
Vidacovich, Deborah 1
Vidacovich, John 1, 17–19, 22, 24–25, 35–38, 40, 44, 47–48, 54, 67–68, 72–74, 82, 85–87, 89–93, 95, 99–100, 102, 105, 108, 110–12, 117, 121, 123, 125–27, 131–34, 138–42, 155, 163–64
Vidacovich, Laura 48
Village Gate (New York) 7, 22–23
Village Vanguard (New York) 6, 116, 150
Virgin Megastore 133
Volz, Nick 142
Voodoobop (Astral Project) 78, 110, 112, 122, 133
Walsh, Tom 2
Walton, Cedar 46
Washington, Grover 23
Watanabe, Marie 142
Waters, Muddy 23
Watson, David Lee 25
The Way it Is (Snooks Eaglin) 126
Weather Report 36
Webster, Ben 110
Webster, Jill Anding 93
Weigel, Jay 91
Wein, George 92
Weinstein, Norman 67
Weinstock, Ron 20
Werner, Kenny 30–32
WGBH 9
Where Will You Be when the Party's over (Archie Bell and The Drells) 13
Whitehead, Kevin 31
Wick, Reid 116
Wide Angles (Michael Brecker) 143
Williams, Buster 46
Williams, Hank 3
Williams, Jamelle 117, 142
Williams, Tony 6, 73
Wilson, Jerome 106
Wilson, John S. 44
Wilson, Nancy 29
Wilson, Phil 7
Windo, Gary 32, 41
Windsor Court Hotel 95, 131, 156
Winds of Change 115
Winold, Allen 2
Winston, Brice 92, 115
Winter Park Jazz Fest (Colorado) 87
Wirt, John 121
Woodenhead 64, 115
Woodenhead Live 65
World Saxophone Quartet 34
World's Fair 39
Wroblewski, Luke 2
WWNO 66, 91, 95, 132
WWOZ 56, 83, 116
Wyatt, Robert 31
WYES 2
Wyckoff, Geraldine 83, 105, 109, 122, 131, 133, 164
X-Ray Vision 115
Yanow, Scott 68, 78
Yasinitsky, Greg 150
York, Coco 25
Young, Alvin 25
Young, Lester 42, 124, 148, 155–56
Zeitgeist Multi-Disciplinary Arts Center 115
Zircon (Boston) 13

www.ingramcontent.com/pod-product-compliance
Lightning Source LLC
Chambersburg PA
CBHW040910020526
44116CB00026B/19